TOURISM ECONOMICS

TOURISM ECONOMICS

Donald E. Lundberg
Emeritus, California State Polytechnic University

M. Krishnamoorthy
United States International University

Mink H. Stavenga
United States International University

John Wiley & Sons, Inc.
New York • Chichester • Brisbane • Toronto • Singapore

Library of Congress Cataloging-in-Publication Data:

Lundberg, Donald E.

    Tourism economics / Donald E. Lundberg, M. Krishnamoorthy, Mink H. Stavenga.

       p.   cm.

    Includes bibliographical references.

    ISBN 0-471-57884-3 (acid-free)

    1. Tourist trade.   I. Krishnamoorthy, M. II. Stavenga, Mink H.

    III. Title.

    G155.A1L797   1995

    338.4'791—dc20

                                              94-20598

Printed in the United States of America

10 9 8 7 6 5 4 3 2 1

Contents

Preface

According to several estimates, and depending upon how it is defined, tourism has become the world's largest business enterprise, overtaking the defense, manufacturing, oil, and agriculture industries. Given that the worldwide gross output for tourism in 1992 was $3.2 trillion (about 6 percent of the world's gross national product), with employment encompassing 127 million people, it is all the more surprising that this is the first textbook written on tourism economics from a U.S. perspective.

Tourism can be defined in a variety of ways, but the broad focus is on travelers away from home and the services they utilize, including transportation modes, food and lodging services, entertainment, and tourist attractions. Tourism economics deals with the economic impact of travel on tourism's various sectors, and the quantitative methods that can be applied to travel forecasting and tourism projects.

This book is intended for two primary audiences. The first audience consists of college students—in the United States and abroad—in the fields of hospitality management and business administration, and in particular, tourism majors. With the increasing importance of the service industry, especially tourism, it seems essential that students who plan to go into business and management understand the economic consequences of tourism, and how it affects a multitude of industries. The second audience consists of individuals who professionally work in, or are planning to work in, any sector of the tourism industry. As competition increases for the tourist dollar, it has become more and more important for the tourism professional to be knowledgeable regarding tourism's economic implications and applications.

This book will also be a valuable resource to government agencies in the United States and abroad, such as national, state, and local tourist offices, hospitality industry associations, tourism marketing firms, convention and visitors bureaus, and libraries (public, university, or other).

A useful aspect of this book is that it is written in an easy-to-read, non-mathematical format. Though tourism statistics change frequently due to the rapid growth of the industry, the basic concepts and perspectives of tourism economics, as presented in this book, remain relevant.

We have drawn heavily for information from, and are indebted to, the World Tourism Organization, The World Travel and Tourism Council, the Boeing Corporation, numerous governmental tourist offices, the *Wall Street Journal*, and *The New York Times*. Most importantly, we are indebted to Somerset R. Waters for permission to draw upon his *Travel Industry World Yearbook: The Big Picture*, published annually by Child and Waters, P.O. Box 610, Rye, New York 10580.

DONALD E. LUNDBERG
M. KRISHNAMOORTHY
MINK H. STAVENGA

TOURISM ECONOMICS

Part I

Introduction to Tourism Economics

1

Introduction to Tourism

According to the World Tourism Organization, an affiliate of the United Nations, tourism is the world's largest industry. The World Travel and Tourism Council, a Brussels-based organization of chief executive officers of major companies representing all sectors of the global tourism business, funded a study produced by the Wharton Economic Forecasting Association that put the total gross output for travel and tourism in 1993 at close to $3.2 trillion, about 6 percent of the world's gross national product (GNP). Tourism, says the study, grows almost twice as fast as world GNP. Worldwide, 127 million people work in the industry. It is a great job stimulator. For every $1 million of revenue generated by the industry, 20,000 new jobs are created. About 31 percent of the industry's total world spending takes place in the European community; the United States and Canada account for about 30 percent of the total spending.

Estimates of tourism's economic impact vary widely according to the definition of tourism used. A 1994 estimate of tourism's economic impact on the U.S. economy made by the U.S. Department of Commerce stated that the tourism industry produces 13.4 percent of the nation's GNP, employs 11 million people, and generates more than $50 billion in tax revenues.

International travel, according to the World Tourism Organization, is expected to reach 935 million people by the year 2010, nearly double the 500 million people who traveled abroad in 1993, and up from the 25 million international tourists in 1950 (*The WTTC Report—1992 Complete Edition: Travel and Tourism*, London, United Kingdom, 1992).

DEFINITIONS OF TOURISM

Tourism, an umbrella concept, has a history dating back to 1811, or before, and continues to change in definition. The term tourism encompasses travelers away from home and the businesses and people who serve them by expediting or otherwise making the travel easier or more entertaining. A traveler is variously defined as someone a specified distance (the distances vary) away from home.

Tourism economics measures the amount of travel and its economic consequences, direct, indirect, and induced. Definitions and methods of collecting travel information vary considerably and are evolving.

Tourism has several dimensions other than economic, among them the complex of interactions and their consequences that occur before, during, and after a tourist trip. There are also psychological, sociological, ecological, and political travel impacts. This book deals with the economic complexities of tourism, including travel forecasting, tourism spending, and the costs and benefits for the bigger travel suppliers (the micro level), and countries and governments (the macro level). Figure 1-1 shows some of the parts of the tourism business.

Job descriptions are available for many of the businesses included under the tour-

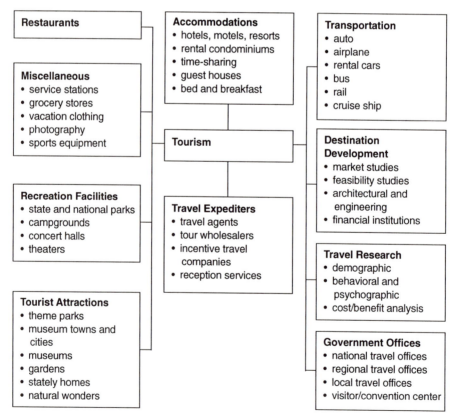

Figure 1-1 The Tourism Business

ism rubric. In 1994 the Council on Hotel, Restaurant and Institutional Education (CHRIE), along with the Convocation of National Hospitality and Tourism Association, published 117 model position descriptions that include hotel and restaurant jobs plus a few other from the field of tourism. A sample of the management jobs found in tourism and the qualifications needed to fill them are shown in the Appendix to this chapter (CHRIE, *Model Position Descriptions for the Hospitality and Tourism Industry*, Washington, DC, 1994).

Tourism as a concept can be viewed from different perspectives. It is an activity in which people are engaged in travel away from home primarily for business or pleasure. It is a business providing goods and services to travelers, and involves any expenditure incurred by or for a visitor for his or her trip. Tourism is an overarching business comprising hundreds of component businesses, some huge but mostly small businesses, including airlines, cruise lines, railroads, rental car agencies, travel marketers and expediters, lodging, restaurants, and convention centers. There are also travel reception services, commercial campgrounds, and parts of retail shops, food stores, and gas stations.

Government has the function of taxing, regulating, and promoting tourism. As governments see the potential for tourism income, economic models and cost/benefit studies are used as a means of forecasting economic impact in communities, states, and regions. The tourist dollar is tracked as it is spent and re-spent in a destination and treated as an export because it is a dollar entering the economy, similar to other exports. As it circulates within an economy its effect is increased and an income multiplier is calculated. Similarly, the impact of the tourist dollar on taxes and employment is estimated.

Tourism can be viewed as an institution with millions of interactions taking place, an institution with a history, body of knowledge, and a constituency of millions of people who feel themselves a part of the institution. For purposes of this book, tourism is an economic activity involving billions of dollars exchanged each month, a social science to be analyzed, trends to be identified, and costs/benefits to be computed.

Today's dictionaries defining tourism are about as much help as that of a nineteenth-century dictionary that defined tourists as "people who travel for the pleasure of traveling, out of curiosity, and because they have nothing better to do," and even "for the joy of boasting about it afterwards" (Gilbert Sigaux, "The History of Tourism," *Dictionnaire Universel du XIXe Siècle*, Geneva, Switzerland: Edito Service Ltd., 1876).

Webster's dictionary continues to limit tourism to the practice of traveling for recreation: "The guidance of management of tourists," "the promotion or encouragement of touring," and "the accommodation of tourists."

Tourist and traveler are virtually the same in the U.S. government's lexicon: anyone who stays more than 24 hours, or makes an overnight stay, away from home. There are some exceptions: Military travel, resident students, resident student immigrants, diplomats, and people working away from home are not regarded as tourists.

Some governmental agencies and researchers may define the tourist somewhat differently. The U.S. Census Bureau defines a trip as "each time a person goes to a place at least 100 miles away from home and returns." The overnight stay is not necessarily a part of the "trip." Statistics Canada, a Canadian government organization, defines a tourist as one who travels away from his or her home for a distance of at least 50 miles beyond the boundary of his or her community. Persons who make border crossings are counted as tourists by some national governments.

Tourism became a significant international item of trade in parts of Europe as early as the 1900s. Before World War I, Switzerland was receiving as many as a half million visitors a year. By 1929, Austria was believed to be receiving about 2 million visitors a year and Italy about 1¼ million. Switzerland was attracting about 1½ million a year (A.J. Burkhart and S. Medlik, *Tourism, Past, Present, and Future*, 1974, p. 71).

According to John M. Bryden (*Tourism and Development*, Cambridge University Press, 1973), the first examination in English of the significance of tourism on a cross-country basis was probably written in 1933. One Italian study appeared as early as 1899. The U.S. Department of Commerce published "The Promotion of Tourist Travel by Foreign Countries" in 1931 (Trade Promotion Series No. 113).

International travel statistics were collected on a worldwide basis in 1947 by the International Union of Official Travel Organizations (IUOTO). This resulted in a publication, *Digest of Tourist Statistics*, a collection of national statistics of tourist arrivals and travel payments of some forty countries. Three years later a permanent IUOTO research commission to study and recommend improvements in statistical methods was established.

In 1961 what had been the Organization for European Economic Co-operation and Development became the Organization for Economic Cooperation and Development (OECD). The OECD has a tourism committee responsible for coordinating studies, organizing meetings of member countries to improve statistical methods of monetary exchange and accounting, and assessing the policies of member countries and their impact upon tourism.

Dozens of types of businesses are tourist-related. Those considered most central include public transportation: airlines, rental car companies, cruise lines, passenger railroads, and motorcoaches. Hotels, convention centers, and other public lodging are included. Other examples are businesses that arrange and expedite travel such as travel agencies and tour operators, and public attractions such as national parks and theme parks that provide entertainment for visitors. Many other businesses share in tourism. Restaurants are an example. Like dozens of other businesses, they serve the traveler as well as others, the percentage of travelers varying according to the restaurant's location.

Though tourism as an industry is made up of hundreds of businesses, integration and concentration is taking place in some sectors via ownership, cross-ownership, marketing agreements, and franchising. Several airlines own all or parts of tour companies in Europe. Some airlines are cross-owned and a number of airlines own part or all of hotel chains. British Airways is an example of an airline engaged in several tourism ventures. British Airways Holidays Ltd., Atla Holidays Ltd., and British Airlines Ltd. are all owned by British Air. So is the Sovereign Group Hotels Ltd., Kenya Safari Lodge & Hotels Ltd., Pegasus Hotel of Jamaica Ltd., and Penta Hotels and Sun Resorts Ltd. in Mauritius. Thompson Corporation includes tour operators, travel agents, and a charter airline. Alitalia owns a large share of a tour operator. Air France owns two tour operators and the hotel chain, Société des Hotels Meridien.

The Carlson Travel Group (Minneapolis) is an example of the synergism possible between tourism segments. It spreads a wide business net as it owns, franchises or manages for a fee a number of travel/tourism businesses including hotels, restaurants, travel agencies and cruise ships. The company owns or franchises some 4000 travel agency locations found in 25 countries. Carlson Travel Academies train travel employees.

Radisson Hotels International, Colony Hotels and Resorts, and Country Hospitality Inns represent Carlson's lodging group. TGI Friday's restaurants and the Country Kitchens are another sizeable tourism segment. Incentive travel produces complete travel packages for corporations to award sales winners, packages that include travel arrangements, entertainment, and meeting planning. Carlson Tours create and market short-stay travel packages to Europe and the Caribbean.

Necessarily the definition of tourism will continue to be imprecise because so many businesses, governments, and researchers are involved, and because of the rapid changes taking place in the travel world. The economic impact of tourism is only beginning to be seen. The automobile industry, for example, has a tremendous stake in tourism, but just what percentage of General Motors sales is attributable to tourism is not known. The same unknowns can be applied to a camera and film company like Eastman Kodak, a maker of sunblock lotion, a sporting goods manufacturer, and hundreds of other companies whose products are economic components of tourism. It has been estimated that more than a million businesses in the U.S. are in some way part of tourism. Some, like the Boeing Company and other airlines, are high profile. Others, like many motor coach tour companies, are less well known. Large hotels are obvious big-time players. Thousands of motels, travel agencies, bed-and-breakfast homes serve travelers but each employ relatively few people.

Tourism economic analysis is somewhat limited by the reliability and validity of the numbers developed by primary research, be they collected privately or by government. Tourism definitions and sampling techniques for collecting data are variables liable to induce errors. Tourism statistics typically appear as numbers of arrivals, expenditures, and tourist nights. International arrivals and receipts are usually treated separately from those generated by travel within a resident's own country (domestic travel). Considerable economic data is collected by private organizations and is proprietary.

John Latham, a specialist in tourism statistics, characterizes them as being estimates, subject to several errors and produced with differing levels of accuracy. Sources or estimates of errors are rarely given in reporting tourism statistics. The cost of collecting large samples is prohibitive for most large-scale tourism economic studies, making the results of economic analysis less than precise (John Latham, "Statistical Measurement of Tourism." In C. P. Cooper, editor, *Progress in Tourism Recreation and Hospitality Management*, New York: Belhaven Press, 1989).

Tourism statistics are fraught with problems of definition partly because tourism is a composite industry, made up of several other industries. The temptation for tourism directors and others is to state that tourism is responsible for so many dollars of income and give it a rank and compare it with other industries such as automobiles, agriculture, petroleum, or chemicals.

The California Office of Tourism employs outside contractors to estimate tourism income for the state. Their estimate exceeds $60 billion a year, but the Office of Tourism wisely refrains from calling tourism the number one industry in the state because tourism estimates are composite figures, aggregates drawn from several other businesses, some of which are parts of other businesses. Some parts, the hotel industry, for example, are obviously businesses serving travelers; the restaurant business, however, serves both travelers and non-travelers; non-travelers contributing the most to sales. Parts of gasoline sales are made to tourists, however defined.

Food store spending by visitors is difficult to identify and tabulate. How much money is spent by visitors for sporting goods, vacation clothing, and a long list of sundries and gifts for friends back home? The fragmented nature of tourism tends to reduce public recognition of its enormous importance.

THE SCOPE AND MAGNITUDE OF TOURISM ECONOMICS

Tourism, says the U.S. Travel and Tourism Administration, is the nation's third largest retail industry, following food stores and automotive dealers. As the nation's largest private employer, it accounted for $641 billion in receipts from domestic travel and international arrivals in 1992. In 1989 tourism became the United States' largest export industry and, according to the U.S. Commerce Department, will increase 75 percent by the year 2000. The United States experienced a travel surplus in 1992, $20 billion more were spent by visitors to the United States than was spent by U.S. citizens traveling outside the country. The dollar amounts in 1992 were huge: $50.8 billion spent by U.S. citizens on foreign travel; $71.2 billion spent by foreign visitors to the United States. Germany, Japan, and the United Kingdom have had the largest travel deficits for several years. Austria, France, Greece, Spain, Portugal, Italy, Turkey, and Switzerland exhibit sizable travel surpluses.

Tourism receipts from international visitors (those staying overnight) are published annually by the World Tourism Organization. The 1992 world total (excluding international transport) was $278.7 billion as seen in Figure 1-2.

The United States has been the largest recipient of tourist travel income for several years, and will probably continue to be, receiving more than twice as much in international tourism income as its nearest competitor, France. Tourism continues to be America's biggest service export (*Travel Industry World Yearbook, 1993*). Figure 1-3 shows U.S. international tourism receipts and payments for the period 1985–1992.

The United States spends the most tourist dollars abroad, followed by Germany, Japan, the United Kingdom, Italy, and France. The top tourism spenders as reported by the World Tourism Organization for 1992 are seen in Figure 1-4. The U.S. international tourism receipts shown in Figure 1-2, and tourism payments shown in Figure 1-3, are not identical to the 1992 travel receipts and payments shown in Figure 1-4 since they are taken from two different sources. Different reporting agencies, as explained earlier, do not necessarily use the same data collection methods.

The Europeans and the Japanese continue to be the big travel spenders in the United States as seen in Figure 1-5.

Figure 1-6 shows the U.S. international tourism receipts and payments by country or region. The far right column indicates the total travel balance (positive or negative) for the United States compared to these countries or regions. It can be seen that here, too, the largest positive balance is with Europe and Japan. The U.S. Travel and Tour-

International Tourism Receipts (excluding international transport)

Rank 1992	Country	Millions of Current U.S. Dollars 1992	Average Annual Growth Rate % 1980/92	Share of World Total (%) 1992
1	United States	$49,000	14.11%	17.58%
2	France	22,190	8.61	7.96
3	Spain	21,035	9.64	7.55
4	Italy	20,013	7.70	7.18
5	Austria	14,804	7.18	5.31
6	UK	13,600	5.83	4.88
7	Germany	11,100	4.47	3.98
8	Switzerland	7,590	7.61	2.72
9	Singapore	5,782	12.33	2.07
10	Canada	5,750	8.00	2.06
11	Hong Kong	5,275	12.26	1.89
12	Netherlands	4,967	9.52	1.78
13	Mexico	4,550	0.99	1.63
14	Australia	4,230	13.09	1.52
15	Thailand	4,057	13.72	1.46
World Total		$278,705	8.74%	100.00%

Source: World Tourism Organization

Figure 1-2 World's Top Tourism Earners, 1992

ism Administration expected a record 47 million international arrivals in the United States in 1994 and they would spend $80 billion. The 42.7 million international arrivals in 1991 were broken down as follows: Canadians (18.9 million), Mexicans (7.6 million), and overseas (16.2 million). Overseas visitors do not, by definition, include Canadian and Mexican nationals.

New York City received almost a quarter of the 17.2 million overseas visitors in 1992, followed by Los Angeles, Orlando (home of Disney World), Miami, San Francisco, Honolulu, Washington, DC, and Las Vegas.

The economic impact to the United States as a result of international visitors' spending varies widely depending on the spending habits of the visitor and length of stay. The Japanese are big spenders per capita partly because of their custom of returning home with gifts for friends and relatives.

Tourism Income and Impact Studies

Child & Waters estimate tourism spending in their annual *Travel Industry World Yearbook* (Child & Waters, Inc., New York City) and break out the amounts of income generated for total taxes, federal taxes, state and local taxes. Their totals include trips to places more than twenty-five miles from home. Foreign visitor spending is included. Estimates for the years 1988–2000 are seen in Figure 1-7.

Per capita income and the amount of travel undertaken within a country and travel abroad are correlated with the gross national product. The correlation is not perfect because travel propensity is partly cultural, partly a result of a country's location, and partly based on its wealth. On a per capita basis, international travel by Scandina-

U.S. International Tourism Receipts and Payments Trend Analysis, 1985–1992

	1985	1986	1987	1988	1989	1990	1991	1992
Tourism Trade								
Balance ($mil)	($8,829)	($6,450)	($6,027)	($1,434)	$5,197	$10,426	$18,904	$20,399
% Change	19.2%	26.9%	6.6%	76.2%	—	100.6%	81.3%	7.9%
Receipts								
Total ($mil)	$22,173	$25,967	$30,566	$38,409	$46,863	$58,305	$64,237	$71,214
% Change	4.4%	17.1%	17.7%	25.7%	22.0%	24.4%	10.2%	10.9%
Travel ($mil)	$17,762	$20,385	$23,563	$29,434	$36,250	$43,007	$48,384	$53,861
% Change	3.4%	14.8%	15.6%	24.9%	23.2%	18.6%	12.5%	11.3%
Transportation ($mil)	$4,411	$5,582	$7,003	$8,976	$10,613	$15,298	$15,854	$17,353
% Change	8.5%	26.5%	25.5%	28.2%	18.2%	44.1%	3.6%	9.5%
Payments								
Total ($mil)	$31,002	$32,418	$36,593	$39,843	$41,666	$47,879	$45,334	$50,815
% Change	8.2%	4.6%	12.9%	8.9%	4.6%	14.9%	−5.3%	12.1%
Travel ($mil)	$24,558	$25,913	$29,310	$32,114	$33,418	$37,349	$35,322	$39,872
% Change	7.2%	5.5%	13.1%	9.6%	4.1%	11.8%	−5.4%	12.9%
Transportation ($mil)	$6,444	$6,505	$7,283	$7,729	$8,248	$10,530	$10,012	$10,943
% Change	12.4%	0.9%	12.0%	6.1%	6.7%	27.7%	−4.9%	9.3%

Travel (Receipts) equal spending by international visitors in the U.S. on travel-related expenses, i.e., lodging, food, entertainment, etc.

Transportation (Receipts) equal spending by international visitors traveling to the U.S. on U.S. flag carriers, and other misc. transportation.

Travel (Payments) equal spending by U.S. citizens outside the U.S. on travel-related expenses, i.e., lodging, food, entertainment, etc.

Transportation (Payments) equal spending by U.S. citizens traveling outside the U.S. on foreign flag carriers, and other misc. transportation.

Source: U.S. Travel & Tourism Administration.

Figure 1-3 U.S. International Tourism Receipts and Payments Trend Analysis, 1985–1992

International Tourism Payments (excluding international transport)

Rank 1992	Country	Millions of Current U.S. Dollars 1992	Average Annual Growth Rate % 1980/92	Share of World Total (%) 1992
1	United States	$43,684	12.72%	16.19%
2	Germany	37,166	5.04	13.77
3	Japan	26,982	15.90	10.00
4	UK	19,485	9.05	7.22
5	Italy	16,200	19.52	6.00
6	France	13,866	7.19	5.14
7	Canada	11,617	11.57	4.31
8	Netherlands	9,277	5.85	3.42
9	Austria	8,341	9.37	3.09
10	Belgium	6,700	6.15	2.48
11	Sweden	6,270	14.50	2.32
12	Switzerland	6,111	8.26	2.26
13	Taiwan	6,075	18.19	2.25
14	Spain	4,749	11.92	1.76
15	Australia	4,037	7.22	1.50
World Total		$269,825	8.61%	100.00%

Source: World Tourism Organization

Figure 1-4 World's Top Tourism Spenders, 1992

vians, the British, and the Dutch is much higher than for North Americans. New Zealanders and Australians undertake international travel more than their per capita gross national product would suggest. Travel, as determined simply by the number of border crossings, is much higher in Europe (with its many countries). It is interesting to note, however, that the countries with the highest per capita GNP all show high travel propensities. The top ten per capita GNPs of the world for 1992 were:

Switzerland	$33,510
Luxembourg	31,080
Japan	26,920
Sweden	25,490
Finland	24,400
Norway	24,160
Denmark	23,660
Germany	23,650
United States	22,650
Iceland	22,580

(United Nations data)

The citizens of all of these countries are known for their high rate of travel. Coincidentally, these countries also have the highest life expectancy at birth, all above 76 years, except Denmark and Luxembourg, at 75 years.

Because of the different definitions used, and the question of whether or not to include the indirect spending effects of tourism, it is difficult to arrive at a total spend-

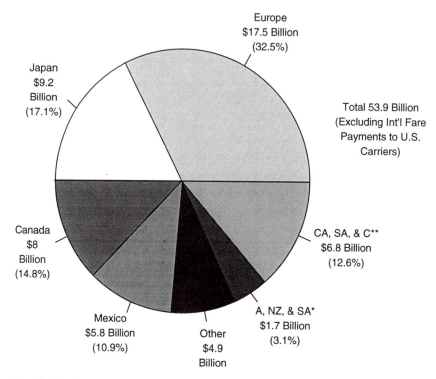

Europe
$17.5 Billion
(32.5%)

Japan
$9.2
Billion
(17.1%)

Total 53.9 Billion
(Excluding Int'l Fare
Payments to U.S.
Carriers)

Canada
$8
Billion
(14.8%)

CA, SA, & C**
$6.8 Billion
(12.6%)

Mexico
$5.8 Billion
(10.9%)

Other
$4.9
Billion

A, NZ, & SA*
$1.7 Billion
(3.1%)

*Australia, New Zealand, & South Africa
**Central America, South Africa, & Caribbean
Source: U.S. Travel & Tourism Administration

Figure 1-5 Sources of U.S. International Travel Receipts, 1992 Revised

ing figure. The U.S. Travel Data Center, using an economic impact model, reported that for 1989 direct and indirect spending for the United States totaled $632.4 billion. This spending produced $186.5 billion in wages and earnings and supported 10.7 million jobs. Taxes generated by tourism exceeded $41 billion. As enormous as these figures are, Somerset R. Waters, who has tracked tourism for a number of years, believes the Travel Data Center underestimates the impact of tourism spending in the United States because it excludes much of the spending for short-haul day trips to cities and resorts outside the travelers' home communities (Somerset R. Waters, *Travel Industry World Yearbook*, 1993).

U.S. Domestic Tourism Income

Nearly every state publishes its own tourism impact study. California, for example, reports that its tourism income exceeds $80 billion a year. The state of New York estimates its tourism income by in-state and out-of-state travelers at $38.0 billion. For 1990 Florida estimated that spending by in-state and out-of-state travelers reached

U.S. International Tourism Receipts and Payments

Country/Region	International Travel Receipts	International Transportation Receipts	Total Tourism Receipts	% Change 1992/1991	International Travel Payments	International Transportation Payments	Total Tourism Payments	% Change 1992/1991	Total Tourism Balance
Europe	17,532.4	6,567.2	24,099.6	18.9%	13,689.0	5,577.0	19,266.0	16.1%	14,311.8
Japan	9,159.5	4,559.1	13,718.6	7.5%	3,160.0	558.0	3,718.0	12.3%	10,000.6
Canada	7,974.8	1,306.0	9,280.8	-2.7%	3,507.4	275.2	3,782.6	-4.3%	5,498.2
Central America, South America & Caribbean	6,821.8	2,180.0	9,001.8	13.5%	3,553.0	1,542.0	5,095.0	15.7%	3,906.8
Mexico	5,821.9	554.5	6,376.4	8.4%	5,228.9	558.5	5,787.4	2.6%	589.0
Australia, New Zealand & South Africa	1,664.3	873.9	2,538.2	5.2%	1,186.0	429.0	1,615.0	4.7%	923.2
Other	4,885.9	1,312.7	6,198.6	14.0%	5,656.0	2,003.0	7,659.0	12.2%	(1,460.4)
Grand Total	53,860.6	17,353.4	71,214.0	10.9%	39,872.3	10,942.7	50,815.0	12.1%	20,399.0

Source: U.S. Travel & Tourism Administration, Bureau of Economic Analysis, 6/30/93

Figure 1-6 U.S. International Tourism Receipts and Payments by Country/Region, 1992 Revised (millions of dollars)

Estimates of Economic Impact of Tourism Spending in United States (Based on domestic trips to places more than 25 miles from home plus foreign visitor spending)

	1988	1990	1995	2000
Total Tourism Spending in the United States (billions of current dollars)	$579	$671	$973	$1,407
Total Tourism Spending in the United States (billions of 1988 dollars)	$579	$616	$721	$845
Total Taxes Generated (billions of current dollars)	$67.8	$78.6	$113.9	$165.0
Federal Taxes Generated (billions of current dollars)	$35.9	$41.6	$60.3	$87.4
State Taxes Generated (billions of current dollars)	$23.1	$26.8	$38.8	$56.2
Local Taxes Generated (billions of current dollars)	$8.8	$10.2	$14.8	$21.4

Source: Child & Waters, Inc., New York

Figure 1-7 Estimates of Economic Impact of Tourism Spending in the United States

$51.8 billion, an amount that generated about 1.5 million jobs and accounted for 24 percent of the state's civilian labor force. Texas was number four in tourism receipts for 1990 at $33.3 billion.

The *Travel Industry World Yearbook* for 1993 lists tourism spending by state for 1990, shown in Figure 1-8.

In 1990 tourism spending in Illinois generated, directly or indirectly, 644,000 jobs amounting to 11.2 percent of the state's civilian labor force. The Illinois Department of Tourism reports that tourism is the state's largest industry and accounted for $23 billion in spending. Tourism is Hawaii's biggest industry: With a population of about one million, its tourism income is estimated by the Bank of Hawaii for 1991 to have been $9.95 billion, on a per capita basis probably the highest in the world.

The annual economic impact studies made by the Office of Tourism, California Trade and Commerce Agency, include the travel definitions used, a breakdown of spending by business type, and spending by traveler type. California divides spending by type of business into eight categories:

Retail shopping
Restaurants
Lodging
Recreation
Ground transport
Food stores
Air transport
Travel arrangement

Domestic Tourism Spending in United States for Trips over 25 Miles from Home—1990

Date	Tourism Spending in State ($billions)	Rank
Alabama	$6.90	27
Alaska	2.30	45
Arizona	9.77	19
Arkansas	4.60	36
California	79.93	1
Colorado	10.35	18
Connecticut	6.33	29
Delaware	1.73	48
Florida	51.75	2
Georgia	15.53	11
Hawaii	11.50	16
Idaho	2.30	41
Illinois	23.00	5
Indiana	7.48	26
Iowa	5.18	33
Kansas	4.60	34
Kentucky	6.33	30
Louisiana	8.63	22
Maine	2.88	40
Maryland	8.63	21
Massachusetts	12.65	14
Michigan	13.23	12
Minnesota	7.48	25
Mississippi	4.03	38
Missouri	10.93	17
Montana	2.30	42
Nebraska	2.88	39
Nevada	21.85	6
New Hampshire	2.30	44
New Jersey	19.55	7
New Mexico	4.60	37
New York	37.95	3
North Carolina	13.23	13
North Dakota	1.73	49
Ohio	15.53	10
Oklahoma	5.18	32
Oregon	6.33	28
Pennsylvania	17.83	8
Rhode Island	1.15	51
South Carolina	8.63	23
South Dakota	1.73	50
Tennessee	11.50	15
Texas	33.35	4
Utah	4.60	35
Vermont	1.73	47
Virginia	16.10	9
Washington D.C.*	5.75	31
Washington	9.20	20
West Virginia	2.30	43
Wisconsin	8.05	24
Wyoming	1.73	46
Total	$574.00	

Note: Foreign visitors spent $40 billion in the U.S. in 1990, bringing total tourism spending in the U.S. to $615 billion.

*Metropolitan Area

Source: Travel Industry World Yearbook—The Big Picture

Figure 1-8   Domestic Tourism Spending in United States for Trips over 25 Miles from Home—1990

Travelers are divided into five groups:

Hotel, motel guests
Day visitors
Private home guests
Vacation home guests
Campers

Travel expenditures are drawn from a number of sources: local hotel occupancy tax, estimates reported in a number of visitor studies, local visitor surveys, data from the U.S. Bureau of Census and the California Department of Finance, studies of campers, weekend vehicle miles traveled on California highways, and the consumer price index. Data from the Air Transport Association is used to estimate passenger revenues for California as a share of total U.S. commercial airline receipts.

The California tourist spending study estimated payroll as 32 percent of receipts for travel arrangement businesses. Air transport, hotels and motels, and recreation businesses each spent 28 percent of income on payroll. Payroll costs for restaurants were estimated at 26 percent of sales. For commercial campgrounds the figure was 19 percent. Payrolls for retail shopping stores were figured at 14 percent; car rentals at 14 percent; food stores at 11 percent; and gas stations at 6 percent. See Figure 1-9 for the words and phrases used in reports of the California Office of Tourism.

Economic studies done for other states have set up different categories. For its study of economic multipliers Hawaii used thirty-seven tourist-related consumption categories.

The reader of studies in tourism economics is entitled to know how and where the data were collected. Tourism impact studies develop annual estimates based on face-to-face surveys, household telephone surveys, and secondary visitor data such as hotel occupancy rates, hotel room inventory, attraction attendance, and population. Visitors are categorized by type of accommodation: hotel/motel, private home guests, other overnight and day visitors.

Occupancy and room rates are published monthly in most cities. Visitor surveys are conducted monthly to gather information on the average party size, length of stay, and spending. Combining this information gives the formula for estimating hotel/motel visitors to an area or city.

To learn how many guests stayed in private homes over a given period, random telephone surveys are made. A certain percentage of the households typically have visits from at least one overnight guest group. That percentage times the number of groups per household, times the number of people per group, times the average spent per private home guest, gives the dollar estimate spent per month by the visitors.

TOURISM IN DEVELOPING COUNTRIES

About three-fourths of the world's 5.6 billion people live in developing countries, about 38 percent of them in China and India. Tourism is just now becoming a major

The following words and phrases have specific meaning when used within this report.

Air Transport. Air passenger spending attributable to travelers in and to California. The spending total includes air travel spending made outside California, purchases by Californians who travel outside the state, and air travel within the state.

Campers. Travelers staying at **RV** parks and commercial campgrounds, or at public campgrounds such as those in national parks and national forests.

Day Visitor. A traveler whose trip does not include any overnight stay.

Destination Spending. Spending by travelers at or near their destinations.

Food Stores. Grocery stores, supermarkets, fruit stands, retail bakeries, and other businesses selling food for consumption off the premises.

Ground Transport. Spending on car rentals, gasoline, and other vehicle operating expenses.

Hotel and Motel Guests. Travelers staying in hotels, motels, and cabins at resorts where the Transient Occupancy Tax is collected.

Hotel Tax. A local tax charged on lodging. Also referred to as the Transient Occupancy Tax or Bed Tax.

Jobs. Industry employment generated from travel spending.

Local Tax Receipts. Hotel tax and local sales tax revenues accruing to cities and counties as a result of traveler spending.

Lodging. Spending for accommodations by hotel and motel guests, campers, and vacation home users.

Payroll. Wages and salaries resulting from traveler spending. Does not include partnership or proprietors' income.

Private Home Guests. Travelers staying as guests with friends or relatives and not incurring a lodging expense.

Recreation. Spending on amusement and recreation, such as admissions to tourist attractions (Referred to as Entertainment in prior reports).

Restaurants. Business serving prepared food and drinks for immediate consumption. In addition to table service restaurants, this category includes fast-food outlets and refreshment stands.

Retail Shopping. Spending for gifts, souvenirs, and other items. Excludes spending listed separately, such as food stores or recreation.

Spending Distribution. Information from visitor surveys showing how spending by each type of traveler is divided between various business categories.

State Tax Receipts. The state corporate and personal income tax resulting from traveler spending, as well as the state share of the sales tax.

Travel. A day or overnight trip that is not of a local or commuting nature. Travel may be for business or pleasure.

Travel Arrangement. Spending for fees paid to travel agents and tour operators.

Traveler. A person traveling in California. The traveler may be a California resident, or a resident of another state or country. The terms traveler and visitor have the same meaning in this report.

Vacation Home Users. Travelers using their own vacation homes or renting vacation homes, condominiums, or privately owned cabins where Transient Occupancy Tax is not collected.

Source: California Travel, Its Economic Impact, California Trade and Commerce Agency, Nov. 1992.

Figure 1-9 Travel Terms Used by California Office of Tourism

factor in places like China and much of South America. The brightest prospects for tourism are found in the developing world, according to one knowledgeable travel analyst. Asia's economy in 1993 was expected to grow 6.6 percent; the Middle East's at about 4.4 percent; and Africa's about 3.3 percent. During the first half of 1993, the People's Republic of China showed a tourism growth of 14 percent, the world's fastest (Somerset R. Waters, *Travel Industry World Yearbook 1993*, New York, 1993).

Put in perspective, these figures are comparatively small. The World Tourism Organization estimated that Africa gets about 4 percent of the world's arrivals and 2 percent of the world's total tourism receipts. South Asia gets only 1 percent of the world's receipts and 1 percent of the arrivals. The Middle East has about 2 percent of the world's arrivals and 2 percent of the receipts. All of South America in 1993 received 9.8 million international visitors who spent $6.4 billion (much less than that received in 1993 in Hawaii for visitors).

With a few exceptions, Africa's fifty countries and 650 million people are desperately poor. Egypt, which was a bright spot touristically, is plagued by a group of Islamic militants whose avowed purpose is to cripple Egypt's tourist business. Much of Africa, especially West Africa, experiences a high incidence of malaria, foodborne and other diseases, decided deterrents to tourism. Political and police corruption in many countries interfere with or block investment. Several African countries have only one or a few good hotels, often overpriced.

Travel distance and cost dissuade travel to South America from North American and European markets, and compared to the many architectural and other cultural attractions of Europe and North America, South American and African attractions are minimal. Domestic travel within South America, however, is growing rapidly.

For those who seek a tropical climate, the Caribbean region and Hawaii are more appealing and safer. Hawaii receives almost 7 million visitors and over $9 billion in tourist receipts each year.

The less developed countries rely heavily on loans or grants from world funds to develop tourism facilities and for foreign expertise to develop and manage tourist enterprises such as hotels and tour operations. Kenya is an example: A Swiss grant helped build the government hotel school.

International hotel chains are eager to operate first-class hotels in developing countries as long as their investment and risk are minimal. The hotel owners, government or private, need the marketing expertise and the chain affiliation to be successful in attracting the potential traveler. For international investors in tourism facilities for developing countries the risk is high. Transnational airlines, hotel chains, and tour companies are reluctant to take more than small equity positions in tourism ventures, and many will not get involved without up-front investment by the nationals or their governments. Even with carefully drawn management contracts there are problems. Work permits for experienced expatriates who are needed to manage hotels are difficult to obtain. Repatriation of profits may be difficult. Unwarranted political influence can be a problem. In several developing countries, including Russia, two employees are needed to perform the work of one elsewhere. In many countries payoffs and bribery are necessary to stay in business. As a rule, management contracts to operate hotels call for 3 to 6 percent of gross income as a management fee.

CHAPTER 1: APPENDIX

Sample Position Descriptions

POSITION TITLE   RESTAURANT MANAGER (FULL SERVICE)

REPORTS TO: Owner/District Manager

POSITION SUMMARY: Coordinates foodservice activities of restaurant, or other similar establishment. Estimates food and beverage costs and requisitions or purchases supplies, equipment, and food and beverages. Confers with food preparation and other personnel from the dining room, bar, and banquet team to plan menus and related activities. Oversees cleaning and maintenance of equipment and facilities and ensures that all health and safety regulations are adhered to. Directs hiring, assignment, training, motivation, and termination of personnel. Investigates and resolves food quality and services complaints. May develop marketing strategy and implement advertising and promotional campaigns to increase business. May review financial transactions and monitor budget to ensure efficient operation and to ensure expenditures stay within budget limitations.

TASKS:
- Periodically meets with food production, dining room, bar, and banquet personnel to plan menus and related activities, plan special events, share information, etc.
- Estimates food and beverage needs and requisitions or purchases produce, meats, poultry, fish and seafood, supplies, beverages, and equipment. Receives and checks orders to ensure that they adhere to specifications.
- Supervises inventories and estimates food and beverage costs. May use computer to facilitate collection and analysis of information.
- Directs hiring, assignment, training, motivation, evaluation, and termination of personnel.
- Investigates and resolves food quality and services complaints.
- Inspects dining room, food receiving, preparation, production, and storage areas to ensure that health and safety regulations are adhered to at all times.
- May be responsible for developing marketing strategy and for implementing advertising and promotional campaigns.
- May review financial information such as sales and costs and monitors budget to ensure efficient operation and that expenditures stay within budget limitations. Takes action to correct any deviations from the budget. May use computer for review and analysis of information.

PREREQUISITES:

Education: Two (2) year associate's degree or a bachelor's degree from a four (4) year college desirable. Must be able to speak, read, write, and understand the primary language(s) of the work location.

Experience: Knowledge of service and food and beverage, generally involving a minimum of three (3) years in front-of-the-house operations as a food server, host-hostess, or dining room manager.

Physical: Must be able to exert well-paced mobility for periods of up to four (4) hours in length and have the ability to lift 10 pounds frequently and up to 50 pounds occasionally. Must have the stamina to work a minimum of 50 to 60 hours a week.

Source: CHRIE, *Model Position Descriptions for the Hospitality and Tourism Industry,* Washington, DC, 1994

POSITION TITLE: HOTEL GENERAL MANAGER
REPORTS TO: Corporate Regional Manager/Corporate VP of Operations
POSITION SUMMARY: Oversees all aspects of property management in accordance with corporate mission statement including maximization of financial performance, guest satisfaction, and staff development.

TASKS:

- Achieves budgeted sales and maximum profitability.
- Actively manages the financial statement, reviews and critiques performance in a timely fashion. Teaches the process to all members of the management team.
- Assesses and reviews the job performance of subordinates and maintains personnel records of assigned employees.
- Closely monitors solicitation and booking activity through the sales activity reporting process and periodical spot checks.
- Communicates effectively within the property and with the Executive Offices.
- Coordinates internal training and development programs.
- Creates and maintains a "guest first" priority throughout the property.
- Creates new programs in response to market conditions and revenue opportunities.
- Develops a goal-oriented business plan to support the financial goals.
- Develops and supports the sales promotion plan in accordance with the Business Plan process.
- Develops accurate and aggressive long- and short-range financial objectives consistent with the company's mission statement.
- Ensures that effective cash and asset controls are in place throughout the property.
- Ensures good safety practices of employee and guests.
- Fully utilizes and follows through a guest comment programs.
- Responds quickly to deficiencies and takes corrective action.
- Ensures regular assessment and review of all hotel personnel by appropriate management staff.
- Maintains a high personal visibility throughout the property.
- Maintains an appropriate level of community public affairs involvement.
- Maintains knowledge of local competition and general industry trends.
- Maximizes sales potential of the property and the management company.

PREREQUISITES:

Education: College degree, Hotel/Restaurant Management preferably or in business management. Must be able to speak, read, write, and understand the primary language(s) used in the workplace. Must be able to speak and understand the primary language(s) used by guests who visit the workplace.
Experience: Previous hotel-related experience, minimum of three years experience as an assistant General Manager, budgetary and financial experience.
Physical: Requires fingering, grasping, writing, standing, sitting, walking, repetitive motions, hearing, visual acuity, and good verbal skills.

Source: CHRIE, *Model Position Descriptions for the Hospitality and Tourism Industry*, Washington, DC, 1994

POSITION TITLE: CONVENTION SALES MANAGER

REPORTS TO: Director of Convention Sales

POSITION SUMMARY: Markets destination and its meeting facilities to corporations, associations, and other organizations as a convention/meeting venue.

TASKS

- Represents destination in a professional manner to the clients and the public.
- Markets city as destination at trade shows and conventions.
- Assists in planning and implementing special projects: familiarization tours, site tours, and sales missions.
- Contacts clients and prospects by telemarketing, and in person.
- Prepares and conducts sales presentations.
- Assists with preparation of marketing plan and budget.
- Prepares activity reports as required.
- Responsible for achieving annual sales goals.
- Responsible for managing telemarketers and sales assistants.

PREREQUISITES:

Education: Two years of college and one year of convention sales experience or three years of progressive national sales experience.

Experience: Convention or hotel sales experience desired. Excellent verbal and written skills necessary.

Physical: Must be able to travel. Must be able to communicate clearly and effectively in written and verbal formats.

Source: CHRIE, *Model Position Descriptions for the Hospitality and Tourism Industry*, Washington, DC, 1994

POSITION TITLE: DIRECTOR OF COMMUNICATIONS CONVENTION AND
VISITORS BUREAU

REPORTS TO: President/CEO

POSITION SUMMARY: Oversees the operation of the division. The broad function of communications is to publicize the destination outside the city and publicize the bureau within the city. The division also has a department called visitor services, which disseminates information to visitors and potential visitors.

TASKS:

- Develops and administers communications division marketing plan and budget.
- Directs and supervises staff to work under deadline in the area for news releases and publications.
- Prepares and distributes news releases.
- Organizes committees for promotional and program campaigns.
- Organizes news conferences as appropriate.
- Maintains regular contact with local, regional, and national media.
- Assists with the writing of editorials for bureau publications.
- Evaluates and reports on program performance.
- Develops and conducts oral and written presentations to the board, clients, and prospects.
- Coordinates activities with other bureau division directors.
- Reviews, evaluates, and takes personnel actions with respect to division staff.
- Determines division physical, financial, and staff resource requirements.
- Analyzes and delegates work within division, and motivates staff to achieve established objectives.
- Provides statistical analysis of division production.

PREREQUISITES:

Education: Bachelor's degree in journalism and professional writing desired.
Experience: Experience in journalistic writing. Experience in supervisory or managerial role coupled with demonstrated organizational skills.
Physical: Must be able to travel. Must be able to speak clearly and effectively in both the written and verbal forms.

Source: CHRIE, *Model Position Descriptions for the Hospitality and Tourism Industry*, Washington, DC, 1994

POSITION TITLE: CONVENTION SERVICES MANAGER

REPORTS TO: Director of Convention Sales

POSITION SUMMARY: This position is the main point of contact for meeting planners after convention is booked, and remains the main point of contact for Convention Services (Housing Bureau, bussing, airport arrival coordination, collateral material, bonded registrar coordination, membership referrals, on-site assistance, etc.) throughout the actual convention.

TASKS

- Supervises the Convention Services Coordinator and Housing Bureau Assistant in their duties and responsibilities.
- Supervises volunteers and bonded registrars in duties and responsibilities.
- Provides continual coordination and contact with the Membership Division, members, and hotels aimed at servicing and accommodating meeting planners, exhibitors, and delegates.
- Maintains close contact and coordination with the Convention Center.
- Coordinates scheduling with other divisions to ensure proper convention planning and support.
- Plans bus routes, schedules, bussing costs, and supervision of actual bussing.
- Plans the annual budget for Convention Services Department.

PREREQUISITES:

Education: A bachelor's degree preferably in business administration or related field desired.

Experience: Ability to handle several accounts at once and anticipate client needs. Must have experience in management skills. Must have computer and word processing skills.

Physical: Must be able to travel. Must be able to speak clearly and effectively. Must be able to drive and lift boxes of material weighing up to 40 pounds.

Source: CHRIE, *Model Position Descriptions for the Hospitality and Tourism Industry*, Washington, DC, 1994

POSITION TITLE: DIRECTOR OF TOURISM CONVENTION AND VISITORS
                         BUREAU

REPORTS TO: President/CEO

POSITIONS SUMMARY: Directs the sales, administrative, and budgetary management
of the Tourism Division of the Convention and Visitors Bureau.

TASKS:

- Manages the direction and duties of tourism sales managers, executive secretary, and
  motivates staff to achieve established objectives.
- Develops and administers tourism division marketing plan and budget.
- Evaluates and reports on program performance.
- Acts as liaison with the state tourism division and local travel and tourism industry
  representatives.
- Coordinates all international travel trade department activities.
- Serves as liaison for travel writers.
- Travels to market destination at trade shows and conventions.
- Coordinates activities with other bureau division directors.
- Develops and conducts oral and written presentations to the board, clients, and prospects.
- Reviews, evaluates, and take personnel actions with respect to division staff.
- Determines division's physical, financial, and staff resource requirements.
- Analyzes and delegates work within division being mindful of changing work flows.
- Provides statistical analysis of divisions production.

PREREQUISITES:

Education: Bachelors degree in business/marketing or allied field desired.
Experience: Three to five years in a management capacity, preferably in a bureau or other
             tourism-related entity. Excellent written and verbal skills, and organizational
             abilities.
Physical: Must be able to travel. Must be able to communicate clearly and effectively in
             both written and verbal forms.

Source: CHRIE, *Model Position Descriptions for the Hospitality and Tourism Industry*, Washington,
DC, 1994

POSITION TITLE: PRESIDENT/CEO
                                  CONVENTION AND VISITORS BUREAU

REPORTS TO: Board of Directors*

POSITION SUMMARY: Directs all functions of the Bureau, including sales and marketing, services, tourism, public relations, governmental relations, membership, administration, and other operations.

TASKS:

- Oversees and manages the Bureau's budget.
- Oversees development of marketing plans and all related activities.
- Oversees all programs designed to attract visitors and conventions to the metropolitan area.
- Acts as a liaison to all public and private constituencies.
- Represents Bureau in press and media.
- Sets long-term organizational strategies.
- Leads and develops staff.
- Prepares and delivers reports to the Board of Directors and governmental officials.

PREREQUISITES:

Education: Bachelor's degree in business/marketing or allied field desired.

Experience: At least five years management-level experience in the convention and visitors bureau field of hospitality industry. Must have proven ability to supervise and manage staff effectively.

Physical: Must be able to travel. Must be able to communicate clearly and effectively, possessing excellent written and verbal skills. Must be able to undertake public speaking assignments.

*Some Bureaus are divisions of governmental entities or chambers of commerce. In these cases, reporting lines may vary.

Source: CHRIE, *Model Position Descriptions for the Hospitality and Tourism Industry*, Washington, DC, 1994

2

Economics as Applied
to Tourism

Modern economic thought originated with Adam Smith and his book *The Wealth of Nations* (1776). He presented the concepts of aggregate supply and demand, productivity growth over time, as well as the division of labor and the resultant increase in productivity due to specialization. Other important thoughts developed by Smith and his contemporaries included the theory of distribution of wealth and the importance of gold and the money supply in the determination of the price level.

French economist T.B. Say, in 1803, generated the idea of the circular flow of income known as Say's Law. His theory suggested that in the economy as a whole production generates exactly the right amount of income to allow people to pay for the sale of all of the goods that have been produced.

The neoclassical economists of the nineteenth century focused on microeconomic issues such as the behavior of firms, relative prices, consumer choice, and on other issues related to competitive markets. The ideas developed in this period continue to be used in economic analysis today.

Periods of prolonged unemployment in the late 1800s and early 1900s, combined with the impact of World War I, caused some large fluctuations in the economies of nations that led to new economic thinking.

Englishman John Maynard Keynes presented a new theory of aggregate demand in his 1936 book entitled *The General Theory of Employment, Interest and Money*. Inspired by the Great Depression of the 1930s in the industrialized world, Keynes suggested that increased government spending in the economy was necessary to support struggling economies, due to the lack of self-correcting mechanisms to stimulate aggregate demand. The Keynesian theories obtained considerable support during the post-World-War-II years as governments intervened successfully to moderate recessions and inflation, and keep unemployment levels low.

American Milton Friedman disputed Keynesian views in the early 1960s, arguing that monetary policy could be an effective tool to stabilize economies. Friedman suggested that governments could set stable rates of growth in the money supply, allowing sustained increases in gross national product (GNP), without excessive inflation or government spending adjustments. Friedman's opinions gained strength during the 1970s when a combination of high inflation and high unemployment, known as stagflation, appeared. Under Keynesian policies there was no explanation for stagflation, since higher price levels and output were supposed to create higher employment levels.

The inconsistencies created by stagflation inspired a new direction in economic thought related to the rational expectations of the population as a whole regarding future economic behavior. The assumption was that people do not work more when the government spends more, since the rational expectation is that any increase in wages will be matched by increases in the cost of goods. Hence, the government's increased spending only creates inflation of prices, and does not increase real output.

Although an explanation was given for the stagnation of the economy in the 1970s, the question remained how to bring about the desired increase in the level of real output. U.S. President Ronald Reagan's economic advisors suggested in 1980 that the problem was not only work effort, but also the U.S. tax system, which was biased against saving and investment. The policies for changing the system became known as supply-side economics.

The primary aspect of the supply-side program was a series of cuts in taxes: lower personal tax rates, saving and investment incentives, and a reduction in capital gains taxes. Other measures included regulatory reform in transportation, communications, and financial services, all designed to increase productivity and competition. The result was a strong economic recovery which lasted for most of Reagan's eight-year term in office. During this period and into the 1990s, the U.S. national debt soared to incredible levels, leaving economists perplexed and divided about economic theory and the role of government economic policies.

The more recent experience of recession, which became clear in 1990 and continued through 1992, has been blamed on a change in tax policy (higher personal and corporate taxes) and a continued massive deficit in the federal government's budget. Effecting and overarching economics are the emotional currents of such things as fear, greed, and the desire to dominate, which expresses itself in nationalism.

ECONOMICS DEFINED

Economics is usually defined in terms of scarcity, a situation in which there is not enough of something to meet everyone's wants. Hence, the study of economics has its basis not in money or wealth, but rather in people. Scarcity itself is a human phenomenon, since things do not become scarce until they become the object of human wants.

Economics, therefore, may be defined as a social science that seeks to understand the choices people make in using their scarce resources to meet their wants. The study of these choices are made in a social context. In the realm of tourism economics, one might ask why people choose to travel to one destination instead of another or to remain at home versus travel. Or, why does an individual make a decision to spend (invest) money for travel?

Microeconomics is the branch of economics that studies the choices of specific economic units, including hotel/motels, restaurants, airlines, and other tourism sectors. Macroeconomics is the branch of economics that studies large-scale economic phenomena, particularly aggregate tourist spending, the multiplier effect, and other macroeconomic effects of tourism. Both branches will be discussed in greater detail in subsequent chapters of this book.

Economic Choices

In every economy certain basic choices must be faced. Among these, the most important are what goods and services should be produced, how they should be produced, who should do which jobs, and for whom the results of economic activity should be made available. Each of these choices is made necessary because of scarcity.

In a modern economy the number of goods and services that can be produced is immense. The essential features of the choice of what goods and services to produce is traditionally illustrated using an economy in which as few as two alternatives exist, for example, travel and education. For many students, going without travel (or limiting travel) is a sacrifice that must be made in order to obtain a college education. The same trade-off that is faced by an individual student is also faced by an economy as a whole: Not enough travel services and education can be produced to meet everyone's wants. Someone must choose how much of each service to produce.

The factors of production are the basic inputs of labor, capital, and natural resources used in producing all goods and services. Each one of these resources is scarce. Labor is the contribution to production made by people working with their minds and bodies. Capital includes all the productive inputs created by people, including tools, industrial equipment, and structures. Natural resources include anything that can be used as a productive input in its natural state, such as arable land, water, mineral deposits, and forests.

Productive resources that are used to satisfy one want cannot be used to satisfy another at the same time. Steel, concrete, and building sites used for hotels cannot also be used for classrooms. People who are employed as teachers cannot spend the same time working for an airline. Even the time students spend in class and studying for tests represents use of a factor of production that could otherwise be used as labor in a travel agency, a hotel or another travel-related business.

Because production uses inputs that could be used elsewhere, the production of any good or service entails foregoing the opportunity to produce something else instead. In economic terms, everything has an opportunity cost. The opportunity cost of a good or service is its cost in terms of the foregone opportunity to pursue the best possible alternative activity with the same time or resource. In an economy with many goods and services, opportunity costs are best expressed in monetary terms. For example, the opportunity cost of one month in Hawaii could be $5000, and that of a four-year college education may be $40,000. Care must be taken when opportunity costs are expressed in terms of money, because not all out-of-pocket money expenditures represent the sacrifice of opportunities to do something else. At the same time, not all sacrificed opportunities take the form of money spent.

Money spent for national defense cannot be spent for welfare, although spending for any purpose has broad impacts on an economy, and especially on a particular locale where the spending occurs. The 7 million visitors to Hawaii and an equal number to Venice, Italy, have immediate impacts on these destinations. Tourism spending subtracts dollars from the economy providing the visitors, and ripples through the economy receiving the visitors, creating differences in the balances of trade between regions and nations.

All spending that generates economic activity is generally believed to be salutary in that business is stimulated, more work is available (for those that want to work), goods are created, and economic activity is generated. Optimism stimulates an economy as a whole, and tourism in particular. The reverse is also true: When there is pessimism, an economy can suffer.

SUPPLY AND DEMAND

The basic explanation of economic activity is described in the so-called "law of supply and demand." In economic terms the law of demand states that an inverse relationship exists between the price of a good or service and the quantity of the good or service that buyers demand, other things being equal. The reasoning behind this "law" is that if the price of a good or service increases while other prices stay the same, consumers are apt to substitute that good or service with a cheaper good or service.

The law of demand is usually depicted in graphical form known as the demand curve. Figure 2-1 illustrates the total quantity of hotel rooms demanded in a particular location, at various prices.

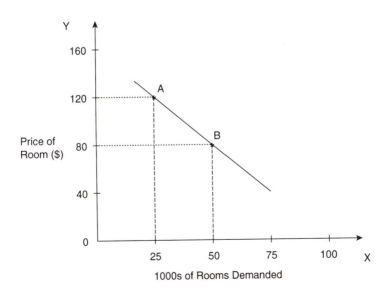

Figure 2-1 Demand Curve

The Y (vertical) axis shows the prices of rooms in dollars, and the X (horizontal) axis shows the quantity of hotel rooms demanded. In the example, point A indicates that an average price of $120 per room would result in 25,000 rooms being occupied. At point B, however, an average price of $80 per room results in 50,000 rooms being occupied. A change in the price results in a change in the quantity demanded, other things being equal.

There are other variables that also have an effect on the demand for the number of rooms in a particular location. Prices of rooms in other locations can have an effect on demand, as can the amount of disposable income available to travelers. There could be many other factors, such as the popularity of the location as a destination spot for conventions, and the population's confidence about the future in general.

A change in demand due to a variable other than the price of the good or service itself will cause a shift in the demand curve as shown in Figure 2-2.

In Figure 2-2, a nearby location raised its prices by 20 percent while the original location in our example maintained its same price schedule. This caused a rightward shift in the demand curve where now the location has 75,000 rooms occupied (point C), instead of the 50,000 rooms previously occupied (point B), at an average room price of $80.

The above example illustrates a rightward shift in demand due to a substitute service; that is, an increase in the demand of one is caused by an increase in the price of another. A leftward shift in the demand curve may be caused by an increase in the price of airfares. As a result fewer people will travel to the destination and now there would only be 25,000 rooms occupied at an average room price of $80 (point D in Figure 2-2).

The demand for a good or service may be effected by a change in consumers'

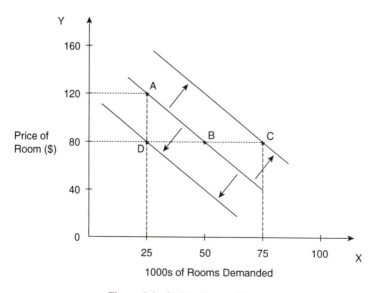

Figure 2-2 Shift in Demand Curve

disposable incomes. A normal good or service is one that will have an increased demand as a result of an increase in consumer income. An inferior good or service is one that will have a decreased demand as a result of an increase in consumer income. In our example a "normal" hotel may have an average room rate of $80, whereas the "inferior" hotel may have an average room rate of $40. If there were to be a decrease in consumers' disposable incomes, inferior services would enjoy an increase in demand and normal services would suffer a decrease in demand.

The law of supply in economic terms states that a direct relationship exists between the price of a good or service and the quantity of the good or service that producers supply, other things being equal. The reasoning behind this law is that if the price of a good or service increases while other prices stay the same, producers are apt to produce a greater quantity of that good or service.

The law of supply is usually depicted in graphical form known as the supply curve. The following example, shown in Figure 2-3, illustrates the total supply of hotel rooms at various prices.

In Figure 2-3, the Y (vertical) axis shows the prices of rooms in dollars, and the X (horizontal) axis shows the quantity of hotel rooms supplied. In the example, point E indicates that at an average rate of $80 per room the quantity supplied would be 50,000 rooms. At point F, however, an average room rate of $120 would result in 75,000 rooms being supplied. A change in the price of a room results in a change in the quantity supplied, other things being equal. As in the law of demand, other variables besides price can determine the quantity of a good or service supplied. For example, if a government wishes to encourage the construction of new hotels by reducing the taxes paid by hoteliers, the cost to provide the hotel rooms decreases. This will cause the supply curve to shift and result in an increase in supply.

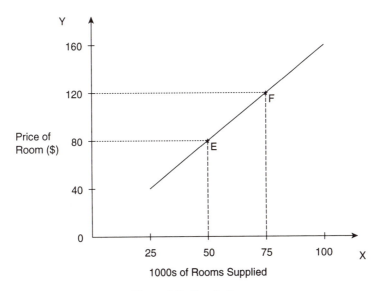

Figure 2-3 Supply Curve

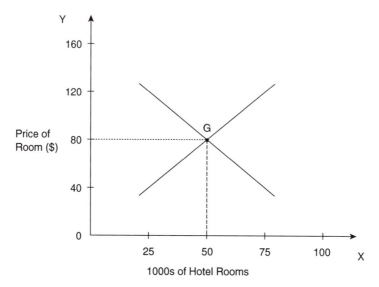

Figure 2-4 Equilibrium Point

The price at which the quantity demanded equals the quantity supplied is called the equilibrium point—the price at which the plans of buyers and sellers match each other. See Figure 2-4 for the graphical illustration. At point G, both the quantity supplied and the quantity demanded is 50,000 hotel rooms at an average room price of $80.

The equilibrium of supply and demand is stationary in the sense that once the equilibrium price is reached, it tends to remain the same as long as neither supply nor demand shifts. If there are no shifts in supply or demand, there are no market prices acting on the price to make it change.

If the price is below equilibrium, the quantity demanded exceeds the quantity supplied, buyers offer higher prices, sellers ask for higher prices, and the price rises. If the price is above equilibrium, the quantity supplied exceeds the quantity demanded, buyers offer lower prices, sellers ask for lower prices, and the price falls.

Supply and Demand of Tourism Products

For many tourism "products," hotel rooms being an example, an additional supply cannot be made quickly. A large hotel may take five years to finance and build. If over a period of time supply does not meet increasing demand, the average price of hotel rooms will rise.

The supply side of the restaurant business is nearly always more than filled. In 1989, the National Restaurant Association estimated that there were 528 people near every commercial food service outlet in the United States. The number had decreased from 800 ten years earlier, indicating fewer people were needed to constitute a restaurant market (or that each restaurant had a lower customer base). Another interpretation: People were eating out more frequently. Whatever the real reason, most restaurant operators could easily accommodate more customers than they have. In most areas the supply of restaurant seats is greater than the demand, one reason the restaurant business shows so many failures. The ease with which new restaurants can open insures that restaurant supply will almost always be met.

The supply of hotel/motel rooms exceeds the demand except for certain days of the week, and for resort hotels during high seasons. Large city hotels usually are full Mondays through Thursdays, mainly because of business travelers. Occupancy drops sharply Fridays through Sundays. The supply/demand equation for hotels is kept off-balance because of the long time required to build and bring a new hotel on line, and by the economic cycle.

Airlines require large capital investments, which would suggest that the supply side would be difficult to keep full. Yet the capital is found to start up dozens of small airlines, most of which fail because the major airlines can outmarket them and have been able to raise huge amounts of money to operate, even with large losses. The belief among investors apparently is that given large load factors the airlines can be hugely profitable. That is true if there were no price wars. But price wars seem to be endemic to the industry. More recently short-haul economy airlines, by offering reduced prices and convenient flights, have found a ready demand in certain markets.

The cruise business is said to be expanding the most rapidly of any major tourist business, largely because of providing a fly/cruise package and tapping into a younger, less affluent market that is thrilled by the inclusive vacation for one price, made available for less than seven days. Much of the demand was created by Carnival Cruises (operating out of Florida) and the heavy use of TV advertising in which cruise passengers are titillated to the point of ecstasy with unending entertainment. It has made Carnival Cruise owner Ted Arison a billionaire. Like hotels, cruise ships take a long time to build and the demand must be anticipated years in advance. Heavy discounting of cruise prices have helped keep demand high.

Supply and demand for rental cars can keep in step by moving cars from one location to another as needed, and by buying or selling cars as required. Rental cars can be kept longer, up to 20,000 miles, according to the demand for the used car market. Auto manufacturers who own large rental car companies can act to buy or sell cars as it suits their economics.

The travel agency business, like the restaurant business, is relatively easy to enter and at any given time the supply of travel agencies is more than enough to meet demand. Most agencies can add personnel, or remain open longer, to meet demand. Hundreds of people seem to be interested in becoming travel agents, either as agents or owners, more than enough to meet the demand. The large franchisors seem ready to add to the supply by adding franchisees.

Factors Influencing Supply and Demand

The "law" of supply and demand suggests that the relationships between supply and demand are inexorable, a change in one results in a change in the other. In some cases this is no doubt true, but other forces, such as advertising, marketing skills and human motivation—with all of its intricacies and convolutions—exert tremendous influence on what people "supply" and "demand." Hamburgers sold by the major chains contain almost the same amounts of fat, protein, and carbohydrates yet the demand for one brand over the others is influenced greatly by image and other factors. Travel destinations come and go based on the way they are perceived by a market. People are attracted to a particular dinner house restaurant if it is perceived as fitting the individual's self-image. Will the restaurant satisfy not only the desire for food and ambiance but also will it enhance the diner's favorable feeling about him- or herself?

Thus, while laws of supply and demand utilize the disclaimer that other things must be equal in order for the laws to work, in the reality of the business world things are not equal. External effects on the quantities supplied or demanded of a service of product are nearly always present. Factors that play in a decision on where to take a vacation include marketing campaigns of a given location and word of mouth—that is, friends or family who may have been to the location.

Another quirk in tourism economics is related to conspicuous consumption, the phrase coined by Thorstein Veblen, a prominent American social theorist and economist who died in 1929. Conspicuous consumption is the practice of purchasing goods or services because of the status they might bring. Being able to say "I spent a week in Tahiti" or "We go to Vail, Colorado every year for the skiing" may be examples of conspicuous consumption. A number of resort hotels, deluxe cruises, and first-class flights are attractive at least partly because of the Veblen effect.

Instead of supply and demand determining the cost of a product, the Veblen effect sets up new demand curves based on exclusivity and prestige. Certainly the purchase of a very expensive Rolls Royce automobile, a huge home, or a diamond ring are examples of conspicuous consumption. The higher the cost of an experience or product, the more desirable it may become—up to a point. The Veblen effect appears on the cruise ship, in the choice of ship, the location of the stateroom, and the length of the cruise. Status seekers want to be seated at the captain's table, and that honor may be worth several thousand dollars. Formal dress evenings are a must so that gowns and jewels may be suitably displayed.

Professor Floyd Harmson devised the Veblen demand curve as shown in Figure 2-5. If price P_1 is charged, quantity Q_1 is purchased. If the price increases to P_2 according to the demand curve D_1, the quantity purchased should decrease to Q_2. This does not happen in the Veblen curve because the buyers attach new importance to the product and actually buy a larger quantity, Q_3. In effect, the new price has enhanced the quality of the service or the experience offered. The demand curve, instead of shifting downward, had shifted to D_2 because of the Veblen effect. Decreasing the price causes only a small increase in the amount purchased since the movement will be along the new demand curve D_2. Increase the price further to P_3, and the curve again shifts. Instead of a decrease in demand to Q_4, the demand actually increases to Q_5.

Economists like to classify goods and services into those that are preferred and those that are non-preferred. Travel is seen as a "preferred superior service" in that more is undertaken as incomes increase. As more families reach higher income brackets, both in the United States and around the world, the demand for a travel experience increases at a faster rate than does income. This phenomenon is described in more detail in the following section.

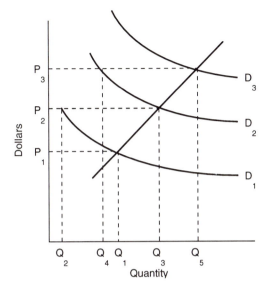

Source: Professor Floyd Harmson, University of Missouri

Figure 2-5 The Veblen Demand Curve

Elasticity of Demand for Tourism

Which travel demand is elastic (sensitive to price changes) and which inelastic varies considerably, depending partly on the affluence of the traveler and the reason or reasons for the trip. The devout Muslim must take the haj (the annual pilgrimage to Mecca) once during a lifetime, just as many devout Catholics travel to Rome. Many trips are made for more than one reason, thereby complicating demand studies.

From an economic point of view, price elasticities are important for the suppliers of tourism products, since they can have an impact on their total revenues. Total revenues (TRs) of sellers in a market are equal to the price (P) of the good or service times the total quantity sold (Q).

When a particular service is price elastic (greater than 1), then TRs increase when there is a decrease in P. This is because the percentage rise in Q is greater than the percentage decrease in P. Conversely, when a particular service is inelastic (less than 1), then TRs decrease when there is a decrease in P. This is because the percentage rise in Q is less than the percentage decrease in P.

Based upon the above rationale, if the price elasticity of a product is known, a tourism product supplier can increase total revenues by making an appropriate adjustment to the price of the product. In practice it is not quite so simple because price elasticities vary considerably and change over time. Price elasticities are impacted by a multitude of factors that are difficult to model. The main determinants of price elasticity are the availability of equivalent substitute products, the relative importance of the product in a spending budget, the amount of time available to adjust to the price change, and the status of the product as a necessity or luxury.

Despite the difficulty of determining specific price elasticities, some studies have estimated actual price elasticities for foreign travel. Hendrick Houthakker and Lester Taylor compiled data on consumer demand in the United States. Two types of elasticities were calculated: price elasticity in the long-run (where the consumers had a longer time to adjust to price changes), and price elasticity in the short-run (where the consumers had a shorter time to adjust to price changes). In the case of foreign travel, the price elasticity increased from 0.14 in the short-run (highly inelastic) to 1.77 in the long-run (elastic) (Hendrick S. Houthakker and Lester Taylor, *Consumer Demand in the United States: Analysis and Projections,* Cambridge, MA: Harvard University Press, 1970).

Houthakker and Taylor also calculated the income elasticities of demand. The income elasticity of demand is the percentage change in the quantity demanded divided by the percentage change in income. Products can be income elastic (greater than 1), income inelastic (between zero and 1), or exhibit negative income elasticity (less than zero). If a product is income elastic, then the quantity demanded increases as income increases, but the quantity demanded increases faster than income. The following tourism-related products were reported: airline travel (5.82), foreign travel (3.08), restaurant meals (1.61), and local buses and trains (1.38). This means that if average incomes grow by 3 percent a year, the demand for foreign travel will grow by 9.24 percent (3 percent times the income elasticity of demand for foreign travel) (*Ibid.*).

According to Witt, Brooks, and Buckley, the main factors affecting international tourism demand by U.S. residents seem to be disposable income and total tourism costs (transportation costs and living costs at the destination combined). In terms of tourists' living costs, tourism demand is price elastic for travel from the United States to France and West Germany, but price inelastic for travel to Canada and the United Kingdom. In terms of transportation costs, demand is price inelastic. It was also determined that overseas travel is regarded as a luxury and is highly income elastic (the higher someone's disposable income the less travel is seen as a luxury) (Stephen F. Witt, Michael Z. Brooks, and Peter J. Buckley, *The Management of International Tourism*, Boston: Unwin Hyman, 1991).

Utility of Tourism Consumption

The demand for tourism is influenced by the economic concept of utility: the benefit or satisfaction that a person gets from the consumption of a good or service. It is, however, an abstract concept and the units of utility for a particular product are hard to define and quantify. Utility is part of a branch of behavioral economics that is mainly based on consumer behavior.

Adrian Bull presented an example of the characteristics that might be important to the tourist interested in a vacation in a sunny destination. The characteristics that could be included are:

- daily sunshine hours at the destination
- per capita beach space at the destination

- similarity of accommodations to known standards
- suitable distance (expressed in travel time) to the destination
- reliability of transportation to the destination

If these characteristics could be quantified, then the tourist's utility would be maximized if each one of these characteristics would rate highly in the consumer's opinion.

To show how different the important characteristics for a conspicuous tourism consumer might be, Bull suggested the following list:

- luxurious accommodations
- gastronomic range and quality of real experiences
- quality and amount of personal service throughout trips
- reliability of transportation
- prestige name suppliers of tourism services

—*(Adrian Bull,* The Economics of Travel and Tourism, *New York: Wiley, 1991)*

In economic terms, total utility is the total satisfaction that a person gets from the consumption of goods and services; it is limited by the amount of disposable income available, the price of the desired goods and services, and in many cases, the time available to consume the desired products. Marginal utility, in economic terms, is the change in total utility resulting from a one-unit increase in the quantity of a good or service consumed. The principle of diminishing marginal utility is that there may be a diminishing satisfaction per additional unit of the product consumed.

In relating this concept to tourism, Chris Ryan suggested that continued increases in travel could make a tourist feel weary, resulting in a greater appreciation for the comforts of home. He suggested that if holiday travel becomes equated with flight delays, traffic jams, violence towards tourists, and long lines at tourist attractions, then the tourist may actually feel that it is better to stay at home.

This is particularly so now that other leisure activities (hobbies and interests practiced in the home area) are competing with tourism for the few valuable hours available for relaxation (Chris Ryan, *Recreational Tourism, A Social Science Perspective*, London, England: Routledge, 1991). Breakthroughs in information technology are turning the home and its surroundings into entertainment centers. The marginal utility of a third or fourth vacation may in one year therefore be diminished.

CURRENCY EXCHANGE RATES

International transactions require buyers and sellers to deal in foreign currencies. The price of one currency in terms of another is called an *exchange rate*. Currency exchange rates are usually floating, with their values determined by demand for, and supply of, currencies in the global marketplace. An increase in the value of a currency is called *appreciation*, a decrease in its value is called *depreciation*.

There are two types of floating exchange rates. When an exchange rate is only determined by open market forces it is termed a *free float*. If a government intercedes in the market to influence the exchange rate, by buying or selling its own currency, it is termed a *managed float*. Changes in floating exchange rates are usually small in the short term, although trends can cause sizable differences over a period of months or weeks.

In the developing countries of the world, the exchange rates are often set by the government at a fixed rate. The central banks of these countries will attempt to maintain its exchange rate versus the "hard" currencies, such as the U.S. dollar, by borrowing from the International Monetary Fund (IMF) , or selling reserves in the form of gold or foreign currencies. Changes in these fixed exchange rates occur infrequently and are usually quite substantial. An increase in the exchange rate is termed a *revaluation*, the more common decrease in the exchange rate is termed a *devaluation*.

Through recent history there have been a variety of fixed and floating currency exchange rate systems. Contemporary international currency systems consists of floating currencies, as jointly floating currencies (known as "the snake"), currencies pegged to a "hard" currency, and currencies pegged to a combination of "hard" currencies. Changes in currency exchange rates can have considerable effects on tourism, and therefore, the economic stability of countries. The following section discusses the impact of these effects.

Balance of Payments

Each country maintains a record of its international transactions known as the *balance of payments*. The statement consists of *in-payment* and *out-payment* items. In-payments include exports of goods and services, unilateral transfers, and inflow of capital in various forms. Out-payments include imports of goods and services, unilateral transfers, and outflow of capital in various forms. Partial balances can be computed from the statement as follows: The balance of trade is the exports minus imports of goods; the balance on goods and services is the exports minus imports of goods and services; the balance on current account equals exports of goods and services minus imports of goods and services and unilateral transfers.

Finally, the overall balance of payments positions, known as the *official reserve transactions balance*, is all private in-payments minus all private out-payments. It is in a *surplus* if in-payments exceed out-payments and in a *deficit* when out-payments exceed in-payments.

In a fixed-exchange rate regime the overall deficit or surplus reflects the country's external position, and it is settled by changes in official international reserves. In a free-float regime there can be no deficit or surplus, since exchange rate variations result from in-payments and out-payments. The country's external position is fully reflected in the movements of its exchange rate. Under a managed float, the country's external position is manifested in a combination of exchange fluctuations and its overall payments imbalance. From a tourism economics point of view the inflow of foreign currencies to pay for tourism services can be critical to the economic well-being of a country.

Freely Floating Rates

In the modern era of freely floating rates, the currency exchange rate is determined by the intersection of demand for (out-payments) and supply of (in-payments) foreign currencies. However, these demand and supply schedules are shifted daily by all developments in the economy as well as by government economic policies. The most important factors include changes in real income, inflation rates, and interest rates—all of which affect the location of the supply and demand curves and therefore the exchange rates. So do various expectations and psychological factors.

A currency may depreciate if there is a rise in income or the rate of inflation, a decline in interest rates, adverse expectations, or decreases in tourism expenditures. A currency may appreciate if there is a decline in income or the rate of inflation, a rise in interest rates, favorable expectations, or increases in tourism expenditures. In all cases, the primary determinants of the currency exchange rate are the domestic circumstances relative to conditions prevailing abroad.

A country on the free float system needs no international reserves since exchange fluctuations always equate in-payments and out-payments, thereby maintaining equilibrium in the balance of payments. A country on the managed float system requires reserves with which to influence the float.

It should be noted that even though the overall balance of payments may be in equilibrium under a free float, partial balances may not be. As an example, the United States had a large trade and current account deficit between 1983 and 1993; this was offset, however, by large inflows of capital. That condition was largely caused by an overvalued dollar (relative to purchasing power parity), triggered by high U.S. real interest rates. In turn, the trade deficit had an unfavorable effect on U.S. output and employment, especially in the manufacturing sector.

Fixed Exchange Rates

A government may choose to keep the exchange value of its currency fixed relative to other currencies. It must then stand ready to buy and sell foreign currencies (usually "hard" currencies such as the U.S. dollar) in exchange for the domestic currency at the fixed exchange rate. To do so it needs to keep sizable international reserves.

In case of excess demand for foreign currencies, the central bank sells "hard" currency in exchange for the domestic currency. Its foreign currency reserves are depleted and the domestic money supply shrinks. This can go on as long as foreign currency reserves last. When they are exhausted, the country may have to devalue its currency. How quickly the local economy reacts to the devaluation may cause a boost in tourism, since it is now less expensive for foreigners to vacation in that country. Recent times of hyperinflation (over 100 percent per year in some countries) have brought about situations where the costs of virtually all goods and services are immediately adjusted after a devaluation. In the case of excess supply of foreign currencies, the central bank buys "hard" currency in exchange for the domestic currency. Its foreign currency reserves and the domestic money supply both rise. This can go on as long as the government is willing to accumulate reserves, or until fears of domestic inflation, triggered by the rise in money supply, become paramount. At that point the government may choose to re-value its currency. This of course would become a deterrent to foreign tourism expenditures and in turn cause a reduction in the country's balance of payments.

Implications for Tourism

A country's exchange rate—the ratio at which the unit of currency of one country is or may be exchanged for the unit of another country—has widespread implications for travel and tourism. In 1993 the exchange rate of U.S. currency made travel to the United States from many other countries a relative bargain. The result was a huge inflow of foreign travelers. Conversely, most European exchange rates were high and made European travel by U.S. residents relatively expensive. Travel to a foreign country tends to increase, sometimes dramatically, as its exchange rate falls. A devaluation of the peso in Mexico, for example, usually increases the number of foreign visitors, at least for a short period of time.

At one point in the 1980s, the British pound sank to about one pound to the dollar and travel to Britain increased sharply. Later the pound climbed to almost two dollars with a resultant decline in travel to Britain. British tourists, however, traveled to the United States in numbers never seen before. Orlando, Florida, was a grateful host for many of the British travelers.

In 1985 the value of the dollar increased so much that the American traveler abroad could travel at bargain rates around the world. Within a year it sank so fast that some foreign banks refused to change it.

Travelers abroad pay the "buy rate" for a currency. When they exchange their currency back, they are paid the "sell rate," a smaller amount unless their own currency has appreciated in the interval.

At any given time, some countries represent travel bargains; other countries are overpriced. The rate of inflation, government policy, and other factors are at play. Spain, under General Franco, decided it would hold down visitor prices to attract tourists. For several years many Britons found they could rent out their homes in England and live more cheaply in Spain. Curves showing currency rates compared with the number of arrivals from Great Britain, Germany, and Japan to the United States can be seen in Figure 2-6.

The U.S. government policy of keeping the dollar weak to increase American exports has been at least partly responsible for the great increase in visitors foreign spending in the United States—receipts climbed from $21.8 billion in 1985 to $58.3 billion in 1991. Figure 2-7 shows the increases. Income from foreign spending was expected to reach $80 billion in 1994.

While statisticians point out that correlations do not necessarily mean cause and effect, common sense says that people travel more when costs go down. The U.S. Travel and Tourism Administration states that the rapid growth of foreign travelers to the United States "is due in large part to the U.S. dollar's continued weakness that makes the U.S. dollar a bargain for many foreign visitors" (*Recap of International Travel To and From the United States in 1989*, Office of Research U.S. Travel Service, August 1991).

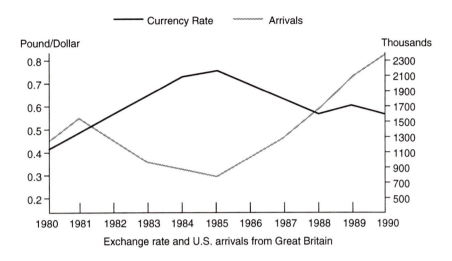

Exchange rate and U.S. arrivals from Great Britain

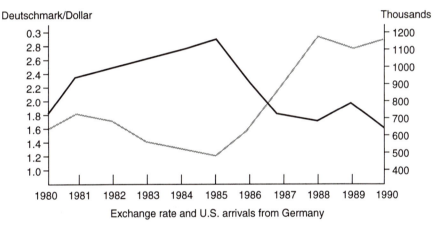

Exchange rate and U.S. arrivals from Germany

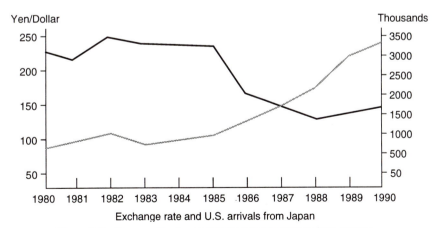

Exchange rate and U.S. arrivals from Japan

Figure 2-6   Currency Exchange Rates and U.S. Arrivals from Abroad

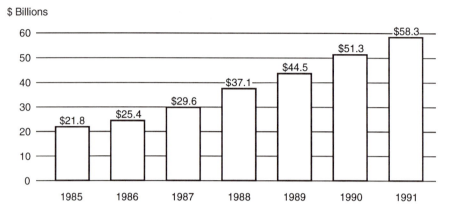

$ Billions

Source: U.S. Travel and Tourism Administration

Figure 2-7 U.S. Receipts from Foreign Visitor Spending

Airlines and other travel providers observe exchange rates closely and price their product and services up or down to avoid losing money. Tour operators try to get guarantees from hotels, ground transportation operators, and other travel providers so that in case an exchange rate makes travel more costly, they are protected from price increases. Without downside protection (guaranteed rates) travel providers can suffer serious losses. The large travel providers such as international airlines sometimes hedge against price increases trying to predict which way exchange rates will move.

TOURISM COSTS

Where tourism is a major industry, critics are quick to point out the dangers to the economy of excessive dependence on tourism. This criticism applies to such places as Bermuda, the Bahamas, and the South Pacific island states. The same can be said for numerous communities that are heavily dependent upon any one industry. For the advanced industrial nations, tourism accounts for an average of 6.3 percent of total GNP. The worldwide figure is higher, 12 percent. For particular regions, the Bahamas and the Cayman Islands for example, the percentage of income attributable to tourism is much higher and can be a cause for concern if alternative sources of income are small.

Some social costs of tourism are obvious; others are not. At one time Amsterdam, Holland, was a magnet for drug users and hippies. The city's reputation suffered, a social cost. Before Disney World was built Orlando, Florida, was a sleepy town with a few hotels. The residents seemed quite happy with the place. After Disney World was built, dozens of hotels and motels were built. The area now has more than 80,000 guest rooms, one of the highest densities of guest rooms in the world. It is plain that Disney World has spurred development and economic growth, and has brought billions of new dollars into the area and made first-class entertainment and restaurant choices accessible. The old-time residents may have preferred Orlando as it was. Highway crowding in the area is massive, a social cost.

Tourism as an industry is seen through different prisms when tourism development is being proposed. Residents who have a comfortable income and are quite satisfied with the quality of life in an area are often opposed to tourism development, predicting that tourism growth will increase highway crowding, air pollution, real estate prices, food prices, and the cost of government services such as police protection. Tourism may attract new residents with lower income and require additional schools and welfare services. Crime may increase. Tourism, say tourism opponents, reduces per capita income rather than increasing it.

The views of the San Diego Association of Governments (SANDAG) may be typical of tourism opponents. When the Convention and Visitors Bureau of Carlsbad, California, was courting the owners of LEGO Park, the Danish Company that was considering building a LEGO World Theme Park in Carlsbad, the San Diego Association of Governments came out strongly against it. They argued that tourism would bring income that cannot compare with income generated by light industry and aerospace. During 1990, said SANDAG, local governments spent $1616 per person to provide citizens, visitors, and businesses with essential government services. Employees in manufacturing contributed an average of $2412 per person to local government. In the service sector, employees contributed an average of $1413 person, a loss of $203 to local government. According to the Association, it takes eighteen employees in manufacturing to create $1 million in goods, and forty-six service sector employees to create $1 million in services provided. The eighteen manufacturing employees contribute a profit of $14,364 to local government, while the forty-six service sector employees only create $9338. If LEGO brought between 800 and 1200 service type jobs to Carlsbad, local government would experience $243,000 in loss, according to SANDAG. The citizens of Carlsbad, the location selected for LEGO PARK, did not buy the arguments against LEGO PARK and voted in favor of the PARK in June, 1994.

Granted that service jobs pay less, perhaps as little as half that of manufacturing and light industry, they include management salaries that can be high. Tipped employees may receive income exceeding $100 a day. The question then must be asked, Are there industrial job vacancies and would service jobs—jobs needed by the local economy—be created? Will the new service jobs take people off welfare? In many places most service jobs in hotels and restaurants are filled by young people, students, and persons living with their families who contribute to family income with little additional cost to the community. A community considering tourism can compare income from tourism versus income from other sources. The assumptions made should be clear. The assumption is often made that other industries will provide full employment at higher wages and salaries. If this were true, the "other industries" would probably already be there.

Nearly every Chamber of Commerce would like to see its community become a Silicon Valley—with lots of research, highly paid jobs, little air and noise pollution, a low crime rate—and avoid all the negatives of the industrialized world. Financial services, computer services, educational services, with a highly skilled, highly educated work force, in a year-round, pleasant climate are desirable.

If the area being considered for tourism development has high unemployment, the virtues of tourism are more apparent. Tourism income, though perhaps less than from other sources, may be the best possible choice under existing conditions, serving to produce tax revenues, reduce unemployment, and enhance the quality of life for many residents. The opportunity cost of tourism under these circumstances is small or may not exist.

Social costs rise for governments when immigrants are employed and remit much of their revenue to their homes abroad. In the U.S. Virgin Islands, for example, immigrants from other Caribbean islands where wages are lower, take hotel jobs. Some bring their families, raising education, police protection, and other government costs.

Tourism critics point out that tourism brings cultural change. Divorce may increase as gender relationships change. Women may not be as dependent upon spouses as before and divorce may rise. Prostitution and drug use may increase, as has happened in Honolulu.

Though Hawaiian tourism brings in close to $9 billion a year and is responsible for 40 percent of the state's jobs, the government tries hard to diversify the economy. The average home cost in Hawaii is the highest in the United States, $350,000 in 1994. Thousands of residents find it necessary to work two jobs. Japanese real estate investment in Hawaii drove up land and home costs. Of all of the major hotels built between 1985 and early 1991, Japanese investors bought or partially financed all but two. Investments were inordinately high in many of these hotels. The Grand Waiolea Hyatt Resort in Maui was built at a cost of $600 million. It was estimated that the hotel would need a room rate of $1000 a night at a 75 percent occupancy to break even.

Too Many Tourists?

Aside from income comparisons, can there be too many tourists? Definitely yes, as seen in several of the U.S. national parks during summer periods. "Crowding," however, is at least partially subjective. Holland has one of the highest population densities in the world. Yet its quality of life seems satisfactory to most residents.

What is considered crowding is subject to the income level, the public services available, especially transportation, and the total environment as perceived by the individual. The urge to live close to others may be partly cultural. In Costa Rica, people want to live within "the sound of the bells." Someone growing up in the Bronx, New York City, may miss the hustle and bustle of a city. Rural or small town residents may feel crowded in any highly urbanized environment.

People living in Sutton Place in New York City get around quite nicely by cab compared to those traveling by subway. The crowds in Hong Kong seem to have adapted to living as a part of a mass population. Hawaii has several times as many visitors each year as residents. So do the Bahamas, the Cayman Islands, the U.S. Virgin Islands, Austria, and Switzerland.

Tourists are seen as invaders by some people; their dollars and influence a source of fear, as seen in the prayer read from Greek Orthodox pulpits throughout Greece in the 1970s.

"Lord Jesus Christ, Son of God, have mercy on the cities, the islands, and the villages of our Orthodox Fatherland, as well as the Holy Monasteries, which are scourged by the worldly touristic way. Grace us with a solution to this dramatic problem and protect our brethren who are sorely tried by the modernistic spirit of these contemporary western invaders."

—*(David Ogilvy,* Blood, Brains and Beer: An Autobiography, *New York: Athenaeum, 1978, p. 155)*

Even where tourism is a prime source of income, there are critics. In Hawaii, where sugar and pineapple once reigned supreme, tourism has become the number one income resource. In Hawaii critics point out that tourism has brought illegal drugs and an increase in crime. Robbery of visitors has become so common that the government has set up a special "restitution" fund for reimbursing visitors for losses suffered from theft.

Tourism and increased social costs are not clearly associated in some places. In Spain, where in 1991 tourists spent $19 billion during their visits, crime has increased. Women are often robbed of their purses and satchels by pairs of men racing by on motor scooters. One drives, the other snatches. One reason for the increase in crime has been the relaxation of police control, a far cry from the days of Franco, the dictator, who died in 1975. Widespread political corruption in Italy and the mafia influence are major correlates with crime, influences which cannot be blamed onto an increase in tourism.

Comparative Advantage

Comparative advantage in economic terms means that there are differences in opportunity costs between various parts of the world, cities, regions, and nations. A place has a comparative advantage in producing a particular good and can produce that good at a lower opportunity cost than competitors. As described earlier in this chapter, the opportunity cost of any action is the best alternative foregone. The best thing chosen not to do—the foregone alternative—is the cost of the thing that is chosen to do.

Many places, like parts of the Caribbean with those lovely beaches, Hawaii, parts of California, Florida, and destination cities such as New York City, Paris, and London, have a comparative advantage in destination tourism. The opportunity costs of developing tourism in the Bahamas, for example, are negligible. Many developing countries have arrived at this conclusion and turn to tourism to provide jobs, taxes, and revenue.

The comparative advantage of some tourism, however, may be more fictitious than real. Cost/benefit and market studies can help make reasonable decisions as to the advisability of making tourism investments. What constitutes comparative advantage for tourism can be difficult to ascertain. Transportation, culture, climate, marketing skill, and other factors are part of tourism's comparative advantage. Hawaii and Fiji both have desirable destination climates and beautiful beaches. Both are thousands of miles from potential tourist markets. Hawaii receives almost 7 million visitors a year; Fiji fewer than 200,000. Yet tourism gives both places a comparative advantage. At the moment, Fiji's other choices are to produce sugar, the world price of which is only a few cents a pound, and other low income agricultural crops.

The debate over whether tourism is a desirable industry is often framed in terms of either/or, either favoring tourism or not. Tourism, in fact, fits nicely into many economies, as one of several parts of the economy, a part that is likely to continue growing. In New York City, the largest tourist destination in the world, it is only a small part of the economy; in Las Vegas, the major part. Tourism has a comparative advantage in both places. Surprisingly, tourism may be viable to a certain extent in remote places such as Tibet when part of a package tour.

In some locations the opportunity cost of tourism is virtually zero. In other words, at the moment there are no viable alternatives. The Seychelles, an island nation in the Indian Ocean, is a case in point. Until the jet plane made the islands accessible for tourists, its economy hung on the coconut palm, the nuts used for making copra that were also pressed to make coconut oil. In the early 1970s an airport, and later several hotels, brought tourist dollars that raised educational and health standards, encouraged social mobility, and the development of a middle class. This nation of 70,000 residents is now reached from London (via Bahrain) or Paris. Air Seychelles has its own Boeing 767. In 1991 tourism brought in $88 million, far and away greater than that from agriculture.

In most tourism locations, tourism complements other existing industries. Without tourism, the U.S. government would need to subsidize Puerto Rico with more food stamps and provide higher federal government subsidies. Economics is a beady-eyed taskmaster. Industries come and go. This is especially true of several agriculture crops such as sugar, pineapple, and bananas, which in some locations cannot be produced competitively for the world market.

Cost/Benefit Analysis

Cost/benefit analysis is an attempt to quantify and compare the pros and cons of a tourism or other venture. The method is as old as Ben Franklin, who suggested that any major decision should be viewed as having some benefits and some negatives. Questions such as whether to marry could be laid out, pros on one side, cons on the other.

In weighing many tourism decisions, especially the major ones such as to build or not to build a resort, it is helpful to try to break the big decision into smaller ones, and to quantify each part.

It quickly becomes apparent that cost/benefit analysis covers more than economic consequences of a decision. For example, the benefits of building a resort hotel are probably seen as a job and tax creator, a means of reducing unemployment and providing increased entertainment choices for the area. Land owners probably benefit; renters do not. Increased police and fire protection and road maintenance will probably be costs.

Psychological and sociological as well as economic costs are involved. Established social hierarchies will change. Some people will gain status, others will lose. If wages increase, some employers will have to pay more. Skilled tradespeople may benefit; unskilled persons may only find that their cost of living increases. Many residents like the status quo. "Crowding" is partly a perception and can be seen as a major reason not to encourage tourism growth.

Example of Costs/Benefits

Pros for Tourism Development	Cons against Development
Increased revenues, tax base, and jobs.	Increased costs of social services.
More classrooms, hospital beds.	More roads, bureaucracy, police and fire services.
Increase in status for some.	Loss of status for some.
Increase in restaurants and entertainment choices.	Increase in crime and prostitution.
Training for youth.	

The example above illustrates the fact that tourism and its perceived costs or benefits cannot be quantified easily and manipulated into an economic model. The quantitative models need to have descriptive elements in order to tie them into economic reality. As we are able to gather more data on tourism, and are able to gain a better understanding of the behavioral aspects of tourism, the applications of tourism economics will continue to expand.

Part II

Economics of Tourism Sectors

3

Hotel Economics

The economics of the public lodging field closely reflect the general economy and in particular the regional economy where located. Heavily capitalized public lodging is as much a business of real estate and finance as it is of lodging operations. The cost of money and the exuberance of developers and investors have exaggerated the cyclical nature of the business, making it largely responsible for much of the overbuilding that inevitably leads to periods of heavy losses because of "too many rooms at the inn."

Hotels and motels comprise the bulk of the rooms available for rent to the public. Related lodging enterprises are all-suites, resorts, conference centers, inns, and bed-and-breakfast hostelries. Timeshare condominiums can be included, and retirement homes that offer meals and other services are also related businesses.

The World Tourism Organization, an affiliate of the United Nations, put the total number of rooms suitable for international travelers in 1991 at 11.3 million, with an annual growth rate of 2.5 percent. The United States offers 3.1 million hotel and motel rooms, or about one-quarter of the world's total. Europe accounts for 45 percent of the rooms. The commercial lodging business in the United States generates more than $63 billion in sales each year, representing about one percent of the country's gross national product, and employs 1.6 million people, full and part time. The American Hotel and Motel Association reports that 25 percent of today's lodging customers are traveling for business purposes, 24 percent are attending conferences, and 31 percent are vacationing. The rest are traveling for a variety of other reasons.

The hotel business by its nature is international, and is growing more so as the major hotel/motel chains and marketing/referral groups expand in number and in transnational ownership. Airlines own or are affiliated in one way or another with hotels. Airline and travel agency computerization has produced a worldwide network of travel information upon which much of the lodging business depends.

The name on a hotel usually tells little about its ownership or whether it is managed under contract or as a franchise. Figure 3-1 shows the major U.S. lodging chains, the number of properties carrying their banner, and how many are owned, franchised, or managed. Many major hotel/motel chains—Holiday Inn, Hilton International, Intercontinental Hotels, Motel 6, Travelodge, Westin, Omni, and Stouffer—that were originally American owned are now owned by non-U.S. parent companies. Asian-Americans own about 7000 U.S. hotels and have their own 600-member Asian-American Hotel Owners Association (*Lodging Hospitality*, April, 1992).

Illustrating the transnational and shifting ownership of chain hotels was the purchase of Westin Hotels & Resorts (established in the 1930s in Seattle, Washington) from the parent company of United Airlines in October, 1987. Westin was bought at that time by the Aoki Corporation in partnership with the Bass Group of Texas for $1.53 billion, one of the largest hotel deals in history. In 1994 the Aoki company agreed to sell a large portion of the lodging chain to a Mexican conglomerate for $708 million. Under the deal, Westin's brand name, business operations in North America, South America, and Europe will be owned by DSC, a large Mexico City based construction and real estate firm with interests in hotels and travel agencies. Aoki will retain Westin's properties in Asia, six hotels in Canada, and several minority investments in the United States.

HOTEL INCOME

Hotel income derives from operations, and for many hotel companies, from franchise fees and management fees. Developers get income from building and then usually selling the properties. In the 1980s, franchisors negotiated fees of up to 9 percent of room revenue for adding a hotel to its reservation and marketing system. In some cases, this increased room revenues as much as 20 percent. In other cases, the franchise name and system did little for the property's income. The franchisor was largely risk-free and could remove the franchise if the franchisee failed to make fee payments or live up to the franchise agreement. During the 1980s, franchise fees dropped from between 9 to 12 percent of revenues to between 4 and 7 percent of sales. According to Coopers & Lybrand, the New York accounting firm, franchising is 25 percent more profitable than building or operating hotels. ("Why Hotel Rates Won't Take off Yet," *Fortune*, October 4, 1993, p. 126) A few hotel companies, notably Marriott, played both the developer and the franchise game, building hotels and then negotiating a sales and management contract.

Casino hotels can generate huge profits. Hilton Hotels revenue for 1993 reached $1.4 billion of which $502.1 million came from its casinos; room revenue was $440.2 million; and food and beverage sales $236.8 million. Income from management and franchise fees was $85.1 million. (*Wall Street Journal*, September 8, 1994).

Financial Problems

Hotels, like most other businesses, are subject to the whims of the economy, particularly the regional economy: Occupancy rates rise during prosperity, fall in recession. Overlaying the economic curve of hotel occupancy are cycles of overbuilding that
(*Text continued on page 59*)

Rank	U.S. Lodging Chains	U.S. Properties		Status of Properties				Foreign Properties	
		Rooms	Number of Properties	Company owned	Franchised Licensed	Management Contract	Other Properties	Rooms	Number of Properties
1	*Hospitality Franchise System* *Persippany, NJ*								
	Days Inns of America	142,907	1,400	0	1,400	0	0	4,504	41
	Howard Johnson	62,111	565	0	565	0	0	4,907	34
	Ramada	102,673	638	0	638	0	0	0	0
	Super 8 Motels	59,516	970	0	970	0	0	676	12
	Park Inns International	6,000	61	N/A	N/A	N/A	N/A	N/A	N/A
	TOTAL	373,207	3,634	0	3,573	0	0	10,087	87
2	*Holiday Inn Worldwide* *Atlanta, GA*								
	Holiday Inn	294,226	1,522	85	1,437	0	0	0	0
	Holiday Inn Crowne Plaza	22,865	67	13	54	0	0	0	0
	Holiday Inn Crowne Plaza Resort	1,016	4	1	3	0	0	0	0
	Holiday Inn Express	10,298	98	3	95	0	0	0	0
	Holiday Inn Sunspree Resort	632	2	0	2	0	0	0	0
	Holiday Inn Garden Court	0	0	0	0	0	0	3,881	25
	TOTAL	329,037	1693	102	1,591	0	0	3,881	25

Figure 3-1 Major U.S. Lodging Chains

Rank	U.S. Lodging Chains	U.S. Properties		Status of Properties				Foreign Properties	
		Rooms	Number of Properties	Company owned	Franchised Licensed	Management Contract	Other Properties	Rooms	Number of Properties
3	*Choice Hotels International Silver Spring, MD*								
	Clarion Hotels/Suites/Resorts	10,862	60	0	60	0	0	4,209	20
	Comfort Inns/Suites	71,616	824	7	817	0	0	17,787	257
	Econo Lodge	48,827	699	0	699	0	0	241	4
	Friendship Inns	6,469	134	0	134	0	0	139	3
	Quality Inns/Hotels/Suites	50,273	390	9	381	0	0	16,726	141
	Rodeway Inns	10,420	104	1	103	0	0	195	1
	Sleep Inns	1,559	20	0	20	0	0	373	4
	TOTAL	200,026	2,231	17	2,214	0	0	39,670	430
4	*Best Western International Phoenix, AZ*								
	Best Western	185,614	1,790	0	0	0	1,790	107,738	1,546
	TOTAL	185,674	1,790	0	0	0	1,790	107,738	1,546
5	*Marriott Corp. Washington, DC*								
	Courtyard by Marriott	30,400	213	193	20	0	0	600	4
	Fairfield Inn	2,250	123	80	43	0	0	0	0
	Marriott Hotels/Resorts/Suites	88,838	208	24	67	117	0	12,859	39
	Residence Inn	22,666	182	73	67	42	0	0	0
	TOTAL	144,154	726	370	197	159	0	13,468	43

Figure 3-1 (Continued)

Rank	U.S. Lodging Chains	U.S. Properties		Status of Properties				Foreign Properties	
		Rooms	Number of Properties	Company owned	Franchised Licensed	Management Contract	Other Properties	Rooms	Number of Properties
6	*Hilton Hotels Corp. Beverly Hills, CA*								
	Conrad Hotels	0	0	0	0	0	0	2,520	7
	Hilton Garden Inns	658	4	0	2	1	1	0	0
	Hilton Hotels	47,530	51	17	0	24	10	0	0
	Hilton Inns	44,334	176	0	176	0	0	0	0
	Hilton Suites	1,246	6	4	1	0	1	0	0
	TOTAL	93,768	237	21	179	25	12	2,520	7
7	*IBL Limited, Inc. Scarsdale, NY*								
	Motel 6	85,197	758	679	0	79	0	0	0
	TOTAL	85,197	758	679	0	79	0	0	0
8	*ITT Sheraton Corp. Boston, MA*								
	Sheraton Hotels/Resorts	58,890	154	13	104	37	0	45,397	131
	Sheraton Inns	20,486	111	0	111	0	0	349	3
	Sheraton Suites	2,502	10	1	2	7	0	0	0
	TOTAL	81,878	275	14	217	44	0	45,746	134
9	*The Promus Companies Inc. Memphis, TN*								
	Embassy Suites	25,612	104	58	46	0	0	332	1
	Harrah's	6,242	5	5	0	0	0	0	0
	Hampton Inn	41,621	345	15	330	0	0	0	0
	Homewood Suites	2,686	24	8	16	0	0	0	0
	TOTAL	76,161	478	86	392	0	0	332	1

Figure 3-1 (Continued)

Rank	U.S. Lodging Chains	U.S. Properties		Status of Properties				Foreign Properties	
		Rooms	Number of Properties	Company owned	Franchised Licensed	Management Contract	Other Properties	Rooms	Number of Properties
10	*Hyatt Corp.* *Chicago, IL*								
	Hyatt Regency Hotels/Resorts	54,891	103	0	0	103	0	15,750	47
	Park Hyatt	809	3	0	0	3	0	1,389	6
	Grand Hyatt	0	0	0	0	0	0	4,103	7
	TOTAL	55,700	106	0	0	106	0	21,242	60
11	*Carlson Hospitality Group, Inc.* *Minneapolis, MN*								
	Colony Hotels & Resorts	5,607	32	0	8	21	3	1,663	7
	Country Lodging by Carlson	1,872	20	0	20	0	0	787	11
	Radisson Hotels International	47,969	196	0	171	25	0	17,535	65
	TOTAL	55,448	248	0	199	46	3	19,985	83
12	*Forte Hotels* *El Cajon, CA*								
	Travelodge	41,250	489	40	310	10	129*	4,200	110
	Thriftlodge	2,050	30	29	1	0	0	0	0
	Forte (various)	1,622	5	N/A	N/A	N/A	N/A	35,990	253
	TOTAL	44,922	524	69	311	10	129	40,190	363
13	*La Quinta Motor Inns, Inc.* *San Antonio, TX*								
	La Quinta Inns	27,002	212	169	3	40	0	0	0
	TOTAL	27,002	212	169	3	40	0	0	0

*Joint venture ownerships

Figure 3-1 (Continued)

Rank	U.S. Lodging Chains	U.S. Properties		Status of Properties				Foreign Properties	
		Rooms	Number of Properties	Company owned	Franchised Licensed	Management Contract	Other Properties	Rooms	Number of Properties
14	*Hospitality International, Inc.* *Atlanta, GA*								
	Downtowner	265	3	0	3	0	0	0	0
	Master Hosts Inns	1,355	21	0	21	0	0	170	2
	Passport Inns	1,465	23	0	23	0	0	0	0
	Red Carpet Inn	10,402	157	0	157	0	0	123	2
	Scottish Inns	10,858	166	0	166	0	0	37	1
	TOTAL	24,345	370	0	370	0	0	330	5
15	*Red Roof Inns* *Columbus, OH*								
	Red Roof Inns	23,256	209	209	0	0	0	0	0
	TOTAL	23,256	209	209	0	0	0	0	0
16	*Westin Motels & Resorts* *Seattle, WA*								
	Westin Hotels & Resorts	22,749	38	18	2	16	2	10,676	23
	Caesar Park Hotels	0	0	0	0	0	0	1,075	6
	Camino Real	375	1	0	0	1	0	3,296	12
	TOTAL	23,124	39	18	2	17	2	15,047	41
17	*Economy Lodging Systems, Inc.* *Cleveland, OH*								
	Arborgate Inn	920	10	0	10	0	0	0	0
	Knights Court	1,875	15	10	5	0	0	0	0
	Knights Inn	19,619	155	15	106	34	0	0	0
	Knights Stop	86	2	0	2	0	0	0	0
	TOTAL	22,500	182	25	123	34	0	0	0

Figure 3-1 (Continued)

Rank	U.S. Lodging Chains	U.S. Properties		Status of Properties				Foreign Properties	
		Rooms	Number of Properties	Company owned	Franchised Licensed	Management Contract	Other Properties	Rooms	Number of Properties
18	R&B Realty Group Los Angeles, CA								
	Oakwood Corporate Apartments	21,084	40	25	0	15	0	0	0
	TOTAL	21,084	40	25	0	15	0	0	0
19	Preferred Hotels Oakbrook Terrace, IL								
	Preferred Hotels	16,774	89	0	0	0	89	7,749	30
	TOTAL	16,774	89	0	0	0	89	7,749	30
20	Stouffer Hotels & Resorts Scion, OH								
	Stouffer Hotels & Resorts	15,540	40	31	0	9	0	0	0
	Stouffer Presidente Hotels/Resorts	0	0	0	0	0	0	1,834	6
	TOTAL	15,540	40	31	0	9	0	1,834	6

Source: Lodging Hospitality, August 1993

Figure 3-1 (Continued)

occur with prosperity, when easy credit is available and/or tax laws provide rapid depreciation, making hotel construction attractive. At times, money is there for the asking from banks and other financial institutions, pension funds, insurance companies, and to a lesser degree, private investors. In the 1980s another factor favored excessive hotel building—the foreign investor. Japanese, French, British, and Hong Kong money poured into the United States to purchase hotels because of the U.S. government policy of favoring a cheap American dollar. The Japanese yen and the British pound almost doubled in value versus the U.S. dollar, thereby making U.S. hotels inexpensive. American hotel and motel owners were pleased to sell for prices that had increased dramatically. In the late 1980s, several megaresort hotels were built with foreign capital in Hawaii and a number of golf courses around the country were bought or built with international money.

Easy money made it possible for hotel developers to borrow vast sums for construction, and as a result, too many hotels and resorts were built. Many were overleveraged: too much debt for the earning capacity of the property. Leveraged buyouts made possible by the sale of junk bonds made fortunes for a few but put unwary investors who were attracted by high yields on the bonds at risk. Many hotel companies had such large debts that even with relatively high occupancies and good management, interest payments were difficult to meet. Small drops in occupancy were enough to place the properties in financial jeopardy.

By 1993 the hotel industry in the United States had experienced eleven consecutive years of losses totaling more than $33 billion, a record reminiscent of the Great Depression of the 1930s when as many as 80 percent of hotels were in financial trouble ("Hotel Business is Waking Up," *The New York Times*, Oct. 2, 1993). In several American cities, hotels had market value declines of up to 50 percent in 1993. The reasons for the losses were several, but the most serious resulted from hotels being built as tax shelters rather than in response to market demand. The hotel business is cyclical. When hotel occupancies rise and investments look promising, too many hotel rooms are built. A period of time is then necessary for demand to catch up with supply.

Real estate developers were encouraged by financial institutions to borrow money and build even though many of the projects were not feasible. Some feasibility studies conducted by accounting firms projected unrealistically high income. The economic recession, which started in 1989, kept hotel occupancies low even though hotel rates were stable or declined. Hotel customers benefited but hotel profits vanished.

By the end of 1993, the overbuilding cycle appeared to have passed. Very few new rooms were built. Thousands of rooms had been taken off the market. The average number of employees per 100 guest rooms dropped to 50, according to Smith Travel Research, a company that compiles occupancy data for the American Hotel & Motel Association. This figure is probably much too low for large hotels. Large full service hotels, in all likelihood, have at least 70 employees for every 100 hotel guest rooms. Hotel occupancy on a national basis was expected to increase from 62 percent in 1992 to 64 percent in 1994. Further cost reductions were realized due to lowered property taxes and management fees, as well as tighter management controls. Group meeting and convention sales were also increasing in volume as the economic recession appeared to have ended by 1993.

In the 1980s hotel developers dreamed big, built big, and profited royally. The most flamboyant, Chris Hemmeter, built such Hawaiian properties as the Hyatt Regency Maui, the Westin Maui, the Westin Kauai, and the Hyatt Regency Waikoloa (on the island of Hawaii, the "Big Island"). Hemmeter's imagination was boundless—he proposed building seven pyramids in Atlantic City, each larger than the Grand Pyramid at Giza outside of Cairo, Egypt. Each pyramid would be seventy stories tall and be sheathed in golden glass. "Lighted at night," said Hemmeter, "you'd be able to see the pyramid for hundreds of miles." The pyramid project, however, was never built.

Mr. Hemmeter's developments that did come to fruition paid off handsomely. He netted about $188 million when he sold the Hyatt Regency Maui and his Waikiki Beach Hotel in Honolulu. Another $72 million came from a 12.5 percent equity he retained in those hotels along with various concessions and ground leases he kept in Waikiki. His formula: Conceive a grand plan, promote the financing, build the property, and then sell the project for a handsome profit. Much or most of his financing came from Japanese investors whose conceptions of real estate values were based on the Japanese market, and whose deep pockets were enlarged by the weak American dollar. In 1993, after the disastrous 1992 hurricane on Kauai, the Westin resort on that island was repossessed. The $350 million resort, and the U.S. arm of Westin International, was up for sale. In 1993 the hotel sat totally empty.

Mr. Hemmeter's grandiose plans of the 1980s did not seem too far-fetched in 1993 when the Luxor hotel was opened in Las Vegas. The $390 million megaresort is shaped like a pyramid, with a glass exterior, and fronted by a ten-story sphinx. It features futuristic amusements, lasers, and waterways, all built to entertain and attract casino patrons. The $1 billion MGM Grand Hotel Casino and Theme Park is even grander in concept and scale than the Luxor.

KINDS OF HOTELS

Hotels in the broad sense include any public lodging establishment ranging from the bed-and-breakfast family operation of a few rooms to the megahotel of several thousand rooms. Hotels can be classified according to the rate structure, location, and type of guest. Convention hotels cater to the convention visitor but also welcome the leisure traveler. Resort hotels may concentrate on attracting group business but advertise as a vacation property. All-suite hotels, a relatively new hotel concept, with complimentary breakfasts and cocktail hours, may seek both the business and the pleasure traveler. Casino hotels are built for one purpose: to attract the person who will engage in gaming, be it slot machines, craps, or other games of chance. Airport hotels are built to serve the air traveler. The 20,000 bed-and-breakfasts in the United States usually have only a few rooms for rent, some quite expensive.

Budget (economy) hotels attract about 30 percent of hotel guests because of the low prices offered. The average daily rate for budget hotel rooms in 1990 was $28.56 (*Hotel/Motel Management*, April 29, 1991, p. 35). Personnel costs for the typical budget property are low. Chains like Motel 6 often hire a husband-and-wife team to run the property; an apartment is provided for their use to compensate for their relatively low salaries. Non-family-owned motels will have few management personnel: usually a general manager and a food service manager.

Up a notch from the budget hotels are the so-called limited service properties represented by the Comfort Inns, Hampton Inns, and La Quinta chains. The limited service chains are the modern successor to the highway motels built in the 1950s and 1960s. With the economic recession, beginning in 1989, hotels caught with huge debt loads and low occupancies tried to reduce payrolls, and many of the newly built hotels were designed to limit the number of personnel needed to operate them. Hampton Inns, a subsidiary of the Promus Companies of Memphis, Tennessee, is an example. A staff of about twenty to twenty-four can run the typical Hampton Inn, which has no restaurant but is built close to a full-service independent restaurant. A free continental breakfast is served in the lobby. The mini-size Hampton Inn requires only the equivalent of 12 full-time employees, from desk clerks to maids. The basic Hampton Inn costs about $31,000 (excluding land) a room to build, compared to $80,000 or more a room for a full-service business hotel ("Limited-Service Chains Offer Enough to Thrive," *Wall Street Journal*, July 27, 1992).

The better known hotels frequented by the business traveler and sometimes called "upscale" are the Hiltons, Hyatts, Sheratons, and Marriotts; properties in the tradition of full-service hotels with at least one restaurant. Many of these hotels offer concierge service. Labor costs are high, in the range of 34 percent to 38 percent of gross income.

Resort hotels can be any property that offers sports facilities. At one time resorts catered largely to vacationers; now many resorts depend heavily on conventions and other group sales for income.

The so-called megahotels, hotels with 1000 or more rooms, are scattered around the world but with a heavy concentration in the United States. Of the 151 megahotels in 1991, 100 were located in the United States. Las Vegas alone had 18 such properties. Asia and the Pacific Region had 30 of these very large hotels, 12 of which were in Japan and 11 in the Peoples Republic of China. Europe had 14 of the 1000-plus room hotels (*Hotel*, August 1991). The MGM Grand Hotel and Theme Park in Las Vegas contains just over 5000 rooms, and according to its owners, is the "world's largest hotel." It could also be called a megahotel with a casino and a theme park.

Trophy Hotels

A new term entered the hotel vocabulary when, beginning in 1987, some luxury hotels with prestigious locations were bid up to prices that broke all valuation rules. These became trophy hotels, properties such as the Hotel Bel-Air in Beverly Hills and the Beverly Hills Hotel. The owners of the Hotel Bel-Air received $1.1 million a room. The Sultan of Brunei paid $757,000 per room for the Beverly Hills Hotel. The reasons for these astronomical prices are said to involve the egos of the buyers and the fact that over time the land they sit on will exceed the purchase price.

Japanese buyers place a much higher value on real estate than do most Americans. Paying over a million dollars a room for a hotel takes on some of the same rationale as paying $50 million for a van Gogh painting. Donald Trump, the New York real estate tycoon, paid $496,000 a room for the Plaza, a New York City landmark, probably as much for the gratification of owning this historic building as for its financial value. Whoever owns it takes on a certain prominence. Like public stock buyers, these hotel owners expect to sell for an even higher price. Hotel chain presidents buy or operate trophy properties partly because they bring status to the entire chain.

Some developers and owners made large profits by selling trophy hotels. The Hotel Bel-Air, for example, was bought in 1982 for $23 million by the Dallas-based Rosewood Company, another $20 million was spent on renovations and the addition of thirty rooms and suites. The owners sold the property (including 11.5 acres of prime real estate) seven years later for $110 million to the Tokyo-based Sekital Keihatsu Company ("Was the Bel-Air Worth It?" *Lodging Hospitality,* October 1989, pp. 144-146).

Lodging Only a Part of the Luxury Hotel

The large luxury hotels located in major cities around the world are more than lodging establishments. Most represent a high-society lifestyle and are the venues of business deals, the meeting places of diplomats, and the intersections of various cultures. Hotels like the Oriental in Bangkok, the Waldorf Astoria in New York, the Portman of London, and the Ritz of Paris cater to high-level business and affluent pleasure travelers. Major hotels play a large role in Japan, Korea, Thailand, and Hong Kong. Most major hotels—especially those with an international clientele—offer excellent food service, including room service and a choice of several cuisines. The afternoon tea, once the province of a few luxury European hotels, is being served in many hotels worldwide. The concierge, also European in origin, is found in most major international hotels.

Casino Hotels

Casino hotels are a breed apart from the usual commercial hotel. They are highly profitable when well located and marketed. Casino hotels exist first and foremost to provide glamour, entertainment, and excellent, yet inexpensive, food and beverage— all with the purpose of enticing the visitor into the casino. The odds favoring the house means that the visitor, if he or she plays long enough, will inevitably depart minus 10 to 20 percent short of what is bet at the slot machines, bingo games, crap tables, roulette wheels, and other gaming devices. What is remarkable is that most visitors, despite losing money, feel they have a good time and are willing to pay for the world-class entertainment found in many casino hotels. Casino hotels are more aptly called hotels with casinos because the hotel's construction and its main reason for existence is the casino. Many casino hotels charge low room rates in order to fuel the urge to get something for nothing. Gaming, the more genteel name for gambling, is fast becoming one of America's leading sports (or addictions). As of 1994 Las Vegas casinos have made that city the largest proprietor in the world with 86,000 hotel guest rooms. Orlando, Florida follows with 79,000 guest rooms.

Profits for casino hotels can be enormous. Casino hotels can also declare bankruptcy as did the Taj Mahal in Atlantic City. Up to 40 percent of Hilton Hotels' profit is taken from its Las Vegas hotels. Nevada's gambling revenue in 1992 topped $6 billion, with Las Vegas-area casinos alone reporting $4.23 billion from gaming income. Las Vegas is the archetypical hotel casino city, leaving its ancestors like Baden Baden (Germany), Monte Carlo (Monaco), and Biarritz (France) as small-time players in glamour and imagination. Casino hotels in Las Vegas provide guest rooms that are less than half the price of comparable quality hotels, a weekday room sells for less than $60. High-rollers (heavy gamblers) are given complementary suites and some are flown free of charge from their homes.

The casino business is highly competitive. Superlatives describe each new hotel, each more glamorous. "The" Las Vegas hotel in 1993 was the previously mentioned megaresort, the Luxor. Transport to some guest rooms is by barge on the Luxor's indoor river that carries the guest to one of four elevator banks built into the corners of the pyramid-shaped hotel. The Luxor has its sphinx' eyes shooting lasers towards a towering obelisk and a lagoon. The waters of the lagoon "boil," producing a steaming water screen on which Egyptian images are projected. In case anyone misses the Luxor in the Las Vegas area a light beams seven miles into the sky, brightly lit by 45 xenon units, said to be the world's most powerful light. The Luxor also has slot machines that accept $5 and $10 bills.

Like the Luxor, the MGM Grand Hotel Casino and Theme Park is a combined casino-hotel-entertainment complex. Its theme park, patterned after a movie studio, contains twelve attractions, one a special effects show that puts the audience into movie scenes. The 33-acre park should keep the kids happy for at least two days while their parents are gambling. To help insure that the high-rollers will get to the casino, there is the MGM Grand Air Charter service. A 15,000 seat arena features championship boxing matches. The MGM Grand's casinos are expected to generate revenue approximating $700 million in its first year of operation. Each of its slot machines is expected to clear as much as $135 a day. The new hotels create employment for thousands of people. Between them, the Luxor and Excalibur (a Circus Circus property) operate some 7500 guest rooms, and have about 7000 employees, or about one employee per guest room.

Operating a casino hotel is more complicated than the usual hotel. Many of the guests feel it is perfectly fine to cheat the house. Consequently security abounds: plenty of security personnel (plainclothes police) and "eyes in the sky" (TV cameras trained on the players from openings under the ceiling). Security employees check on other security personnel.

Call it gaming, gambling, recreation, tourism, or what have you, gambling is growing more widespread and there will be more, and a greater variety of, casino hotels. For casino hotel operators it is a hard-headed business with entertainment costs and other expenses computed to keep profits coming, even though top-notch entertainers are paid in the millions. The La Mirage Hotel in Las Vegas claims its "Siegfried and Roy" stage show was created at a cost of $50 million, including a $25 million, 1500-seat theater. The show features two dozen wild animals, of which nineteen are rare white tigers. One illusion turns a woman into a 600-pound white tiger; another makes an elephant disappear into thin air.

The Las Vegas Convention Bureau reports that tourists spend nearly $500 per person per visit, and conventioneers spend nearly $1000 per person per visit. Non-gambling visitors in Las Vegas spend over $10 billion a year. About 25 percent of the state's workforce is employed directly in the gaming industry while 69 percent work in tourism (Tom Powers, *Introduction to Management in the Hospitality Industry*, New York: John Wiley & Sons, 1992, p. 362).

Casino operators study their market. The high-roller's average bet is between $150 and $250. To receive casino credit the high-roller is expected to have a line of credit of $15,000 available during a typical three-day visit to Las Vegas. The average slot machine player bets $3 per pull and averages 300 lever pulls on a machine (or several machines as is often the case). The total input in each machine is therefore $900 per player. From an economic aspect, these averages work out nicely for the casinos, since they make between 5 and 8 percent profit on each machine. The mathematics is straightforward: The average player will put $900 in the slot machines and the casino will keep between $45 (five percent) and $72 (eight percent). Fifty-five percent of the total dollars bet in a casino is in the slot machines, yielding an average of 80 percent of a casino's profit. Conversely, the remaining 45 percent of the bets placed (on blackjack, roulette, craps, etc.) only yield 20 percent of the profit.

Atlantic City has its high-rollers, but a majority of visitors come by bus (known as bus junkets). Bus junketeers usually get a roll of coins, inexpensive meals, and a diversion from the usual routines in their lives. On a typical day between 1000 and 1500 charter buses arrive and stay between four and twelve hours. This proved to be unfortunate for the general economy of the city which has had little economic benefit, in terms of infrastructure growth, from the gambling.

Food service in many casino hotels is not expected to make a profit, the low prices bring customers who are potential gaming customers. Some forty Las Vegas hotels offer all-you-can eat buffets that are some of the world's best food bargains. For high-rollers all costs are complimentary (commonly referred to as "compted"): free rooms, food, beverages, and entertainment. Casino hotels hope to make the most of picking up, transporting, and "comping" all high-rollers, who must have a good line of credit.

The general sentiment against gambling seems to be passing. *Las Vegas Advisor* publisher Curtis feels that gambling's negative stigma has been removed since even the government encourages gambling (through state-sponsored lotteries) ("Casino Slot Clubs a No-Lose Situation in Vegas—Sort of," *San Diego Union*, March 27, 1994). Riverboat gambling, and casinos operated by Native Americans (who can legally bypass state laws governing gambling) is increasing. The control of much of casino gambling by the mafia has disappeared, at least on the surface. Legalized gambling rose from two states (Nevada and New Jersey) in 1989 to sixteen in 1993. Five states now allow casino gambling and a number of states have agreed to gaming on Native American lands.

Since the Indian Gaming Regulatory Act of 1988, 176 bingo parks and casinos have sprung up, the biggest and most successful being operated by the Mashantucket Pequot Nation in Ledyard, Connecticut, which owns some 3000 acres and operates Foxwood High Stakes & Casino, a theme park and golf course. As many as 25,000 visitors per day come on a Saturday or Sunday, 18,000 per day on weekdays. The

9000-employee operation is well managed: Slot machines, video poker, video craps, and video blackjack ring up huge profits by always allowing an average payoff of 92.4 percent. Some $32 million is taken in each month from the slot machines alone.

Foxwood may be the most profitable casino in the world, guaranteed by a monopoly granted it by the state of Connecticut in return for a guarantee of $100 million a year plus one quarter of the income from slot machines. Of course, Donald Trump, known for his deals, thinks it unfair. Foxwood got its financing from UBAT, an Arab-American bank, and from the Lim family of Malaysia who invest in casinos in Australia and the Bahamas, and in commercial shipping, cruise ships, and rubber production (Julie Baumgold, "Frank and the Fox Pack," *Esquire*, March 1994, pp. 89–96).

Several factors related to the volume of casino gambling are listed below.

- The regional and national economy, especially those regions close to the casinos (California is believed to provide half, or more, of the visitors to Las Vegas and Reno).
- The national sentiment for legalized gambling which, in the 1990s, has been increasingly tolerant about gambling in its many forms.
- Airfares, and the cost and availability of gasoline (fuel shortages raise the price of gasoline and aviation fuel).
- Exchange rates (favorable rates for Europeans and Asians increase travel to U.S. casinos).
- Casino marketing and glamour (worldwide coverage of casino openings has increased the number of foreign visitors to Nevada and Atlantic City).
- The numbers of retired people who casino gamble is rising as are the number of "junkets" (expense-paid trips paid for by the casinos).

The Lodging Leaders

Until the 1980s it was fairly easy to keep track of the large lodging chains worldwide. The names Sheraton, Hilton International, Intercontinental, Westin, Holiday Inn, and Marriott were well known and U.S.-based. By 1994 lodging ownership had become much more international and the list of the top lodging chains changes frequently. British, French, and Japanese names are among the top twenty lodging chains. The fifty largest lodging chains as of December 1992, are presented in Figure 3-2. Motel 6, the typical American budget motel chain, is part of Accor, a French company which, with the addition of some 600 Motel 6 units, is the largest of the non-U.S.-owned lodging chains.

Most of the large hotel companies have moved out of ownership to become management, franchise, or marketing/referral companies. The large chains represent a mixture of ownership and franchised operations. Many also operate hotels under management contract. Holiday Inn Worldwide and ITT Sheraton do not own most of the hotels that operate under their names. Neither does Days Inns of America. Most of the Choice Hotels International are franchisees. Best Western International is a marketing/referral organization whose members are independent owners.

The 50 Largest Corporate Hotel Chains in the World, 1992

Rank 1992	Organization	Company Headquarters	Rooms 1992	Hotels 1992
1	Hospitality Franchise Systems	USA	354,997	3,413
2	Holiday Inn Worldwide	USA	328,679	1,692
3	Best Western International	USA	273,804	3,351
4	Accor	France	238,990	2,098
5	Choice Hotels International Inc.	USA	230,430	2,502
6	Marriott Corp.	USA	166,919	750
7	ITT Sheraton Corp.	USA	132,361	426
8	Hilton Hotels Corp.	USA	94,653	242
9	Forte Pic	England	79,309	871
10	Hyatt Hotels/Hyatt International	USA	77,579	164
11	Carlson/Radisson/Colony	USA	76,069	336
12	Promus Companies	USA	75,558	459
13	Club Méditerranée SA	France	63,067	261
14	Hilton International	England	52,979	160
15	Sol Group	Spain	40,163	156
16	Inter-Continental Hotels	England	39,000	104
17	Westin Hotels & Resorts	USA	38,029	75
18	New World/Ramada International	Hong Kong	36,520	133
19	Canadian Pacific Hotels	Canada	27,970	86
20	Société du Louvre	France	27,427	398
21	La Quinta Motor Inns Inc.	USA	25,925	209
22	Red Roof Inns	USA	23,443	210
23	Tokyu Hotel Group	Japan	22,671	102
24	Hospitality International Inc.	USA	22,425	345
25	Husa Hotels Group	Spain	21,500	98
26	Knights Lodging System	USA	21,300	180
27	Prince Hotels Inc.	Japan	20,249	70
28	Meridien Hotels	France	18,261	58
29	Omni Hotels	USA	18,148	45
30	SAS Intl. Hotels/Sunwing	Belgium	16,507	46
31	Scandic Hotel AB	Sweden	16,000	97
32	Stouffer Hotel Company	USA	15,767	41
33	Fujita Kamko Inc.	Japan	14,891	65
34	Queens Moat Houses Hotels	England	14,697	126
35	Mount Charlotte/Thistle	England	14,320	114
36	Red Lion Hotels & Inns	USA	13,910	53
37	Nikko Hotels International	Japan	13,590	33
38	Reso Hotels	Sweden	13,350	61
39	Cubatur	Cuba	12,455	100
40	Southern Pacific Hotels	Australia	12,346	70
41	Four Seasons Hotels/Resorts	Canada	11,894	34
42	Interhotels	Germany	11,668	31
43	Ana Enterprises Ltd.	Japan	11,210	33
44	Circus Circus	USA	11,145	5
45	Park Inns International	USA	11,006	80
46	Maritim Hotels	Germany	10,900	41
47	Orbis Co. Inc.	Poland	10,788	55
48	Walt Disney Company	USA	10,642	13
49	U.S. National Park Service	USA	10,223	164
50	National 9 Inns	USA	10,200	172

Note: Rankings are based on total rooms open as of December 31, 1992.

Source: Hotels, July 1993, a division of Reed Publishing, USA

Figure 3-2 The Fifty Largest Corporate Hotel Chains in the World, 1992

The Value of "Location"

One of the widely quoted statements made by Ellsworth M. Statler, premier hotelman of his time, concerned the value of a hotel's location. When asked the three most important things about a hotel, he replied: "First, location; second, location; third, location." The answers depend upon the market(s) being sought by management and a variety of other factors. A hotel located in Fiji is of little value without regular and relatively inexpensive air service. A resort hotel's value depends in large part on its surroundings—ocean, mountains or other attractive setting. A convention hotel is enhanced by a convention center nearby. A highway motor hotel must be on or close to a highway; an airport hotel must have rooms in or near a busy airport.

Prestige hotels gain prestige by catering to prestigious guests. It does not hurt to be located on the Champs Elysees in Paris or Central Park in New York City. The Plaza Hotel in New York City has had its favored location since 1907. The Waldorf Astoria hotel in New York City gained prestige by having General Douglas MacArthur as a long time guest (free, of course, to the General and his family, who overstayed their welcome). The really prime hotel locations, even though they decline at some time, can reincarnate themselves with new ownership. Railway stations were once highly desirable locations for hotels in the United States. This is no longer the case, but innovative new owners have been able to turn some of these "relics of the past" into desirable, nostalgic, hotels.

A hotel's location can be enhanced by its management. The Four Seasons hotels and the Ritz Carlton chain add to the character and the éclat of the hotels they manage by carefully selecting appointments and staff, and providing outstanding food and beverage service. A prestige hotel must be careful that its rates are not so low as to attract the "wrong" kind of guests. No bus tour groups, please.

Location as an abstraction is an ambiguous term until spelled out in terms of market, management, accessibility, and kind of guest. In the last analysis, a location's value is what the market value of the hotel is at any given time. For most investors market value is what the hotel can produce in profit, appreciation, or can be sold for later.

HOTEL ROOM RATES

Room rates are set according to what management believes can be charged and still attract the maximum number of guests. The advertised room rate is the rate established for, and quoted from, the "rack rate," the rate that is published as being the standard rate for each of various kinds of rooms offered by the hotel. The Average Daily Rate (ADR) is what the hotel actually receives in revenue, computed by dividing room revenue by number of occupied rooms. Published rates are discounted to corporate travelers (corporate rate), and to senior citizens, students, and other groups. Convention groups get a negotiated convention rate. Airline employees and travel agents usually receive sizable discounts. Casino hotels give complimentary rooms to high-rollers and usually heavily discount weekday rooms. Tour groups negotiate special rates. Other groups, such as the military and tour groups, may be given reduced rates. Most resort hotels charge rates that change with the seasons. In the end the ADR can be 20 to 50 percent lower than published rates. Management's goal is to raise the ADR and the occupancy rate, while holding constant, or reducing, expenses.

Establishing a "right" room rate can be complicated, dictated in large part by what competitive hotels charge, and is dependent on costs and "what the market will bear." Peter Drucker, the well-known management consultant, argues against pricing at "what the market will bear." Mispricing, he says, creates a risk-free opportunity for the competition (Peter Drucker, "The Five Deadly Business Sins," *Wall Street Journal*, October 21, 1993). Management of new hotels seem well aware of this caveat. When a new property opens it offers rates below the prevailing market. Newly opened Marriott hotels, for example, not only offer low rates but also low meal prices, later raised when the hotel is established.

Others argue that "price" is in the eyes of the guest. If the guest thinks it is too high, it is. It can be too low. Price is a symbol of quality. A low price can signal poor quality regardless of reality (Margaret Shaw, "Hotel Pricing," In *VNR's Encyclopedia of Hospitality and Tourism*, New York: Van Nostrand Reinhold, 1993, pp. 435–457).

When occupancy is low in an area, and has been for some time (as was the case in the late 1980s and early 1990s), hotel management tends to forget the admonition to hold prices steady. When occupancy rates drop below 60 percent hotel managers may cut prices to levels at which few hotels, especially those with large debt loads, can make a profit, no matter how excellent the management.

Should a hotel charge less than enough to meet fixed costs? The answer in many cases has been yes, because management must meet competitive pricing even though the hotel is operated at a loss. Hundreds of hotels did just this during the late 1980s and early 1990s. The alternative was to sell the property or continue to operate as tightly as possible by cutting staff and expenses.

During the 1930s many hotels closed down whole floors, rented rooms to permanent guests at very low rates, and did other things to reduce losses. The Waldorf Astoria was bought by Conrad Hilton with bonds at five cents on the dollar. Later, with the onset of World War II, Hilton profited greatly as hotels reached occupancy rates of 97 percent. Rooms were sometimes rented three times over a 24-hour period.

Fixed costs in a hotel run roughly 70 to 75 percent of income; variable costs, 25 to 30 percent. Logically it makes little sense to sell a room at less than enough to cover fixed costs. But what if the "marginal" room (the last room sold) could not have been sold at a rate sufficient to cover the fixed costs? Is it better to get the extra guest or to leave the room vacant? Variable costs are relatively low. According to one estimate, $25 to $45 for full service hotels in metropolitan areas (*Ibid.*, p. 455).

In the past, accountants for the hotel industry likened rate cutting to the wages of sin, and produced statistics to prove it. Figure 3-3 shows that to compensate for cutting rates by 20 percent when a hotel had a 64 percent occupancy rate, it would be necessary to raise the occupancy level to 77.2 percent.

Intense competition may set aside the merits of holding or raising rates, leaving management in the position of having to join in the rate-cutting melee. If you do not join in you may be left with very few guests. Yield management, described later in

Occupancy Required at Various Room Rate Reductions

Present Occupancy Level	Room Rate Reduction			
	5%	10%	15%	20%
78%	81.6%	85.6%	90.0%	94.9%
76	79.5	83.4	87.6	92.4
74	77.4	81.1	85.3	89.8
72	75.3	78.9	82.9	87.3
70	73.2	76.7	80.5	84.8
68	71.1	74.4	78.1	82.2
66	70.0	72.2	75.8	79.7
64	66.9	70.0	73.4	77.2

Source: The U.S. Lodging Industry.

Numbers are for a 352-room suburban hotel. Monthly fixed expenses were $396,349 and variable expenses were $13.46 per occupied room. The percentage of net income to total sales expected at each occupancy level was added to variable expenses.

Figure 3-3 Occupancy Required at Various Room Rate Reductions

this chapter is a kind of sophisticated melee, using computer models to forecast sales by the hour, day, and kind of guest.

The Hubbart Formula

Provided there is little or no cut-throat competition, an accountant or hotel finance officer can rationally arrive at a "correct" ADR. The Hubbart Formula lays out the steps needed to cover all costs and provide a 15 percent profit on investment. The process works backwards: Find the total annual revenue needed to cover all costs and provide a 15 percent return (including desired profit) on investment, then divide by the projected number of rooms that will be sold in the coming year.

The Hubbart Formula, the best known of the room rate formulas, was developed by two national accounting firms, Horwath & Horwath and Harris Kerr Forster (now defunct), and is named in honor of Roy Hubbart of Chicago, who was the major proponent of the plan. As an example, suppose that in a 100-room hotel the total annual income needed for all expenses is $400,000. On a predicted occupancy of 70 percent, the number of rooms that will be sold in the year is 25,550. Suppose the hotel costs $4 million and that the owner expects to make an annual 15 percent return on the investment, or $600,000. The owner needs to take in $1,000,000 (all expenses plus return on investment) divided by 25,550, which gives him an ADR of about $39.14. Other factors may be more important than the mathematical computation, but the Hubbart Formula is still worthwhile as a guide.

The Dollar per Thousand Rule

Another guideline for determining rates is that $1 should be charged for each $1000 dollars invested per room. If a 100-room hotel costs $4 million, the cost per room is

$40,000. The room rate necessary of a fair return on the investment would be $40 ($40,000 per room cost divided by $1000). The usual Holiday Inn costs $40,000 to $50,000 a unit, so the rate based on this formula would be $40 to $50 per room.

The J.M. Pei-designed hotel in New York City was reported to have cost $1 million a room. If so, that hotel, according to the $1000 formula, requires the room rate to be $1000 a night to break even (*Wall Street Journal*, September 4, 1994).

Calculation of the dollar-per-thousand building cost assumes a 70 percent occupancy over the life of the hotel, and management good enough to show a 55 percent house profit on room sales. House profit is defined as all profits except income from store rentals, and before the deduction of insurance, real estate taxes, depreciation, and other capital expenses. It assumes that store rentals will offset real estate taxes and interest charges on the land. The calculation further assumes that the hotel will show an annual 6 percent return on the total investment.

As said earlier, the average rate being discussed is not the rate advertised by the hotel. It is the ADR (total room revenue divided by number of rooms sold). As the percentage of occupancy increases, so does the ADR. Less expensive rooms sell first and as they are sold out, higher priced rooms are sold, raising the ADR.

Several of the large city hotels built in the mid-1970s were part of the urban redevelopment plans—usually in downtown areas—of various cities. The developers were able to secure money at less than the going rate through the economic redevelopment administration of the cities involved. In some cases the land cost them nothing. Feasibility studies and the determination of a room rate had to be tailored to the particular property. The dollar-per-thousand guideline was not relevant. That rule probably applied to the motor hotels, which could still be constructed at somewhat reasonable cost on the outskirts of cities and towns. The dollar-per-thousand guideline was modified to include the cost of land, building, and equipment. A return of 10 percent on invested capital was considered a minimum goal.

Occupancy rate and the ratio of food and beverage sales to room sales vary from one hotel to another. Generally speaking, the greater the ratio of restaurant sales to room sales, the higher the occupancy or room rate needed to achieve a desirable return on the investment. The reason for this is that food and beverage sales do not produce the high percentage of profit generated by room sales.

Other Determinants of Room Rates

For certain areas, and for a limited time, price fixing may occur. This was demonstrated in 1977 when the Hotel Association of Hawaii pleaded "no contest" to criminal charges of conspiring to fix Hawaiian hotel room rates. The price fixing took place during 1971–1972 when visitor totals had dropped and competition had forced room rates below the breakeven point. Tour operators and travel agents were pitted against hotel operators who believed some kind of price fixing was necessary to survive (*Travel Weekly*, May 1977).

With the hotel overbuilding experienced in the late 1980s, competition forced many hotels to operate at a loss. Due to the room rules for most locations there does not seem to have been any price fixing (or price collusion). Prices go up during high seasons, and during major events such as political conventions, football bowl games, or baseball playoffs. Even in those cases hotels will merely charge the published rack rate for as many rooms as possible, and there can be no case made for illegal business practices. Since most hotels have high fixed costs, and price wars tend to hurt every hotel within an area, there is a strong incentive for hotels to not cut prices, even if business is slow.

Throughout the 1970s, hotel rates increased at about the same rate as the consumer price index (CPI), then increased at a higher rate than the CPI throughout the 1980s. Figure 3-4 shows the trends in occupancy rate and ADR for hotels in the United States and abroad from 1985 to 1991. It can be seen that the occupancy rate in U.S. hotels has remained steady while the ADR peaked in 1990 and started to drop by 1991. This trend has continued through 1993—the room rates in budget properties like Motel 6 have dropped below $30 for an individual traveling alone. Package deals for vacation travelers and for "weekend specials" are common. It is interesting to note, as shown in Figure 3-4, that in the same time period of 1985 to 1991 non-U.S. hotels suffered a substantial decline in occupancy rates while the ADR continued to increase. Most of these trends were due to the European hotels.

International and U.S. Hotel Trends, 1985 to 1991

| | Percent of Occupancy | | | | |
	1985	1986	1989	1990	1991
United States of America	66.9%	65.6%	67.2%	66.2%	65.2%
All International Hotels	70.0	67.1	69.0	67.2	63.0
Canada	70.7	68.2	67.6	66.3	60.2
Mexico	60.3	65.9	60.1	61.7	63.7
Latin America	63.5	66.9	61.6	62.9	63.9
Caribbean Region	70.9	69.6	71.7	71.3	70.1
Europe	72.4	66.8	70.8	68.7	62.3
Africa	68.0	64.5	69.0	66.6	60.7
Middle East	56.3	53.0	55.7	60.6	58.1
Pacific Basin	74.9	73.7	77.0	71.4	67.1

| | Average Daily Rate per Occupied Room* | | | | |
	1985	1986	1989	1990	1991
United States of America	$62.60	$66.56	$73.23	$78.76	$75.14
All International Hotels	59.57	64.53	81.54	94.45	96.83
Canada	48.56	53.97	73.07	77.95	78.37
Mexico	42.55	40.96	59.66	64.78	68.24
Latin America	44.35	34.07	61.75	66.76	69.56
Caribbean Region	86.46	100.81	88.03	146.20	114.30
Europe	60.48	73.61	93.52	116.79	116.46
Africa	41.70	51.22	57.69	65.05	74.38
Middle East	72.69	79.19	74.97	83.02	92.06
Pacific Basin	66.06	69.81	87.91	97.02	103.60

*Expressed in U.S. dollars

Source: Pannell Kerr Forster

Figure 3-4 International and U.S. Hotel Trends, 1985 to 1991

ECONOMIC ANALYSIS OF HOTEL OPERATIONS

Hotel Economic Life Expectancy

Hotels experience economic lifecycles: start-up, mid-life, and decline. A few properties like the Willard Hotel in Washington, DC, the Hotel Del Coronado in San Diego, the Sheraton Palace in San Francisco, and the Plaza in New York City have gone on with the help of renovations for some eighty to ninety years. Most, however, have much shorter lifespans. Characteristically, new hotels experience rapid growth in occupancy and income during the first five to ten years. According to Stephen Rushmore, a hotel consultant, income then remains fairly level for eight to fifteen years after opening. After that the revenue-producing capacity declines. Studies show, says Rushmore, that a hotel's economic life averages about forty years.

Many of the factors that play on the lifecycle are beyond the control of management. Changing demographics and changes in neighborhoods, traffic flows, and hotel overbuilding are examples (Stephen Rushmore, "Hotel Life Expectancy," *Lodging Hospitality*, May 1992, p. 16).

Forecasting Sales

Hotel management necessarily forecasts occupancy to be able to schedule the number of employees needed to serve the guests, and to have the appropriate amount of food, beverages, and other supplies on hand. In the past room sales forecasting was done in four steps.

1. Use past sales, reservations, and group bookings as a base for the forecast.
2. Apply current economic trends (for example, trends in occupancy rates).
3. Reflect special conditions that will augment sales (for example, the booking of a convention).
4. Subtract from the forecast a number that represents any negative factors, such as the opening of a competing hotel.

A particular hotel may be primarily concerned about its regional economy, citywide occupancy percentage, or the number of new hotel rooms under construction. Most hotels are affected by the national economy. New York City hotels may get as much as 25 percent of their occupancy from foreign visitors. An island location is concerned about the number of flights coming in and the airline load factors. Each hotel identifies the conditions that affect it, local, other regional, national, or international.

The rooms forecast is updated daily or weekly and used to schedule the number of personnel needed for each job for each day covered by the forecast.

Forecasting hotel sales is done by market segment. In a large hotel the segments could be: (1) individual business travelers, (2) pleasure travelers, (3) conventioneers, (4) corporate meeting groups, (5) tour groups, and (6) rooms booked for airline personnel. Each market segment can be affected differently by a recession or an upswing in the economy, changing airfares, or the number of flights being scheduled into the area. A hotel might reduce the forecast for pleasure travelers and raise the one for the business travel segment.

Yield Management

Since about 1986, room sales forecasting has become a basic part of "yield management" programs, used to discount or increase room rates to maximize income, a management tool adapted from airline experience in adjusting fares to fit demand (Terry Breen, "Hoteliers Yield to Yield Management," *Hotels*, November 1991, p. 29).

A yield management program can be set up to automatically project room demand based on historical records. The "rules" for the computer program are made by management and sales personnel. The computer then chooses discount rates to sell room nights that would otherwise be lost during slack periods. Some yield management programs measure group room requests in terms of the projected occupancy on a certain date. High-occupancy weekday reservations for a group may be rejected, and alternate dates can be suggested.

In 1988 Hilton Hotels Corporation began a yield management system that forecasts demand up to 120 days in advance. Room rates can be adjusted up to four months ahead of the actual date in question. If bookings are slow the number of discounts are increased. If it appears the hotel will be sold out, bookings can be made at higher rates ("The Big Picture - 1989," *Travel Industry World Yearbook*, New York, p. 133).

The airlines have practiced yield management for many years, discounting fares when necessary to create the maximum load factor and revenue. Hotels try to maximize yield by changing prices as necessary to attract the most customers at the maximum price they are willing to pay. Convention and other group rates are negotiable depending largely on the time of year when convention sales are needed to fill rooms. Group sales in large hotels may be forecast five to ten years in the future. Convention and other group sales are blocked out as contracts are made and current sales fitted around group sales.

Personnel Budgeting

Because the number one cost is labor in most hotels, personnel budgeting and control are part of a management system. Growing out of the sales forecast, the personnel budget is an attempt to predict how many staff will be needed, by the day, or throughout the sales forecast period. In large properties, personnel budgeting is an ongoing process, personnel schedules are updated daily or every few days.

The personnel budget is a control device for scheduling only those personnel who will be needed, no more, no less. Variances from personnel forecasts are expected, and quantified. Basic to personnel budgeting are staffing tables that show how many people in each job classification will be needed. Figures 3-5 and 3-6 are examples of staffing tables for a hotel kitchen and a dining room.

Figure 3-7 shows a payroll comparison for one week. Each job classification has been assigned a "standard" number of employees for the week. The example shows

Staffing Table for Kitchen

Jobs to Be Filled	For 0–49 Guests	For 50–99 Guests	For 100–175 Guests	For 175–plus Guests
Chef	1	1	1	1
Cook	1	2	3	4
Salads—Pantry	1	2	2	3
Dishwasher	1	2	3	3
Potwasher	1	1	1	1
Cleaner	0	1	1	1
Storeroom clerk	0	1	1	1
Baker	0	1	1	1

Figure 3-5 Kitchen Staffing Requirements

that the front office department met the standard while the housekeeping department went over the standard by the equivalent of 1.4 employees. Personnel scheduling in hotels and restaurants involves considerable effort to schedule employees to fit their time preferences. Everyone wants to be assigned the good shifts, in terms of the hours scheduled and opportunities for high tips. Tips in a prestige hotel may run as high as $100,000 a year for some employees.

Hotel Food and Beverage Economics

The full-service hotel has no choice but to offer food and beverage service(s), in large hotels as many as ten separate ones. Budget properties try to locate near restaurants to avoid the need for operating food services. All-suites compromise by offering breakfasts at low prices or give them away. Complimentary beverages may be offered at a "happy hour." Chains like Holiday Inn traditionally included restaurants, but many have had difficulty breaking even. Recently built Holiday Inns have been located next to a separately operated restaurant. The highway traveler has checked out by lunchtime, and may search out a specialty or name restaurant for dinner. Hotel food services usually have higher labor costs than commercial restaurants in the environs.

Breakfast, when guests are in a hurry to get on with their travel or business, has proven to be best served as a breakfast buffet that involves considerable self-service.

Staffing Table for Dining Room

Jobs to Be Filled	For 0–37 Guests	For 38–58 Guests	For 59–75 Guests	For 76–95 Guests	For 96–112 Guests	For 113–129 Guests	For 130–145 Guests	For 146–166 Guests	For 167–plus Guests
Host/Hostess	1	1	1	1	1	1	1	1	1
Waiter/Waitress	2	3	4	5	6	7	8	9	10
Bus person	1	2	2	3	3	3	3	4	5
Cocktail server	1	1½	1½	2	2	2½	2½	2½	2½

Figure 3-6 Dining Room Staffing Requirements

Summary of Departmental Payroll Comparison Reports for One Week

Hotel

Department		Average Number of Employees on Duty		Variance	
		Actual	Standard	Employees	% of Standard
Front Office		5.5	5.5	—	—
Housekeeping		22.1	20.7	1.4	6.8
Uniformed Service		14.6	15.1	[0.5]	[3.3]
Food Preparation		27.0	25.5	1.5	5.9
Steward		25.0	26.0	[1.0]	[3.9]
Food Storeroom		2.5	2.5	—	
Food Service	Dining Room	10.2	10.2	—	
	Room Service	5.5	5.5	—	
	Coffee Shop	12.9	12.4	0.5	3.9
	Banquets	20.2	18.7	1.5	7.4
Total Food Service		48.8	46.8	2.0	4.3
Beverage Preparation		7.2	7.2	—	—
Lounge Service		7.6	7.2	0.4	5.5
Telephone		4.7	4.7	—	—
All Others		47.5	47.5	—	—
Totals		212.5	28.7	3.8	1.8
Volume Statistics					

Total Sales	$50,400.00
Occupied Rooms	2,632
Food Covers Served	10,210
Beverage Sales	$ 6,600.00

Figure 3-7   Summary of Departmental Payroll Comparison Reports for One Week

The typical hotel food and beverage operation takes in about half as much in sales as the rooms department, but generally only provides between 10 and 20 percent as much profit (Tom Powers, *Introduction to Management in the Hospitality Industry*, New York: John Wiley & Sons, 1992, p. 266).

Convention food service looms large in the minds of corporate planners, responsible for corporate meetings and conventions held in hotels. One study found it to be considered the most important factor by 80 percent of corporate planners. Group food service in hotels can be more profitable than service provided in restaurants. Menu prices can be higher and service handled more efficiently. Only one or a few choices are usually offered and prices are often higher than in the hotel's restaurants.

Room service for guests is generally believed to be a loss operation even though menu prices are high. Cost of assembling and transporting food and beverage, and the cost of extra personnel or the interference with restaurant service makes room service an expensive nicety.

Staffing may be required around the clock with three shifts of supervisors, captains, order takers, set-up people, wait staff and porters. Many hotels provide only breakfast for room service, full room service being offered in only first class and luxury properties (L. Taylor Damonte, "Hotel Room Service," In *VNR's Encyclopedia of Hospitality and Tourism*, New York: Van Nostrand Reinhold, 1993).

All hotels follow the Uniform System of Accounts for Hotels, published by the Hotel Association of New York City, in their accounting practices. The Uniform System is flexible enough to meet the needs of any size hotel and is updated periodically to take account of the changes taking place in hotel finance and accounting.

In the past, hotel management may have been misled by accounting practices into thinking the food and beverage department is profitable because it shows a departmental profit. The Uniform System of Accounts for Hotels is set up by department and does not allocate administrative and general expenses, sales and public relations expenses, and property operation, maintenance, and energy costs to the other departments. It is quite possible to show the food and beverage department returning an 18 percent departmental profit when unallocated costs are such that the department actually operated at a loss. Some hotels contract out their food and beverage departments.

Market and Feasibility Studies

Developers, investors, and hotel operators want market and feasibility studies done before a hotel is built. These studies include competition analysis, projected costs and income, and supporting information that indicates the likelihood of profitability for a hotel in a particular location. The studies are conducted by third parties, the findings and recommendations supposedly free of bias. Lenders insist on such studies. Even with the most careful studies conducted by experts, and reviewed by experienced and astute business people, numerous hotels were built in the 1980s that later proved unprofitable. Whether to build a motel on a busy highway would seem a simple question, yet dozens of new motels have failed. To build a resort complex or a large hotel is many times more complicated, requiring financial commitments years in advance of the hotel's opening and prediction of economic and travel trends for up to ten years in the future.

A hotel market analysis collects information about occupancy and room rates, employment data and demographics for the locale and surrounding area. How stable is the economic base? Is employment rising or falling? Three common economic barometers are percentage of office occupancy, employment, and the value of building permits. For a new hotel the lender requires assurance that all of the building and operating permits can be secured and the physical requirements of the hotel—drainage, heat, light, and other energy requirements—will be available. Road and highway access may be a problem. Some of the factors considered are the hotel's visibility (especially for a highway property), sign ordinances, personnel availability, and proximity to offices, businesses, and attractions that may appeal to potential guests. Financial comparisons are made with the operating results of similar properties in the area, and elsewhere, recognizing that cost and convenience of transport may be critical (Harold E. Lane and Mark van Hartesvelt, *Essentials of Hospitality Administration*, Reston, VA: Prentice Hall, 1983). Feasibility studies project room demand and room rates that can be charged and describe the kind of guest (business, pleasure, government, convention, conference, or other group) that will be attracted to the hotel.

Cost elements of a new hotel can be classified into land, construction costs, interest during construction, furniture, fixtures and equipment, inventories required for opening, pre-opening expenses, and working capital. Many hotels are built on leased land. The cost of land varies widely. In most instances land costs exceeding $10,000 per room will make the project unfeasible (William S. Gray and Salvatore C. Liguori, *Hotel and Motel Management and Operations*, Prentice Hall, 1990, p. 38). Land costs in many high-rise and luxury hotels exceed this figure. Resort properties that involve large acreage have much higher land costs. The builders expect to sell condos to carry much of the land cost. Land cost is divided into the number of rooms to be built. A 50-story hotel may occupy a relatively small land space.

Hotel developers and lenders consider the time value of money in figuring cost. Money in hand is more valuable today than it is later. Inflation and what the money could bring in interest makes present day money more valuable today than it will be later. Charts are available to show these relationships.

In the past, principal sources of money for hotel building have been insurance companies, pension funds, real estate investment trusts (REITS), banks, savings and loan associations, and government loans. Foreign investors, largely Japanese, French, and British, have supplied billions of dollars for the construction and purchase of U.S. hotels.

Operating Ratios

Hotel management uses several operating ratios as indicators of efficiency and to compare operating results with hotels of similar character and location. The two most widely used operating ratios are the previously mentioned Average Daily Rate (the number of available guest rooms divided by the total room revenue) and the guest occupancy rate (the number of occupied rooms divided by those available). The ADR takes into consideration the number of rooms sold as doubles, income from suites, and the several discounted rates being offered.

Profit margin (net income compared to total revenue) is the ratio in which investors have the most interest since it indicates the ability of the venture to pay back their investment. Variable cost ratios, those that can be controlled up to a point, are also of interest and watched daily. Cost of labor as a percentage of revenue, cost of food as a percentage of food sales, and the beverage cost as a percentage of sales are key indices in hotel operations.

Lenders and owners are interested in liquidity and solvency ratios, those ratios that indicate the financial soundness of the investment. Current assets divided by total assets indicates the percent of assets that can be quickly turned into cash. Financial officers are careful to see that the cash flow is sufficient to meet cash requirements, and if it is not, to arrange for the availability of credit should it be needed.

FUTURE TRENDS

In the future it is almost inevitable, given a free market society, that hotels will continue to be cyclical in profitability. Because hotel construction depends upon tax laws, the general economy, and investing psychology, there are likely to be too many hotels in some locations and too few in others. Similarly, there will be periods during which there are too many rooms for the current demand, for particular kinds of hotels, at particular locations, during certain seasons. Lead times for the construction of hotels makes it impossible to be certain of the need for hotels when they open.

In 1994 numbers of U.S. hotels were being bought by Chinese investors, mainly from Hong Kong and Taiwan. In a curious switch, some American hotels that had been bought by Japanese investors at highly inflated prices were being bought by Hong Kong and Taiwan investors at a fraction of their replacement costs.

Reflecting the overbuilding, many hotels were on the block, some for as little as 30 to 40 percent of their replacement cost. Orient Hotels Group of Stamford, Connecticut spent $100 million on hotel acquisitions, half in cash. New World Development Co. purchased Stouffer Hotels & Resorts from the Nestlé Company for more than $1 billion. Most of the hotels bought by the Asian groups are American managed ("Ethnic Chinese Companies Find Room at Some U.S. Inns," *Wall Street Journal*, February 1, 1994).

As travel and per capita incomes increase in the United States, and around the world, the demand for hotel rooms is likely to increase at a rate close to the rise in income. No one knows what the effect of the "information highway" will be on hotel demand, but it is likely that the need for face-to-face business meetings will be reduced, replaced by video phones and video conferences. The urge to be with other people of similar interest enjoyed in sports, conventions, gambling, or other exciting events will certainly continue.

4

Restaurant Economics

About 25 percent of the $254.9 billion of restaurant sales in the United States in 1992 can be considered tourism-related (sales made to customers fifty miles away from home). In 1991 international visitors to the United States spent over $8 billion on food and beverage, which accounted for about 274,000 food service jobs and a payroll of $2.3 billion. The California figure for restaurant tourist sales in 1991 was $11 billion. Travelers, says the National Restaurant Association, accounted for $76 billion in food and beverage consumption in the U.S. in 1990. Whatever the real figure, the restaurant business depends heavily on tourists for sales.

The growth of the commercial restaurant industry (excluding institutional and military groups) had slowed to less than 3 percent a year by 1994—a drop from 8 percent growth in 1983 for fast-food restaurants, and a little over 4 percent for full service restaurants in that year. Commercial foodservice in 1992 showed total sales of $225.4 billion (National Restaurant Association). Sales of takeout food from supermarkets, delicatessens ("delis"), and convenience stores grew faster because of lower prices and ready availability to the customer. Expansion abroad, however, was in a growth pattern in downtown locations. In 1992, McDonald's had 4400 of its 13,400 units outside the United States and received about 40 percent of its $21.9 billion in revenues from abroad (*Wall Street Journal*, October 20, 1993). Kentucky Fried Chicken (KFC) is in more than sixty countries, and Pizza Hut is in about sixty-five countries. More than thirty international restaurant chains, mostly fast-food oriented, are headquartered in the United States (*Hotels*, May 1992, p. 82).

Restaurant chains are controlling a larger share of restaurant sales. In 1989, the 100 largest restaurant chains controlled 46.5 percent of restaurant sales, up from less than a third of the market in 1972 (U.S. Chain Restaurant Companies, Technomic Consultants, Chicago, 1990).

FAST-FOOD RESTAURANTS

The big division in restaurant foodservice is between fast-food (also called "quick service") and other kinds of restaurants. Fast-food restaurant sales were reported by the National Restaurant Association to be $75.6 billion in 1992, with additional billions in sales abroad. Sales for the same year for other commercial eating and drinking places were $98.8 billion and $29.4 billion for institutional/military places.

Franchisees for fast-food restaurants are seen all over the world. Sales in 1992 were $21.9 billion, up 10% over 1991. Profits in 1993 topped the billion dollar mark. Ironically, the two largest McDonalds are in Moscow and Beijing. The Moscow McDonald's can serve 25,000 people a day.

The big fortunes in the food service business have been made in fast-food. Hundreds of millionaires and numerous multimillionaires are proud franchisees of McDonald's.

Fast-food franchising builds on three well-established business phenomena: product standardization, economies of scale, and massmarketing. Every established franchise chain has exact standards for buying, processing, preparing, and serving its product. The potatoes, the hamburger, and other menu items have been carefully specified; preparation methods are controlled by training and by the use of selected equipment. The "cookie cutter" (standardized everything) approach to building and operating a franchised unit reduces costs and partially controls quality. A good "cookie cutter" approach is worth a fortune and can stamp out units indefinitely with good locations and other optimum conditions.

Economies of scale brought about by mass purchasing of food, equipment, and advertising means that the large franchisor can assure the franchisee of reduced costs in everything from building blueprints to the cost of a pat of butter. Economies of scale carry over to mass marketing and merchandising, which is critical in meeting the competition with the best advertising firms, TV advertising, and imaginative promotional schemes. The independent fast-food operators face considerable odds. McDonald's is the paradigm for the fast-food business and its franchise is eagerly sought.

There are approximately 13,000 McDonald's in sixty-six countries. More than 2000 potential owners apply each year, but only about 150 or so are selected: those "with ketchup in their veins," that is, owners willing to work long hours and commit themselves to the business. Those between the ages of 35 and 45 with at least ten years of business experience are preferred. McDonald's sends in field consultants if there are problems at franchised units. Successful franchisees—which includes most of them—are given first call on additional locations. The average number of restaurants per licensee is a little over three. A typical franchisee with six stores realizes annual sales of $9 million and a net return before taxes in excess of $500,000 a year.

McDonald's is a built-on system—a system for doing everything: high profile advertising, low labor costs (about 30 percent of sales), strict purchasing and portion control, disposable plates, cups, and utensils. Intensive training is given to managers and workers. Simplicity rules the day: a limited menu, self service, assembly-line production, and cooking equipment requiring a minimum level of skill.

Franchisees pay an initial franchise fee and continuing royalty fees that include advertising assessments, equipment purchase, and rent. McDonald's owns the land and the restaurant building, which in 1993 averaged about $1.2 million per restaurant. The franchisee's books are set up and audited, in one way or another, to insure the correct fees are paid.

Some chains are on-line by computer, or report sales and other operating figures every night by phone to a regional or central office. Because of competition, food costs in a fast-food restaurant may run as high as 33 percent of sales, a figure that works well with low labor costs. The goal is to provide 10 to 15 percent of sales to the profit line. Price wars and so-called "value-pricing" that began in the early 1990s forced food costs up. McDonald's food cost percentage in 1991 was 33 percent. Food couponing is widespread during the off-season, January through April. Taco Bell, a unit of Pepsico, became a big player in the fast-food market by cutting prices to the bone and featuring tacos (cheap compared to a hamburger) containing a minimal amount of ground beef.

Fast-food franchisors typically charge licensees an initial license fee, plus a percentage of sales as a royalty fee, and an advertising fee for the duration of the contract, usually twenty years. There are other requirements. Hardee's Food Systems, owned by Imasco, a Canadian firm, charges typical fees and royalties. Net personal wealth required by the company ranges between $700,000 and $1.7 million, excluding the franchisee's personal residence and real estate costs in the area. The Hardee location requires land with a 165-foot frontage and a 210-foot depth. The company charges an initial franchise fee of $15,000, a royalty fee of 3.5 percent of sales the first 5 years, and 4 percent in years 6 to 20. An advertising fee of 5 percent of sales is also charged.

The International House of Pancakes headquartered in Glendale, California, charges an initial license fee of $50,000, a royalty charge of 4.5 percent and an advertising royalty fee of 3 percent. One of the least expensive but well known fast-food franchises is Subway Sandwiches and Salads. Its initial franchise fee is $10,000, its annual royalties are 8 percent and its advertising fees 2.5 percent. Capital requirements, says the company, are $44,400 to $72,400. The company operates none of its units. While most franchisors require their franchisees to have had restaurant work experience, 80 percent of Subway Sandwiches and Salads franchisees have never worked in food service.

Fast food continues to get faster. Portable order entry terminals are being used for faster, more accurate service. With a terminal in hand an employee can take an order from a customer either standing in line or from one in a line of cars. The order is transmitted to a cash register and the production line, where it appears on a viewing screen. Some regular restaurants, such as Stuart Anderson's Black Angus, use this same technique.

Chain operators are linking personal computers, located in each store, to divisional and corporate offices where such time-consuming chores as crew scheduling and inventory monitoring can be done more efficiently. This allows the store manager to concentrate on customer service, personnel relations, and store cleanliness.

Drive-through service at fast-food restaurants speeds the customer in and through the service line. Take-out and drive-through service accounts for 65 percent of Wendy's fast-food chain service. Two drive-through lanes, one on each side of the restaurant, are becoming more common. Some fast-food restaurants have no inside seating.

While most economists warn against high labor turnover, fast-food operators have learned to use it to their advantage. Standardized training and production procedures produces proficient workers quickly. Pension and other benefit costs are reduced because few employees stay very long. Unmotivated and inefficient workers screen themselves out. Labor costs are kept low because short tenure means few pay raises. Wages and salaries are kept low because so many employees are young people with little work experience and few alternatives, who can be replaced easily.

Nearly all wait personnel in table service restaurants rely heavily on tips, not wages, for their income. Salaries for dinner house general managers can be high, sometimes exceeding $100,000 a year, and a large number of managers in all kinds of restaurants work on bonus plans. Bonus plans must be carefully controlled to avoid managers from cutting costs too much in order to increase the bonus.

Not all franchisees do well financially. Hundreds of restaurant franchisees work long hours for relatively small incomes. The well known franchised restaurants have a failure rate of under five percent a year and failed franchises amount to less than one-half percent of total franchise sales (Tom Powers, *Introduction to Management in the Hospitality Industry*, New York: John Wiley & Sons, 1993, p. 90).

It is in the franchisor's best interest to screen out people unlikely to succeed. The better franchisors insist that the new franchisee take pre-opening training. The franchisor helps with site selection and provides operations manuals, and if trouble develops, has troubleshooters for back-up support.

Restaurant operators rely heavily on teenagers, people in their twenties, and recent immigrants as employees. A recent rise in the minimum wage, and a crackdown on illegal immigration has raised restaurant labor costs. Continued price wars in terms of "value pricing" will keep profit margins low among fast-food operators.

Convenience stores offer the usual fast-food restaurant tough competition with self-service, low priced foods like hot dogs, hamburgers, and sandwiches, together with soft drinks. Labor cost is minimal: one employee may work the cash register, re-stock, and clean up.

Pizza take-out stores can be very efficient. Domino's Pizza offers the customer only two sizes of pizza and a soft drink. The pizza store can locate where rent is low. Only two job titles exist: pizza maker and delivery person. Delivery people provide their own cars and insurance. Franchise fees and opening costs are from $50,000 to $100,000 and Domino's, for example, will help with the financing. A store can gross $200,000 or more a year. Some double those figures. Food costs are in the range of 20 to 30 percent of sales. Profits can exceed 20 percent of sales.

Compared to other kinds of restaurants, fast-food restaurants are extremely efficient in the use of labor. The Agricultural Research Service lists comparative labor costs as a percentage of sales among different restaurant styles:

Food Service Type	Direct Labor Hours per 100 Guests
Luxury restaurants	72.3
Family restaurants	20.7
Cafeteria	18.3
Fast Food	10.5

Fast-food restaurants depend heavily on catchy slogans and massive TV advertising. About 8 percent of sales is spent on advertising and promotion by franchised stores. Independently owned luxury restaurants may spend more, either in direct advertising or for public relations. Franchised table service restaurants only spend about half this percentage (that is, about 4 percent) (*Restaurant Industry Operations Report,* Washington, DC: The National Restaurant Association, 1990).

Not all economic ratios favor fast-food restaurants. Moderately priced restaurants offer an advantage over fast-food establishments according to one analysis. Shoney's or Sizzler restaurants have sales that are 1.25 to 1.75 times the restaurant cost. Fast-food restaurants, the analysis points out, have lower sales compared to investment, with ratios between 1.1 and 1.05 to one. In other words, the fast-food restaurant must spread its capital cost over fewer sales. Profit is reduced at a proportionately greater rate (Michael G. Mueller, "Why the Mid-Priced Restaurant is More Attractive than Fast Food," *1989 Restaurant Industry Trends and Analysis*, San Francisco: Montgomery Securities, October 16, 1989).

The fast-food chains take advantage of their size to negotiate purchasing advantages that are impossible for the independent restaurant operator to match. Purchasing can be centralized or agreements can be made with purveyors to have the hamburger, colas, french fries, milkshake ingredients, and other fast-food menu items made to chain specification and delivered to the stores. The chains can do their own in-house research on product and equipment development.

Standardization can give table service restaurants like the Red Lobster and the Olive Garden (both owned by General Mills) some of the advantages enjoyed by the multi-unit fast-food restaurants. Red Lobster, for example, processes most of its shrimp in St. Petersburg, Florida where it is peeled, deveined, cooked, quick-frozen, and packaged daily for shipping to its dozens of restaurants around the country. The chain can cut as much as 10 percent from its food bill through mass purchasing. Sales forecasts are made daily at each store using data fed into a computer that checks sales records each night. Based on sales for the same day, the previous week, and the same day the previous year, the manager can forecast the number of each menu item to be defrosted and pre-prepped, ready to cook, for the next day.

OTHER TYPES OF RESTAURANTS

Family restaurants, including coffee shops, offer waiter/waitress service and often self-service salad bars, breakfast bars, and dessert bars. Most food is cooked to order or made from frozen or chilled prepared foods requiring more labor than fast-food places. Coffee shops usually have one or two sections with counter service. Menu items such as pancakes, hamburgers, fried eggs, and french fries keep prices competitive. Pancakes, for example, have a food cost of less than 20 percent of sales. Coffee and tea have food costs even lower. Chains like Denny's, Bob's Big Boy and Shoney's control about 75 percent of the market. Originally the "family restaurant" was operated by a family. Many still are a family-managed enterprise, often an extended family, with sons and daughters occupying key positions, including that of cashier. Labor costs are low in that family members fill in as needed and may eat many of their meals in the restaurant.

Fine dining (luxury) restaurants are typically under 100 seats. There are far fewer of these than their reputation would suggest. Many of these restaurants depend heavily on attracting people in the public eye. The National Restaurant Association defined them in 1987 as having a per person average check of $30 or more. Places like New York City, San Francisco, Los Angeles, and Chicago have many of these restaurants. Wine sales help these establishments in maintaining a high check average and a comparatively low beverage cost.

Dinner houses are a step below the luxury restaurant. The name dinner house is misleading in that many or most feature lunch as well as dinner. Many of the menus of the leading dinner house chains feature a cuisine such as Italian or Mexican for the reason that they permit a lower than average food cost to be achieved because less solid pieces of meat are served. Chinese restaurants, too, can run comparatively low food costs with rice as a filler and meat and seafood items, accompanied by sauces, being served in small pieces. Other restaurant categories appear from time to time, classifications relating to menu price are an example. Terms like "low-end," "mid-scale" and "up-scale," are seen. Casual dining chains are a category that seem to cut across ethnicity and relate more to colorful decor, laid-back service, and heavy marketing. The International Foodservice Manufacturers Association publishes a list of such restaurants (*Emerging Casual Dining Chains*, Chicago, 1994) and includes 26 chains among them the Lone Star Steakhouses, Hard Rock Cafe, Spaghetti Warehouse, and The Italian Oven.

The biggest competition for restaurant foodservice is the food eaten at home. If food items eaten in a fast-food store were identical to those eaten at home and the time taken to shop, store, prepare, cook, and clean-up was calculated, the cost would probably be greater for the home prepared food (*Nation's Restaurant News*). The fact, however, is that the home food preparer does not price the time involved and may enjoy preparing meals. A steady fast-food menu can be very boring. The home food preparer has better control over nutritional requirements and variety.

RESTAURANTS: HIGH RISK OF FAILURE

Statistically the commercial restaurant business has more chances of failure than of success. There are two big reasons: too many restaurants for the population, and it is too easy to enter the business. A study of restaurant failure found a failure rate of 27 percent during the first year, less than 50 percent by the end of year three, and about 60 percent at the end of five years of operation (Chris Muller and Robert W. Wood,

"The Real Failure Rate of Restaurants," *FIU Hospitality Review*, Fall 1991, pp. 60–65). Other studies place the failure rate even higher. Undercapitalization is common. Many new restaurants fail because they lack a financial cushion to carry them through the several months needed to gain consistent profitability. Prior experience in restaurant operation is a prerequisite for success. The independent restaurant operation competes with the large chains that control almost half of restaurant sales (*Nation's Restaurant News*, August 7, 1990, p. 4).

The leveraged buyout (LBO) of restaurant chains enriched insiders and the financial dealmakers. One example was the LBO of Foodmaker, parent of the Jack-in-the-Box fast food chain. In 1985, the chief executive officer and other insiders at Foodmaker bought the chain from Ralston Purina for $430 million using borrowed money. In early 1987, Foodmaker sold 4 million shares of the stock to the public at $13.50 a share, a move that tripled the market value for the LBO partners. In 1988 the company went private again in a new LBO for $247 million (Elias S. Moncarz, "Leveraged Buyout in the Hospitality Business: Five Years Later," *FIU Hospitality Review*, Spring 1991).

Another instance of a LBO that did not benefit employees, over the long pull, or the stockholders, was that of Flagstar Companies, a Spartanburg, South Carolina company that owns or franchises five restaurant chains, of which 1000 Denny's restaurants are their largest holding. In 1989, Coniston Partners bought a controlling interest in Flagstar. At that time $1.5 billion was paid for the nebulous asset called goodwill, which was part of the huge debt of $2.4 billion incurred in the buyout. Goodwill is the excess over book value that is paid for a company's assets. In 1994 Flagstar took a $1.65 billion write-off for the loss in the value of its goodwill ("Flagstar Loss Is $1.65 Billion in Big Change," *Wall Street Journal*, January 25, 1994). In other words, the LBO partners gained $150 million in the transactions related to goodwill.

LBOs have had a lasting effect on the restaurant business, one that, overall, has been negative. The professional restaurant manager and the employees are given little consideration. The goal of a LBO is to create profits for the insiders and LBO managers. Stockholders may also benefit because generally the stock price rises, at least temporarily. LBOs usually create new debt—sometimes enormous new debt—which may be too much to be serviced. Pressure is placed on managers and employees to maintain dividends even though much of the earnings are required to pay down the debt incurred in the LBO. Stockholders may suffer in the long run because much or all of the takeover money used was raised via junk bonds, bonds that carry a high interest rate but that may be of low quality.

LBO proponents argue that old, incapable, management is swept out and replaced by new management that can realize the firm's potential. This sometimes happens.

ECONOMIC MEASURES IN RESTAURANT OPERATIONS

Prime Costs

The two principal costs in restaurant operations are labor costs and food costs, together called *prime costs*. Most kinds of restaurants can be profitable if prime costs can be kept below 60 to 65 percent of sales. The mix between the two prime costs can vary.

These cost mixes could be profitable:

A steakhouse:
    40 percent food cost
    20 percent labor cost
A family restaurant:
    33 percent food cost
    30 percent labor cost
A luxury restaurant:
    35 percent food cost
    30 percent labor cost
A Mexican restaurant:
    28 percent food cost
    28 percent labor cost
A fast-food hamburger restaurant:
    30 percent food cost
    25 percent labor cost

The National Restaurant Association has assembled a list of key restaurant ratios, comparing fast food, limited service, and table service restaurants. According to their statistics, food costs vary only slightly between the three restaurant styles. Prime costs are lowest in fastfood restaurants. Occupancy and capital costs are highest for fast-food restaurants. The "bottom line" profit before income taxes is almost twice as high for fast-food establishments compared to limited table-service restaurants. Table-service restaurants show the lowest percentage profit. See Figure 4-1 for the comparison of the various operating statistics.

For restaurants with heavy bar sales, the cost mix may be different. The operator may lump food and beverage sales together, raising food costs and giving away hors d'oeuvres in the bar to increase liquor sales. Liquor costs could be as low as 20 percent in a hotel restaurant, food costs as low as 40 percent.

The Uniform System of Accounts for Restaurants

The National Restaurant Association publishes a guide to restaurant accounting, the *Uniform System of Accounts for Restaurants,* that defines account classifications and offers a widely followed accounting system. The system allows one restaurant operator to compare results with industry averages for the same style of restaurant. The results should not necessarily correspond because of menu differences and pricing that fits a particular location and its competition. Figure 4-2 illustrates the accounts recommended by the National Restaurant Association.

Breakeven Analysis

Breakeven analysis helps the restaurant operator approximate the sales volume needed to break even and, roughly, the profit that can be made at various levels of

Comparison of U.S. Restaurant Operating Statistics (as a percentage of sales)

	Quick-Service Restaurant	Limited Menu Table-Service Restaurants	Table-Service Restaurants
Food cost[a]	34.3%	35.6%	36.2%
Beverage cost[b]	32.3[f]	28.2	27.8
Product cost[c]	34.6	34.2	34.5
Payroll and related cost[d]	29.2	31.1	33.4
Prime cost[e]	63.8	65.3	67.9
Other operating costs	13.7	15.9	16.5
Occupancy and capital costs[g]	14.4	12.1	12.4
Profit before income taxes	8.2	4.3	3.2

[a]Food cost as percentage of food sales.

[b]Beverage cost as percentage of beverage sales.

[c]Total food and beverage cost as percentage of total food and beverage sales.

[d]Includes employee benefits.

[e]Total of product cost and labor cost.

[f]Applies to some operations.

[g]Includes "other deductions."

Source: Restaurant Operations Report (Washington, DC: National Restaurant Association, 1990); median figures are used.

Figure 4-1 Comparison of U.S. Restaurant Operating Statistics

sales. Figure 4-3 shows a theoretical breakeven chart. The same relationships can be computed mathematically. One value of drawing a breakeven chart is to identify and separate fixed, variable, and semi-variable costs. Costs can be seen as variable (changing with the volume of sales), semi-variable (partially a fixed cost, and partially a variable cost). Those costs that do not change with sales volume are called fixed. The semi-variable costs can be allocated into those that are fixed and those that are variable before drawing the breakeven chart.

Controllable (variable) expenses include:

Food costs

Payroll

Employee benefits

Telephone (variable portion)

Music and entertainment

Advertising and promotion

Utilities (heat, light, water, and power)

Repairs and maintenance

Capital costs (fixed costs) include:

Occupancy costs (debt service if building is owned)

Interest

	Amount	Percentage
Sales		
Food		
Beverage		
Others		
Total sales	_____	100.00
Cost of Sales		
Food		
Beverage		
Others		
Total cost of sales	_____	
Gross profit	_____	
Other income	_____	
Total income	_____	
Controllable Expenses		
Salaries and wages		
Employee benefits		
Direct operating expenses*		
Music and entertainment		
Marketing		
Energy and utility		
Administrative and general		
Repairs and maintenance		
Total controllable expenses	_____	
Rent and other occupation costs		
Income before interest, depreciation, and taxes		
Interest		
Depreciation		
Net income before taxes	_____	
Income taxes	_____	
Net Income	=====	

*Telephone, insurance, accounting/legal office supplies, paper, china, glass, silvers, menus, landscaping, detergent/cleaning supplies, and so on.

Source: Adapted from Raymond S. Schmidgall, *Hospitality Industry Managerial Accounting*, 2nd ed. (East Lansing, MI: Educational Institute of the American Hotel & Motel Association, 1990) p. 94.

Figure 4-2 Sample of Restaurant Accounts

Depreciation (if building is owned)

Insurance

Real estate taxes

As seen on the breakeven chart, once the breakeven point is reached (with sales of $60,000 and 6000 guests) profits can increase at a fairly rapid rate. The chart does not show that there is a point where profits stop increasing and may decrease because the restaurant is operating at maximum capacity. The chart shown here exaggerates the

Sales ($10,000)

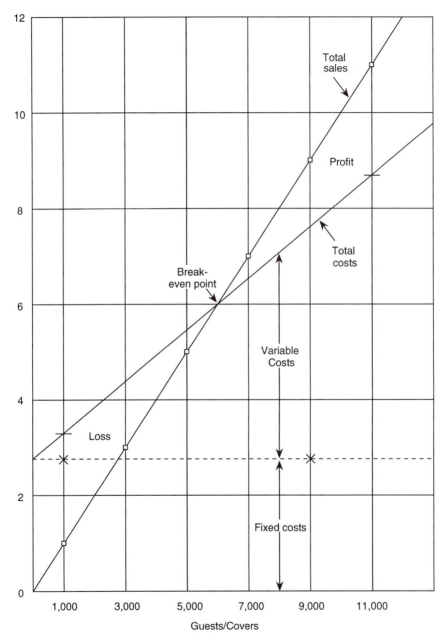

Figure 4-3   Breakeven Chart

rate of profit growth once the breakeven point is passed, but it is clear that once the fixed costs are met, profits rise disproportionately fast. Food costs as a percentage of sales may not decline much but labor costs do decline because personnel are more fully utilized.

Seat Turnover

The number of times a table "turns over" (is reoccupied by a customer) is a widely used measure for the restaurant operator. Turnover ranges maybe up to seven times during the rush lunch hour in some counter and stool restaurants to a low of once or twice an evening in a luxury restaurant. The fast-food operator wants the customer in, served, and out as soon as possible, preferably using a drive-through window, where the order has been given before the window is reached, the customer is served in a minute or two, the bill paid, and the customer leaves, then next customer, please. The In-and-Out Burger chain says it all. Fast-food restaurants hurry the customer by offering hard seats, bright colors, and a limited menu.

At the other end of the service spectrum is the luxury restaurant that wants the customer to linger, select an expensive wine, and order a complete meal. The seats are comfortable and restful. There are soft lights, quiet music, a frequently filled water glass, and an experienced server. The ambiance includes the other patrons. The Four Seasons restaurant in New York City raises and lowers the lighting according to the time of day and the type of guest present.

Serving speed correlates with check average. Restaurants priced in the mid range are geared for seat turnover of two to three times in the course of an evening. A 75-seat luxury restaurant must have a high check average, perhaps as much as $100. The fast-food establishment attains dollar volume by rapid turnover. The objective is the same: maximize sales income and concentrate on sales that produce the highest profit.

Depending upon location, market, and menu a restaurant may do 40 percent of its sales on Fridays and Saturdays. The 1500-unit Denny's chain has 40 percent of its sales during the breakfast period.

Menu selection also correlates with speed of service. A dinner house can feature roast beef and other items that have been wholly or partially prepared, waiting to be served. The concept is called "stored labor," preparing as much as possible during slow periods for service during rush periods.

Employee training expedites service and makes possible the quick service required during rush hours. Team service in which one server helps others during rush periods eliminates some trips between kitchen and customer. A waitress going into the kitchen may bring food items for other team members and wait personnel may step in to clear tables if bus personnel are otherwise occupied. The menu, the kitchen personnel, the layout of kitchen and dining room, the service style, and the type of customer help determine an appropriate target figure for seat turnover.

Employee Theft

Employee theft in restaurants is widespread, necessitating tight cost controls, especially on bartenders. Collusion between vendors and chefs to steal is fairly common.

Restaurant operators keep close tabs on cost percentages. Variance of one or a few percentage points from a standard is cause for immediate concern and corrective action. For example, if utilities normally run 4 percent of gross sales and increase to 6 percent of sales, the net profit may have been reduced by as much as one-fourth. If net profit were 8 percent of sales, a 2 percent increase in a cost represents one-quarter of the net profit. The restaurant business is a business of percentages, one or a few percentage points can result in a large difference in what is left as profit.

Forecasting Restaurant Sales

Sales for most restaurants vary throughout the week and with the season. For table service restaurants, weekends are usually high sales volume days; for some restaurants these two days may account for one-half of all weekly sales. Depending upon location, fast-food restaurants have slower sales during the spring. The restaurant operator plots sales using past experience, and estimates sales for the week ahead and for the season. Thanksgiving and Easter are peak volume days for many restaurants. Effort is made to increase sales for particular meal periods. Offering Sunday brunch with champagne is an example; offering a breakfast special is another.

Sales forecasts are compared with actual sales, and variances from the forecasts examined. Figure 4-4 is an example of a budget forecast for a table-service restaurant that includes bar service. Food, labor, and other costs are predicted and compared with actual costs. In large restaurants and hotels, sales figures may be on line with a computer and the percentages checked daily. The sales forecast for customer count is used for scheduling personnel—the number of hours of work that will be needed in each job for the week:

Supervisor hours	_____
Cashier hours	_____
Waiter/waitress hours	_____
Bus personnel hours	_____
Cook hours	_____
Utility (clean-up)	_____
Bartender hours	_____
Lounge service hours	_____

A sales and personnel forecast can be installed as part of a system and is routinely monitored. The forecast can be then translated into the number of steaks, chicken breasts, and other menu items that can be pre-prepped each day, ready for cooking. At the end of the week the hours forecast are compared with actual hours worked.

Personnel scheduling must fit the peaks and valleys of sales, which in some cases means scheduling employees on split shifts, asking them to work at odd hours and to divide work hours within the course of a day. Another solution: employ part-time workers.

Budget Forecast of Restaurant Sales, Period _____ Week _____ 19XX

Day	Forecast No. of Guests	Actual No. of Guests	% for (−)	Forecast Amount of Average Check	Actual Amount of Average Check	% for (−)	Forecast Amount of Food Sales	Actual Amount of Food Sales	% for (−)	Forecast Amount of Beverage Sales	Actual Amount of Beverage Sales	% for (−)	B	L	D	Total Forecast Sales	Total Actual Sales	% for (−)
Mon																		
Tues																		
Wed																		
Thur																		
Fri																		
Sat																		
Sun																		
Week's total																		

Note: B = Breakfast; L = Lunch; D = Dinner

Figure 4-4 Budget Forecast of Restaurant Sales

Restaurant Finance

The larger restaurant chains raise capital through stock sales. The independent restaurant operator gets funds wherever possible, from friends, or from loans for which the lender demands collateral. Many restaurants have been started with home loans. Banks have been notably reluctant to lend money for restaurant ventures unless the loan is guaranteed by a federal government agency such as the Farmer's Home Administration, the Economic Development Administration, or the Small Business Administration.

Restaurant buildings and equipment are more often leased than purchased. The cost of leasing a building, or parts of it, is in terms of cents or dollars per square foot per month. The restaurant operator forecasts the amount of sales to determine if the lease cost is fair. A choice location could be suitable for one restaurant concept, much too expensive for another. Sales per square foot or sales per seat depend upon the average customer check amount and the speed of seat turnover.

Lease costs are whatever the restaurant operator can negotiate. Leases are for a fixed dollar amount per square foot per month and usually contain a clause that includes a percentage of gross sales to the landlord. The percentage may be based on a sliding scale. Triple net leases put the burden of upkeep, taxes, and insurance on the restaurant operator. In highly desirable locations, such as a busy airport, the lease cost can go as high as 20 percent of sales. On average, most restaurant leases are in the range of 5 percent to 8 percent of sales to the landlord. The restaurant operator needs a lease long enough to get established and a clause that protects against exorbitant increases in rent.

Many restaurant leases are made on a sliding scale—the landlord receives a greater percentage of sales as restaurant sales rise. In 1993 the $225 billion commercial foodservice market had slowed its growth to less than 2 percent a year. One reason for the slower growth was a general slowing in the rate of women joining the work force. Takeout food from grocery stores and delis also cut into sales. Convenience store food grew because of its lower price.

It is clear that the restaurant business keeps in step with the economy, especially the local economy. The big financial winners have been the chains with regional and national marketing clout and programs for purchasing, controlling costs, and training personnel.

5

Airline Economics

Worldwide there are about 800 carriers who together employ more than 3 million people and fly some 9000 commercial jet aircrafts from 14,000 airports. Within the United States just eight airlines carry 90 percent of the nation's air traffic. The largest of them are American, Delta, United, US Air, Northwest, Continental, Southwest, and Trans World. The U.S. airports serving the most passengers are O'Hare/Chicago, Dallas/Ft. Worth, Los Angeles, Hartsfield/Atlanta, and JFK/New York. Overseas the largest airports are Heathrow/London, Narita/Tokyo, and Frankfurt/Germany. The figures change frequently.

While most non-business air travelers have paid low prices, most airlines have experienced huge losses in recent years. In 1992 U.S. airlines lost $4.4 billion, bringing total losses for the previous three years to over $10 billion. In those three years the industry lost more than accumulated industry earnings between 1945 and 1992 (*The Big Picture*, 1993, p. 151). Among the large carriers in Europe only British Air has been profitable. Figure 5-1 shows that very few of the world's top fifty airline companies, as reported by *Fortune*, made profits in 1992. American Airlines (AMR) and United Airlines (UAL) continue to be the world's largest airlines in terms of revenues and passenger miles.

U.S airline costs and earnings fluctuate widely depending upon the economy, labor costs, fuel prices, operating efficiency, and price wars. Nearly all of the U.S. airlines carry huge amounts of debt. Relations between airline management and unions have been a large factor in airline profit and loss. Union wages have been high, especially for the cockpit crew. For the amount of work and stress involved U.S. flight attendants are especially well paid. JAL, the large Japanese airline may be overpaying flight attendants at an average of $85,000 a year (*Wall Street Journal*, August 9, 1994).

Pan American and Eastern are examples of the devastation suffered when management and unions collide. Pan Am was once America's flag carrier and the world's

Rank by Revenues 1992	'91	The Top 50 Airline Companies		1992 Revenues $ Millions	% Change from 1991	Profits $ Millions	Rank	Traffic Passenger miles in Billions	Rank
1	1	AMR	U.S.	$14,495.0	11.6%	($935.0)	45	97.4	1
2	3	UAL	U.S.	$12,889.7	9.7%	($956.8)	46	92.7	2
3	2	Air France Group	France	$12,299.6	4.0%	($616.8)	44	34.5	9
4	5	Lufthansa	Germany	$11,074.6	14.0%	($248.7)	33	38.1	7
5	6	Delta	U.S.	$10,836.8	18.2%	($506.3)	43	72.7	3
6	4	Japan	Japan	$10,421.1	(1.9%)	($383.6)	40	33.7	10
7	7	British Airways	Britain	$9,416.0	9.9%	$301.1	3	46.0	5
8	8	Northwest	U.S.	$7,963.8	5.7%	($386.2)	41	58.7	4
9	9	All Nippon Airways	Japan	$7,158.8	7.9%	($9.4)	16	23.7	12
10	10	USAir Group	U.S.	$6,696.3	2.5%	($1,228.9)	47	35.1	8
11	12	Scandinavian Airlines System	†	$5,909.1	10.6%	N.A.	—	9.8	30
12	13	Alitalia	Italy	$5,672.6	19.8%	($11.9)	17	17.0	18
13	11	Continental Holdings	U.S.	$5,575.2	0.4%	($125.3)	27	43.1	6
14	14	Swire Pacific	Hong Kong	$5,029.5	16.2%	$570.9	1	17.6	17
15	16	KLM Royal Dutch	Netherlands	$4,662.8	11.6%	($343.7)	37	20.5	15
16	15	Swissair	Switzerland	$4,414.9	3.1%	$80.3	8	10.1	28
17	17	Iberia	Spain	$4,389.2	15.5%	($339.0)	36	14.8	19
18	18	Trans World	U.S.	$3,634.5	(1.4%)	($317.7)	35	28.9	11
19	20	Singapore	Singapore	$3,465.2	13.8%	$522.4	2	23.5	13
20	21	Qantas	Australia	$3,104.1	2.5%	$105.6	6	17.9	16
21	22	Korean Air	South Korea	$2,980.3	9.3%	$1.5	15	13.5	21
22	19	Air Canada	Canada	$2,895.4	(7.0%)	($375.0)	38	21.6	14
23	23	PWA Corp.	Canada	$2,379.3	(5.0%)	($449.0)	42	13.3	22
24	26	Saudia	Saudi Arabia	$2,352.0	12.5%	($39.0)	21	11.4	26
25	27	Varig	Brazil	$2,181.2	9.4%	($380.3)	39	12.7	23

† Denmark, Norway, Sweden

Figure 5-1 The Top 50 Airline Companies

Rank by Revenues 1992	'91	The Top 50 Airline Companies		1992 Revenues $ Millions	% Change from 1991	Profits $ Millions	Profits Rank	Traffic Passenger Miles in Billions	Traffic Rank
26	25	Japan Air System	Japan	$2,180.2	8.9%	($42.0)	23	7.5	34
27	24	Thai Airways International	Thailand	$2,156.2	6.3%	$120.6	5	12.6	24
28	28	Garuda	Indonesia	$2,150.0	N.A.	N.A.	—	11.2	27
29	32	Ansett Transport Industries	Australia	$1,880.6	2.3%	($70.1)	25	5.2	43
30	31	LTU	Germany	$1,831.0	20.7%	N.A.	—	9.0	32
31	30	Sabena	Belgium	$1,702.2	10.5%	$11.1	14	3.8	48
32	35	Southwest	U.S.	$1,685.2	27.3%	$103.6	7	13.8	20
33	29	China	Taiwan	$1,649.9	4.8%	$145.0	4	8.3	33
34	36	Malaysia	Malaysia	$1,468.9	12.2%	$57.2	10	10.0	29
35	34	Aer Lingus	Ireland	$1,368.6	1.3%	($315.0)	34	2.5	49
36	33	America West	U.S.	$1,294.1	(8.8%)	($131.8)	30	11.8	25
37	38	Air New Zealand	New Zealand	$1,222.1	4.6%	$63.7	9	7.2	35
38	41	Australian	Australia	$1,166.8	8.0%	($37.9)	20	5.1	44
39	37	Finnair	Finland	$1,131.0	(12.2%)	($16.8)	18	5.6	39
40	40	Alaska Air Group	U.S.	$1,115.4	0.0%	($84.8)	26	6.0	3
41	42	TAP Air Portugal	Portugal	$1,100.0	1.3%	($150.0)	29	4.8	46
42	43	Mexicana	Mexico	$1,068.6	6.7%	($160.8)	30	6.5	36
43	47	Aeromexico	Mexico	$1,029.3	33.7%	($52.6)	24	5.4	41
44	44	South African Airways	South Africa	$1,029.0	(17.7%)	($26.7)	19	6.0	38
45	39	Austrian	Austria	$955.6	18.7%	($39.8)	22	2.3	50
46	45	El Al	Israel	$937.8	6.8%	$31.5	13	5.3	42
47	•	Gulf Air	††	$930.9	13.3%	$47.6	12	4.8	45
48	•	Britannia Airways	Britain	$922.9	22.2%	$56.1	11	9.6	31
49	48	Olympic Airways	Greece	$920.0	11.3%	($222.1)	32	4.7	47
50	46	Aerolineas	Argentina	$917.7	15.7%	($188.8)	31	5.5	40

†† Bahrain, Oman, Qatar, United Arab Emirates

Source: Fortune Magazine, December 13, 1993.

Figure 5-1 (Continued)

	Salaries & Benefits	Commission	Fuel	Aircraft Rentals & Landing Fees	Depreciation	Aircraft Maintenance	Other Expenses	Profit
UNITED	33.2%	16.3%	12.5%	10.1%	5.4%	2.8%	17.4%	2.3%
AMERICAN	32.4	8.9	11.8	9.5	7.2	4.1	17.6	8.5
SOUTHWEST	28.8	6.5	13.2	9.7	6.8	6.8	15.4	12.8

Sources: 1) "The Bully of the Skies Cries Uncle," Stephen D. Soloman, *The New York Times*, September 5, 1993.

2) "United Fights For Its Health as Unions Fight for United," *The New York Times*, August 23, 1993.

Figure 5-2 Cost and Profit (as a percentage of sales) for United, American, and Southwest Airlines (Second Quarter 1993)

biggest airline. Eastern Airlines, under Eddie Rickenbacker, was one of the world's leading airlines. Both no longer exist. Continental Airlines went into bankruptcy twice, partly because of a leveraged buyout that saddled the company with huge debt. The price of oil has been a factor in airline economics, at times overriding other cost factors. Airlines, like hotels are cyclical: There are periods of oversupply and weak demand and then periods of high demand and lack of supply.

While it is difficult to describe a normal year for U.S. airlines and therefore estimate what can be expected in cost and profit, Figure 5-2 presents data collected by *The New York Times* for one quarter and provides a breakdown of costs as a percentage of sales for the two largest airlines, United and American, and for Southwest Airlines, the exemplar of a cost-efficient airline.

On a worldwide basis, airline costs as reported by the International Civil Aviation Organization (ICAO), the major world commercial airline organization, are seen in Figure 5-3. Fuel costs in 1991 were 15 percent of total costs. Ticketing, sales, and

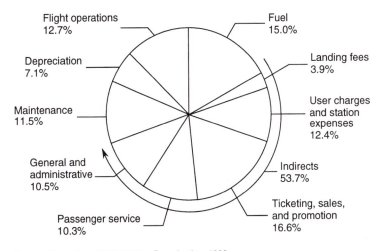

Source: International Civil Aviation Organization, 1993

Figure 5-3 Airline Operating Cost Distribution (ICAO Airlines, 1991, Preliminary)

promotion costs were estimated at 16.6 percent. Passenger service constituted 10.3 percent of total costs.

According to Boeing Aircraft, three categories of costs predominate: fuel, labor, and investment. A new B747-400, the largest commercial jet, costs between $140 and $160 million.

One effective way to cut airline costs is to sell all or parts of the company to its employees who may be more willing to accept salary cuts and agree to necessary changes if done by the employees themselves. In 1992 Northwest Airlines' employees gained 37.5 percent ownership of the airline and helped Northwest avoid bankruptcy. In 1993 employees of United Airlines agreed to buy at least 53 percent of UAL, the parent of United Airlines. The deal was estimated to involve $5.5 billion and make UAL the largest employee-owned company in the U.S. United's employees agreed to make substantial wage and work-rule concessions estimated to save $4.5 billion over six years. Labor/management strife which helped destroy Eastern Airlines and Pan American Airlines was avoided.

ECONOMICS OF AIRLINE OPERATIONS

One measure of airline efficiency is cost per available seat mile. That cost, according to *Financial World* (Sept. 1993, p. 36) for U.S. airlines in 1993 was 9.5 cents. American Airlines' cost per seat mile in 1992 was 8.93 cents. Load factor, the percentage of seats filled, is another efficiency and marketing measure used by airlines. Salaries and benefits run close to the same percentage as hotel labor costs.

United's profit for 1993 was only 2.3 percent of sales, while Southwest was able to bring 12.8 percent to the bottom line. By operating with few management levels, and other cost efficiencies, Southwest underpriced its competitors by at least 25 percent while enjoying higher profits (as a percentage of sales). Fuel prices for 1993 continued to be low because Saudi Arabia, being strapped for cash, insisted on maintaining high petroleum production. According to consultants Morten Beyer and Associates, Southwest gets more flight time from its pilots than American—672 hours a year versus 371—and racks up 60 percent more passenger miles per flight attendant ("Something Novel in the Air," *Newsweek*, August 12, 1993, p. 34).

Southwest has a decided cost advantage in salaries and benefits. The company prides itself on being a lean, no frills airline. From its inception, the company has had a flat organizational structure with little distance between the CEO and front-line employees. Bureaucracy is minimal. The fare structure is simple: only two fare levels, peak or executive, offered during the day, Monday through Friday, and off-peak or pleasure, offered on Monday through Friday evenings and weekends. Salaries for pilots are about the same as those for the major airlines flying mid-size planes but are augmented by a profit-sharing plan. Southwest employees own 12 percent of the airline, and share in the profits. Senior management at Southwest arrive on the job between 7:30 A.M. and 8:00 A.M. (For an interesting comparison of UAL and Southwest see *The Winds of Turbulence* by Howard D. Punam, Harper Business, 1991.)

Sales commissions for Southwest constitute only 6.5 percent of sales while UAL commissions were 16.3 percent of sales. Sales commissions on some transatlantic flights, where competition is intense, go as high as 20 percent. Travel agents quite naturally favor the airlines offering the highest commissions. Southwest Airlines has been a cut-rate regional airline and cost-conscious fliers do not mind dialing direct for flights. Southwest prides itself on buying newer planes that require fewer pilots and are fuel efficient. Southwest flies one type of plane, flies point-to-point without benefit of hubs, and offers minimal service including peanuts as a nod at food service. Any Southwest pilot can fly any Southwest plane, which cuts down on training costs and makes for scheduling flexibility among pilots (*Wall Street Journal*, November 4, 1993). Pilots for Southwest earn a little over $104,000 a year for flying mid-size aircraft and fly eighty hours a month compared with American Airlines pilots who also earn an average of $104,000 a year but fly only about forty-eight hours a month. Southwest has no senior pilots earning over $200,000 a year as do UAL and Delta.

The large carriers such as Delta, United, and American have lost money on their shorter routes and dropped many from their schedules. Several regional carriers, often owned or affiliated with the majors, and which share the computer-reservation code and name of the larger carrier, stepped in and did well. United and American both pulled out of many California markets after battling Southwest's low fares. United stopped its service between Fargo, North Dakota and Denver, Colorado and let its United Express, with its nineteen-passenger turboprop planes take over. Continental has its low-cost subsidiary, CALite, a low cost, quick turnaround carrier, linking fourteen cities in the Southeast (*Wall Street Journal*, October 19, 1993). The regional airlines fly with lower labor, fuel, and maintenance costs, and smaller, more efficient, turboprop planes that better fit market demand. The breakeven point for some of the smaller planes is as low as 35 percent of seats filled. Competition may be nonexistent on some routes (*Wall Street Journal*, September 15, 1993).

Fuel Prices

OPEC, the Organization of Petroleum Exporting Countries, has waxed and waned in its power to control oil prices. The average price of fuel paid by members of the International Air Transportation Association (IATA) during one period, September 1973 to January 1974, doubled in four months. By mid-1976 airlines were paying three times as much for fuel as they had two years earlier (Rigas Doganis, *Flying Off Course,* Boston: Allen & Unwin, 1985, p. 18).

Because of political differences, it is difficult for the OPEC nations to agree on price policy and individual members are prone to cheat on their assigned quotas of oil production. If and when Iraq is allowed unrestrained oil export by the United Nations, the cartel will be further weakened. Russia is a wild card that, if its productive capacity is realized, will serve to dampen oil prices. Fuel and oil prices as forecasted by the Boeing Company are shown in Figure 5-4.

Boeing sees jet fuel prices increasing to over $1.20 a gallon by the year 2010. Predicting oil prices is a dicey game—fortunes have been made and lost in playing it. Plainly, other energy sources are available. Coal can be used to generate the electricity needed for electric cars and synthetic oil can be produced if need be. In the long-

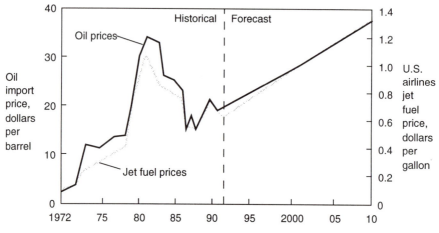

Source: Boeing Corporation, 1993

Figure 5-4 Fuel and Oil Prices (Current Terms)

run an alternative may be available for aviation fuel, but for now airlines' fortunes are partially linked to oil prices.

Fuel burn efficiency is projected to improve by 2.5 percent per year due to the purchase of larger and more efficient airplanes. Capital costs are increasing as a percentage of total costs because of newer technology, regulatory requirements, and replacement of older planes. Load factors, according to Boeing, will fluctuate around 66 percent and rise above 68 percent by the year 2000. The newer planes make more two-person flight crews possible (*Current Market Outlook, World Market Demand and Airplane Supply Requirements,* Boeing Commercial Airplane Group, Seattle, WA, 1993).

Long-haul flights cost less per mile than short flights. The cost of flying a plane falls per mile once it reaches cruising altitude. Waiting time to take off and land can be very costly. Costs per mile above cruising speed rise as speeds increase. High speeds equal high fuel costs. That is why most commercial jet planes average 540 miles per hour in flight and why fuel costs are high for the Concorde at high speeds.

Airline Statistics

Airline load factor is a measure of productivity that shows the percentage of seats filled. Figure 5-5 presents a graph compiled by the Boeing Company. The load factor for the top 20 airlines shows an upward trend during the 1987 to 1991 period, after which a general decline took place. Asia and Oceania have the highest load factors, ranging above 70 percent. Europe and Canada's load factors fall a few points lower, while the U.S. load factors are 6 to 8 points lower.

Average airplane size grew from 176 seats in 1980 to 193 seats in 1992. Somewhat surprising is the size of the U.S. airline market compared to the rest of the world. Of the 1166 billion Revenue Passenger Miles (RPMs) flown by commercial airlines in 1990, the U.S. held a 42.2 percent market share. In other words, about 40 percent of

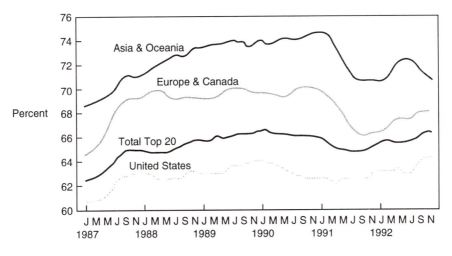

Source: Boeing Corporation, 1993

Figure 5-5 Load Factor Trends, Top 20 Airlines (12-month Moving Average)

the miles flown in 1990 were flown by U.S. airlines. Europe had 27 percent of the airline market. Figure 5-6 shows the breakdown by region.

By the year 2010 the market shares are predicted to change: The U.S. share will drop as a percentage of the total 3138 billion RPMs while Japan and other Asian countries will increase, as seen in the Figure 5-7.

Boeing points out that the 1980s were a period of airline consolidation by mergers

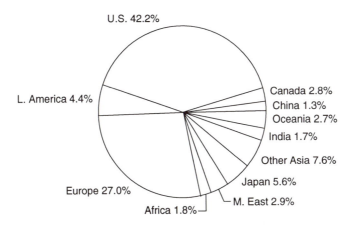

1166 Billion RPMs*

*RPMs = Revenue Passenger Miles
Source: Boeing Corporation, 1993

Figure 5-6 1990 Airline Market Share

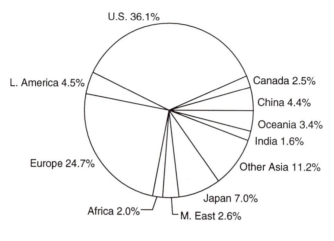

U.S. 36.1%

Canada 2.5%

China 4.4%

Oceania 3.4%

India 1.6%

Other Asia 11.2%

L. America 4.5%

Europe 24.7%

Japan 7.0%

Africa 2.0%

M. East 2.6%

3138 Billion RPMs*

*RPMs = Revenue Passenger Miles
Source: Boeing Corporation, 1993

Figure 5-7 2010 Airline Market Share

and acquisitions. In the future, there will be more cross-shareholding; route and code sharing; more computer links; integration of routes, networks, and scheduling; and combined maintenance and training. In addition, says Boeing, direct operating costs will be lower as airlines operate more efficient planes. Employee productivity will rise as a result of automation and technology. Economies of scale will lower interest costs (*Current Market Outlook*, Boeing, Seattle, WA, 1993).

AIRLINE PRICING

Deregulation of the U.S. airlines was followed by a huge consolidation of major airlines and the startup of dozens of new airlines. The startup of the new airlines and the bankruptcy of others have been disruptive to the airline business and have helped keep airfares low. To gain a foothold in the air travel market, the new airlines have had to underprice their competitors—a risky and costly tactic in that the established airlines usually match the lower airfares. Airlines in various stages of bankruptcy are protected from all their obligations and this helps keep fares lower than is feasible, often to the destruction of other airlines. The leveraged buyout of Continental Airlines made millions for insiders, but eventually forced the company into financial difficulties. The top U.S. airlines (by number of passengers) in 1992 as listed by the Air Transport Association are shown in Figure 5-8.

Airfare wars seem endemic. Small airlines have affiliated with the big ones or lost out. According to *Airline Economics*, 198 new airlines were started between 1978 and 1987. Of these, 160 merged with other airlines or faded. Most were undercapital-

Top 25 U.S. Airlines in 1992

Rank/Airline		Passengers (000)
1	American	85,955
2	Delta	82,911
3	United	66,596
4	USAir	54,654
5	Northwest	43,443
6	Continental	38,359
7	Southwest	31,023
8	Trans World	22,292
9	America West	15,118
10	Alaska	6,167
11	Aloha	4,662
12	Hawaiian	4,654
13	Air Wisconsin	2,864
14	Horizon Air	2,380
15	Simmons	2,341
16	West Air	1,947
17	U.S. Air Shuttle	1,472
18	Trans States	1,322
19	Executive Airlines	912
20	Midwest Express	808
21	Carnival	575
22	Markair	549
23	Braniff International	518
24	American Trans Air	480
25	Tower	463

Source: Air Transport Association

Figure 5-8 The Top 25 U.S. Airlines, 1992

ized. One example was Hawaii Express. Operating with one plane leased from the Italian airline, Alitalia, it flew one route, between Los Angeles and Honolulu. An engine needed replacement so the airline had to rent one at an exorbitant price. The company lasted only a few months.

When not affected by price wars, airlines have a pricing policy of depending heavily on the business traveler for profits. About half of domestic airline travel is done for business reasons. The inflexible business traveler is charged full fare; the flexible leisure traveler is given heavily discounted fares. The fare charged the person who must go tomorrow, or at a specific time in the near future, may be triple or more than the fare for the person who can schedule his or her trip several days or even weeks in advance. Business travelers find ways around the two-tier pricing system and corporations who have huge travel budgets negotiate special rates for themselves. The individual corporate traveler flies as necessary and may select the airline that grants the largest frequent flier bonus points. Many companies require frequent flyer points be given back to the company. To avoid the highest fares, many business travelers take cheaper flights that force them into Saturday night stays.

The "soak the business traveler" policy may boomerang with the telecommunications "revolution." Why fly when you can use a video telephone or take part in a videoconference? Audiographic technology permits simultaneous transmission of voices and graphic images. Teleconference costs for a typical videoconferencing system dropped from $200,000 in 1986 to about $15,000 in 1993 (Ron Taylor, "Videoconferencing: Building Ubiquity, Cutting Cost and Communicating Easily," *Telecommunication (U.S.)*, August 1991, pp. 46–48; also in "Teleconferencing Technology: Recent Developments and Implications for the Hotel Industry," *FIU Hospitality Review*, p. 2).

Premium Fares

First-class fares typically cost three to four times as much as coach fares. Up to 85 percent of the travelers flying at these premium fares are traveling at business expense ("Airlines Revamp The Front Cabin," *The New York Times*, October 17, 1993). The Pan American Clipper flights of the 1930s tried to make the expense account traveler and the wealthy as comfortable as possible by offering some seats that could be screened off and made into beds. Ever since, the major airlines have installed larger, better seats and provided more leg room for first-class passengers, and charged whatever the particular market would bear. The number of first-class seats that are added depend upon the flights being offered. Some flights may have as many as 20 percent of the seats in first class. Several airlines have eliminated first-class seating on short flights.

Scandinavian Airlines and Finnair have eliminated first class in favor of "business" class, close to first class in services with slightly smaller seats, fewer amenities and less opulent food and beverage service. Business class is priced between full-fare economy class and first class. On some East Asian airlines, there is little difference between "first" and "business" class. Both are outstanding in service and amenities. Frequent fliers can often upgrade into first and business class if seats are available.

Airline seats can be quickly changed to match demand and newly developed seats can be widened or narrowed in seconds, adding two inches of seat width by turning a six-across row of seats for coach class into five-across for business class.

To attract the luxury market, British Airways upgraded its arrival lounge in London and installed twenty-three private shower and washrooms. Valets are on hand to press a suit for first-class passengers while they wait. A few airlines offer limousine free pickup and delivery service for first-class passengers.

Says one airline analyst "there is virtually no floor below the discounting of fares." Getting whatever is possible for those "last unsold seats" is considered better than leaving them vacant. The marginal cost of taking one additional passenger is less than one-fourth of the full cost. The flight's only costs are for extra meals, commission cost, and a small amount for extra fuel (Ibid., *The New York Times*, October 17, 1993). This assumes that the plane will not be overbooked and that the "marginal" flyer will not take a later flight with the same airline. About 75 percent do.

The large corporation can negotiate steeply discounted fares for its employees' travel. Add to these fares the discounts that pleasure travelers can get during price wars, and some flights will lose money even when all seats are full (Ibid., *The New York Times*, October 17, 1993).

Frequent Flier Programs as a Cost

Frequent flier programs under which many airlines give passengers credits for miles flown have been an inducement to fly more often, but in some cases have been too successful, too much of a giveaway. Credit miles have increased to the point that frequent fliers take seats that could otherwise be taken by fare-paying passengers.

Airlines have partnerships with an assortment of businesses, including hotels, cruise lines, telephone companies, and credit-card issuers, to give mileage credit that can be used for free trips. United Airlines has tie-ins with five cruise lines, four rental-car companies, and a number of hotels. The number of passengers utilizing frequent flier mileage for "non-revenue" trips has risen to about six percent of total passengers.

FORECASTING AIRLINE DEMAND

Almost every tactical or strategic decision taken by management is based on forecasting. Airline forecasting requires both short- and long-term estimates of air traffic on which to base aircraft purchase decisions and operational budgets. An airline tries to forecast overall demand for the market segments it serves, business and pleasure, and further break down fare types. In the United States, fare wars have been particularly disruptive making forecasting and budgeting for cost control extremely difficult. Competition on many routes is high, and even an airline with only one route and one leased plane may find its forecast meaningless because a larger airline can force it out of business.

Where the information is available, forecasting relies heavily on past experience to estimate future demand. Trend projections based on time series are the most commonly used method of airline forecasting. Smaller airlines may use it exclusively. The method assumes that the factors effecting air traffic in the past will continue to apply. The independent variable is time, the dependent variable, air traffic. Forecasts are based on the average rate of growth in the recent past but the data series should be long enough to identify what are random variations and those that represent basic trends.

The larger airlines bolster their trendline projections with a variety of market studies, concentrating on the market segments they serve. Market studies are done both in-house and by outside research firms. Airline forecasts made by Boeing and the other aircraft manufacturers are also used. Though possibly biased in favor of airline growth, these studies provide long-term trendlines based on years of research. Boeing, for example, has a large department devoted entirely to forecasting regional and world economic data.

The judgment and experience of company officers is added to whatever information comes from market research and other sources of information. Executive judgment is often augmented by Delphi studies which call in experts in the field to anticipate future trends. Their forecasts are pooled and may be modified as a result of discussion.

Multiple regression is the technique commonly used to measure relationships between an independent variable, for example, airfare, and a dependent variable, such as distance traveled or exchange rate. When simultaneous multiple regression equations are made, it is called econometrics. These cost more and take longer to use. Many researchers have found that forecasts by econometric models are not necessarily more accurate than those made by time series models (Turgut Var and Choong-Ki Lee, "Tourism Forecasting: State-of-the Art Techniques," *Encyclopedia of Hospitality and Tourism*, New York: Van Nostrand Reinhold, 1993).

According to Rigas Doganis, most airlines use a range of forecasting techniques. Short to medium forecasts tend to be based on time series projections frequently modified by executive judgment and by market research findings. Forecasts beyond three to five years ahead must be thought of as very tentative (Rigas Doganis, *Flying Off Course*, Boston: Allen & Unwin, 1985, Chapter 8).

Time series forecasts can be refined by weighing recent information more heavily and adjusting it to reflect the level of maturity of flight segments. Markets may be in a developmental stage or may have matured; the forecasts are adjusted accordingly.

Several methods of air traffic forecasting may be used, the simplest are those made by experienced executives and others that extend a timeline based on past experience. Thousands of airfares are changed daily and as flight time approaches, more seats may be discounted to attract the most passengers possible. Airlines normally overbook the number of seats available for a flight, expecting a certain percentage of no-shows. Overbooking means more passengers than seats and some passengers with confirmed reservations must be shifted to other flights. Inducements of cash help. On the other hand, revenue from unfilled seats represents revenue lost forever. Discounted fares are used to attract passengers who can plan trips well in advance. Depending upon the time of year, discounted seats may account for 90 percent of the passengers.

Yield Management

Yield management, as a tool for maximizing revenues by the management of seat inventory and forecasting demand and fares charged, became popular among the larger airlines in the early 1980s. Yields are raised by taking as many reservations as possible at the highest possible fares. Yield management means lowering the price of seats according to expected demand and relying heavily on computers and modeling techniques. As departure times approach, discounted seats are added or subtracted, the goal being to fill all seats with the highest possible fares, using booking trends on specific flights to predict the number of seats that will be sold, and at what prices. Overbooking and sales to standby passengers are part of the system. So too is the practice of paying some passengers with confirmed seats as an inducement to take later, less booked flights.

Heavy discounting takes place on most U.S. domestic routes and the passenger may find him- or herself sitting next to a passenger who has paid less than half the published fare. The business traveler without discretionary time pays full fare; the pleasure traveler can schedule the pleasure trip weeks in advance.

Domestic markets typically involve a much higher amount of business travel. In 1990, nearly 50 percent of U.S. domestic travel was done for business reasons and accounted for 68 percent of revenues (Boeing, 1993). Major tourist destinations attract international travelers, resulting in higher percentages of pleasure travel on international routes.

Hub-and-Spoke Economics

The major airlines became enamored of the hub-and-spoke concept in the 1980s, scheduling a number of flights to arrive at an airport within a certain limited time and in most cases requiring a change of planes for the passenger's final destination. In theory, the hub concept worked to the airlines financial benefit. Passengers from San Diego flying on American to New York may fly to the Dallas/Fort Worth hub where they join passengers from several other feeder flights to continue on to New York. American Airlines built seven of the industry's more than two dozen hubs. Some of the major hubs and the airlines that dominate them include American Airlines at Dallas/Fort Worth, Delta at Atlanta, United at Chicago, and TWA at St. Louis.

The hub-and-spoke concept cannot compete costwise with the low-cost carriers like Southwest on point-to-point short flights. The passenger flying to the Dallas/Fort Worth hub is often delayed an hour or more before going on to the final destination. American's combined losses at their hubs in San Jose, Nashville, and Raleigh, NC hubs may have surpassed $100 million a year ("The Bully of the Skies Cries Uncle," *The New York Times*, September 5, 1993). Hubs, it was found, were not feasible unless they were of a size that could carry the cost of maintaining them. Small hubs are inactive much of the time.

Computer Reservation Systems as Airline Assets

Computerized reservation systems (CRSs) have played a large role in airline economics. The CRS was born in the airlines and almost all are airline owned. In 1988 the U.S. Department of Transportation calculated that computer reservation systems profits in the United States have passed the billion dollar mark. TWA put its interest in the Worldspan CRS on the block for $50 million in 1993.

Sabre (Semi Automated Business Research Environment), the world's largest privately owned real-time computer network, began operating as a reservations system for American Airlines in 1962 and later was developed as a travel agency booking tool in the mid-1970s. Sabre serves more than 25,000 travel agency locations and has the schedules of some 650 airlines. It can be used to book more than 27,000 hotels and condos, fifty car rental companies, and thirty-six tour wholesale companies. In 1992 it created 1.2 million passenger name records, the records stored in an airlines reservation system detailing reservation and passenger information. The Sabre system is being used in sixty-four countries on all six continents. American earns a fee on each seat assignment. In 1993 American expected Sabre and American's other data processing service to generate $240 million in profit.

American is designing a CRS for the French railroad's TGV, the superfast trains, and another system for the English Channel tunnel. Holiday Inn Worldwide will buy a version of American's CRS for its hotel reservations.

Nearly all travel agencies lease computers from one or more of the airlines. In 1991, an average of 11,982 schedule changes and 215,396 airfare changes were processed daily for 724 airlines by the Official Airline Guide. Computers allow immediate access to this information. These systems also allow access to most of the cruise lines, hotel chains, and also for AMTRAK and Via Rail (the Canadian rail system).

Travel agencies can use the CRS as part of their accounting system (CRS ownership is covered by Monika Echtermeyer, Chapter 39, *Encyclopedia of Hospitality and Tourism*, New York: Van Nostrand Reinhold, 1993).

Air travel correlates well with income, especially with higher per capita income. Figure 5-9 shows that about 75 percent of U.S. households with incomes over $100,000 a year are air travelers; only 11 percent of households with incomes of $10,000 or less a year are air travelers.

While air travel is increasing most rapidly in the Asia-Pacific area, its total is relatively small compared to Europe and North America. Figure 5-10 shows the revenue passenger miles (RPMs) per capita of air travel in the various regions. North Americans fly most, followed by Europeans. The graph by the International Civil Aviation Organization and published in Boeing's Market Forecast for 1993 is a strong reminder of the importance of air travel in the United States and Canada as compared to other regions of the world.

Gates as Assets

Airport "gates," the airport spaces that are mostly leased to airlines by airport authorities for airlines to load and unload passengers, can be a valuable asset. Depending upon the airport owner, gates can be subleased to other airlines. Gates and slots (the term referring to the space of time during which a plane lands, remains at a gate, and departs) can give an airline a predominant position at an airport. United Airlines and American Airlines have preferential positions at Chicago's O'Hare International Airport, the world's busiest. Delta has the most gates at Atlanta's Hartsfield International

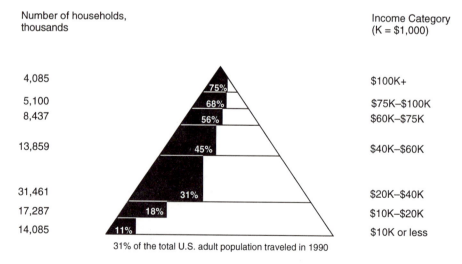

Figure 5-9 Penetration of Air Travel by Income Category, United States

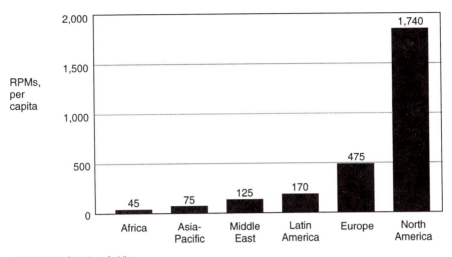

Note: By ICAO region of airline
Source: Boeing Corporation, 1993

Figure 5-10   Per Capita Travel, 1990

Airport. Airport landing fees can be costly, running up to $10,000 per landing at some airports for the largest planes fully loaded.

Airlines must buy or lease the planes that fit their routes and schedules. The Boeing 747s, the huge wide-bodied planes, are needed for heavily traveled routes, usually long-haul flights. They are very cost efficient where load factors are high. Airlines with newer planes operate with a cost advantage even though the price of planes continues to rise. A Boeing 747-400, the latest long range behemoth, with spare parts, costs in excess of $150 million.

Concorde, the aircraft used in supersonic flight by British Air and Air France, has proved uneconomical since its first flight in 1969. Though it can travel at Mach 2 (twice the speed of sound) its cabin is a long, slender tube that seats only 105 passengers and is an aviation fuel guzzler. Added speed increases costs per mile. Fares are about four times regular first-class fares. Eighty percent of the passengers are business travelers. The huge advantage of the SST (supersonic transport) is lost when the plane flies over land and is forced by most nations it overflies to slow down to subsonic speeds to avoid producing the ear-shattering sonic booms that sometimes damage buildings in the plane's path. Another disadvantage is its high fuel consumption and flight range of less that 4000 miles. Only sixteen Concordes have been built.

Boeing, the largest of the aircraft manufacturers, offers a series of planes to fit various markets. The B-737 series are fuel efficient and best suited for short haul markets. Boeing's biggest plane, the 747-400, has the longest range and can fly non-stop using the polar route from New York City to Tokyo. Figure 5-11 shows the various Boeing planes, their number of seats and the number of nautical miles each can fly non-stop.

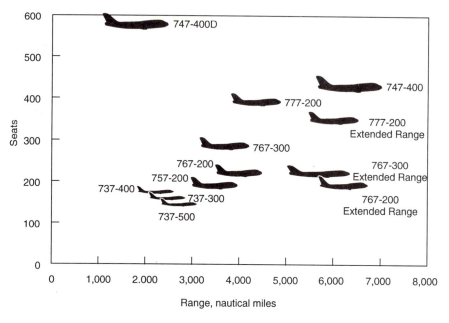

Source: Boeing Corporation, 1993

Figure 5-11 Characteristics of Boeing Planes

More than 3000 of the world's best selling jetliners, the Boeing 737 series, have been manufactured since the first 737 flew in 1967. Seating configurations range from 100 to 172 seats. The Boeing 757 and 767 are medium capacity, fuel efficient twinjets. The 757 can carry 186 passengers in mixed class seating about 4000 nautical miles. The 767 has a range in excess of 6000 nautical miles. (A nautical mile is about 6067 feet compared to 5280 feet in land miles.)

Boeing's newest plane, the B-777, is being developed internationally: The flight computers are supplied by the General Electric Company and Aironics Ltd. of Kent, England; Korean Airways supplies the flap faring; rudders are produced by Aerospace Technologies of Australia; outboard flaps are produced by Alemmia of Naples, Italy; as well as products provided by a number of other suppliers. The 777 will be the largest twin-engined airliner certified to fly long-range routes directly across oceans. With 400 seats, it will meet the need for a jet plane larger than the 767 but smaller than the 747 jumbo jet (*The Economist*, April 13, 1991). The 777 should cost 25 percent less to operate than the older models of the four-engine 747. The 777's range will be extended to 7250 miles and will be able to carry 440 passengers. Its development costs were $4 billion. More powerful engines and 3000 pounds less weight than the 747 will increase operating efficiency (John Holusha, "Can Boeing's New Baby Fly Financially?", *The New York Times*, March 27, 1994).

Boeing is by far the largest airplane manufacturer and seller of commercial aircraft. In 1992 the company served about 60 percent of the world market for commercial jets with sales of $17.8 billion for that year. About half of its orders are from non-U.S. airlines, which helps it attain the title of the U.S.'s largest exporter. The European Airbus Consortium is Boeing's archrival; Boeing claims unfair competition because of large government subsidies to Airbus. In 1992 the European community reached an agreement to limit direct subsidies to 33 percent of development costs for new models. Airbus is, however, studying the development of a 600- to 700-seat jumbo plane (*Boeing 1992 Annual Report*, 1992).

ECONOMIC FUTURE OF AIRLINES

By extrapolating airline growth, Boeing forecasts air travel to continue to grow at an average annual rate of somewhat more than 5 percent through the year 2010. See Figure 5-12 for Boeing's projections. Greatest growth will continue to be in international travel and East Asia will grow faster than the world average.

The airline industry in the United States has already been compressed into about five or six major airlines which, far from forming a monopoly, fight viciously for market share, a fight that makes profitability uncertain. As a result the consumer benefits with low fares. British Air continues to fly the largest number international route miles and is profitable. A number of airlines in other countries are government subsidized.

The next generation of airplane being studied is a new 550- to 800-seat jetliner.

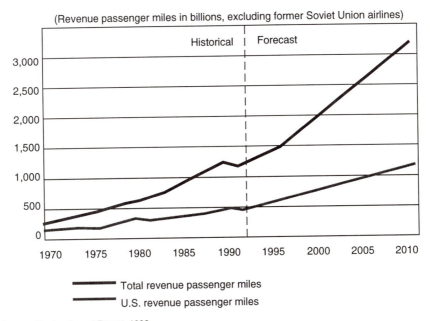

Source: Boeing Annual Report, 1992

Figure 5-12 Future World Air Travel

Also under study is another supersonic transport known as the High-Speed Civil Transport, an attempt to produce a larger supersonic plane that, unlike the Concorde, is economically feasible.

As of 1994 the real battle within the U.S. airline industry was being waged between the major airlines, with their relatively high costs, and the low-cost airlines. American, United, and Delta were being forced to cut costs by the low-cost, shorter flight airlines that can fly for about 6 cents per mile versus about 9 cents a mile necessary for the big airlines to survive.

The major airlines had bet on a strategy of more planes, more flights, and more hub airports. By 1993, it was clear that strategy had failed. The new strategy pushed for wage and salary cuts, and work rules that would mean greater efficiency.

Code sharing agreements among airlines, a practice by which a single flight number is assigned to a trip in which more than one airline is used, was in effect between Northwest and KLM; British Airways and U.S. Air; Delta and Swissair; American and British Midland; Continental and Air France; and United and Lufthansa. With two airlines selling seats for the same flight the chances of filling most or all seats increase (*The New York Times*, December 5, 1993). More alliances, transnational ownership, and marketing agreements between airlines were being planned.

Cross-ownership of major airlines is growing. British Airways has approval to invest 750 million in U.S. Air and owns 25% of Qantas, the largest Australian airline; Scandinavian Airlines owns 9.9 percent of Texas Air; Swissair has 5 percent of Delta; KLM owns 10 percent of Northwest. KLM, Swissair, and Austrian Airlines were planning to merge. While the airlines continue dogfighting among themselves, new, more cost effective planes are being developed, operating costs are being reduced, and for the public willing to sit in crowded planes, airfares continue to be a bargain.

As we approach the end of the millennium, the airline industry continues on the path of consolidation and transnational ownership; air travel continues its rapid growth and is the primary mode for long-distance travel. Despite the several airline bankruptcies and huge airline financial losses experienced by most large American and European airlines, investors continue to buy airline stocks. Continental, American, and Delta are countering the short-haul, low-cost airlines by setting up their own low-cost lines. It was found that hubs must be of a certain size to be feasible, so some hubs are being cut back. An airline hub has fixed costs that continue even though the hub may be active only a few hours a day. Airport cost is skyrocketing as was evident when building the new Denver airport. The new Kansai airport built as a 1300-acre atoll off the coast of Osaka, Japan is reported to have cost $14 billion.

6

Economics of Other Tourism Sectors

CAR RENTAL ECONOMICS

The car rental business as it effects tourism is a multibillion dollar business largely controlled by Hertz, Avis, Budget, and National, who borrow heavily, have thousands of employees and licensees, and are international in scope. Ford, General Motors, and Chrysler either own or have major stakes in the large U.S. car rental companies. In 1992 the industry grossed $11.5 billion (*Auto Rental News*).

Hertz, Avis, Budget, and National controlled about 80 percent of the U.S. market, in terms of number of locations. The top ten U.S. car rental companies are shown in Figure 6-1. These companies offered cars at about 7000 locations. The other 19,000 locations were mostly car dealers and service stations. In Europe the car rental business is divided among some 6000 companies, with a fleet of about 430,000 cars (*Travel Industry World Yearbook*, 1993).

Eighty percent of car rentals originate at airports where the rental car companies lease space. Travel agencies generate between 25 and 50 percent of the bookings of major companies. Commissions to the agents are 5 percent of sales for corporate business, 10 percent for leisure sales. Some companies pay 10 percent on all bookings and 15 percent or more in some markets where competition is keen. Tie-ins with airline frequent-flier programs are common as many fliers select rental cars based on the number of frequent-flier miles available.

A significant part of making a profit in the car rental business is the difference between prices paid for cars and the prices they are sold for after being used by customers. Fleet purchases of cars are acquired at discounts of 30 percent or more below retail prices. Auto manufacturers who may own parts of the car rental companies

U.S. Car Rental Companies - 1992
Ranked by Number of Cars
(some figures are estimates)

	U.S. locations	Number of Vehicles	Revenue (miles)
Hertz	1,500	230,000	$2,860
Avis	1,100	170,000	1,400
Budget	1,150	159,000	1,300
Alamo	104	127,000	840
National	1,000	115,000	920
Dollar	486	61,500	595
Thrifty	400	37,000	287
General	54	20,000	N.A.
Payless	120	15,000	45
Advantage	55	6,000	55

Source: Auto Rental News

Figure 6-1   U.S. Car Rental Companies, 1992

have their own reasons for the prices charged. Such as getting a new model car seen and used by car renters.

Car location managers and other managers have the responsibility of keeping cars available where needed and ensuring that cars are sold at times most favorable to the company. Sometimes it may be best to keep cars rented for 20,000 miles before selling them; at other times rental cars are sold with as few as 12,000 miles.

Car rental economics are closely tied to the general economy, rising and falling as the economy moves up or down. The major costs in the car rental business are the purchase or lease of automobiles, the cost of borrowing money, and labor costs. Vehicle manufacturers supply over 1.5 million cars to the industry annually. Like the airlines, car rental seats must be kept occupied, and a measure of company performance is fleet utilization. The Avis record of fleet utilization, for example, rose from 63.7 percent in fiscal year 1988 to 75.3 percent in 1993. Figure 6-2 shows the fleet utilization curve from 1988 to 1993.

The length of time cars are kept in service is a factor in containing costs, as vehicles must still bring a good price in the resale car market. With proper maintenance, the cars retain a high resale value. Rental cars are ordinarily purchased as the new model cars come out, then are operated for up to 20,000 miles before being sold, mostly to wholesale buyers.

A close alliance or overlapping ownership with a major auto manufacturer has advantages. The car rental company is assured of car availability and possible favorable prices. Ford has a large stake in Budget Rent-A-Car. General Motors owns National Rental Car. Chrysler has the Thrifty, Dollar, and Snappy car rental companies.

Avis is 26 percent owned by General Motors and features GM cars. The mainstay of Avis income comes from its U.S. Rent-A-Car division. Corporate and joint venture holdings in ten countries and licensee operations in sixty countries around the world account for 14 percent of revenue; the U.S. Rent-A-Car division accounts for 85 percent of income. Avis also has a subsidiary communication company called Wizard with a worldwide network span of leased communication lines of over 190,000 miles. Avis is unusual in that its employees own 74 percent of the company stock, held in trust via an employee stock ownership plan (ESOP).

Like so many companies in the 1980s, Avis was subject to a leveraged buyout at a purchase price of $1.785 billion; the 11,500 corporate U.S. employees bought the company. Both the fleet debt and the purchase price of the company were borrowed under ESOP regulations, which enabled the new company to secure favorable interest rates.

As of 1994 Avis had paid off most of the $785 million acquisition debt four years ahead of time. The company stresses employee participation and holds monthly meetings of employee-participation groups at national and regional levels (*Wall Street Journal*, November 23, 1993).

Hertz, the largest of the rental car companies, is represented in about 130 countries and operates approximately 420,000 vehicles from 5000 locations. The annual investment in vehicles is about $3 billion. In 1985 Hertz was part of UAL, parent of United Airlines, but was bought in 1987 by an investor group formed by the Ford Motor Company and certain members of Hertz's senior managers. Volvo (North America) also became an investor in Hertz. The "fly-drive" car rental was pioneered by the company. Hertz International coordinates a network of more than 3900 corporate and licensee locations in Europe, Asia/Pacific, Canada, Latin America, and the Caribbean. Including both corporate employees and licensees, Hertz employs some 18,000 people worldwide. In 1994 Ford began increasing its 49 percent stake in Hertz to 54 percent.

Chrysler bought Thrifty in 1989, and, a year later, Dollar Rent-a-Car. Ownership by auto manufacturers has kept the rental companies alive by providing subsidies.

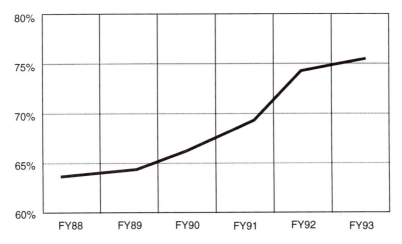

Source: The Avis Corporation, 1993

Figure 6-2 Fleet Utilization

Prices paid by rental car companies to the auto companies increased in 1993. Detroit, said the *Wall Street Journal*, had decided to move away from subsidized car rental sales after years of using no-profit or low-profit sales (to car rental companies) to keep factories running ("Prices for Rental Automobiles Will Increase Sharply Once Again," *Wall Street Journal*, September 29, 1993). In 1994 the industry was more influenced by the car manufacturers' policies than by the number of people arriving at airports. Profitability was the name of the game instead of aiming to gain market share by expanding the number of locations or fleet size (*Travel Industry World Yearbook*, 1993).

Airport car rentals correlate well with the amount of air travel. A half-price seat sale in June 1992 caused car rental sales to break previous records and resulted in fleet shortages in some resorts and cities. The increase in foreign visitors to the United States has helped car rental sales. Leisure travel has grown in importance, a fact favored by the car rental companies; leisure travelers keep their cars longer, which reduces transactions, servicing, and labor costs. The leisure market fits in well with the business market: More rentals can be made on weekends, periods when the business market drops sharply.

Car rental companies must constantly protect themselves against possible legal liability, not the least of which are claims made by renters who have suffered an injury. Jury trials can result in wildly exorbitant awards. In 1993 a New York jury awarded $163 million to a renter who was involved in an accident. Car rental companies have moved to change the rental contracts to make the renter's insurance company liable in case of an accident involving a liability claim that injures or kills other people, or damages others' property. When the car renter has no auto or home policy that covers accidents, a liability insurance supplement is charged. This charge is in addition to the rental contract provision that, for a fee, absolves the renter of responsibility for losing or damaging the rental car (*The New York Times*, August 8, 1993).

CRUISE LINE ECONOMICS

Cruise lines in North America experienced spectacular growth since the fly/cruise was introduced in 1971 (when some half a million passengers boarded cruise ships). That figure in 1992 reached 4.4 million, making the cruise business the fastest growing in the travel business. Total world spending for cruises in 1991 was about $9 billion, according to the International Council of Cruise Lines. The cruise industry in the United States directly or indirectly created 63,168 core section jobs. Altogether—through direct, indirect, and induced effects—the cruise line industry generated 450,166 jobs, $14.5 billion in wages, and $6.3 billion in tax revenues during 1992. North America is the center of the cruise business with a lion's share of the cruises sailing from Florida and California ports. Some 122 cruise ships are based in North America. Unfortunately for American business, only a few are registered in the United States.

Cruise ships vary in size from small exploration-type vessels to megaships that carry more than 2600 passengers ("Against the Tide," *Time*, February 17, 1992). In

1994 the Carnival Cruise Lines was building a new megavessel of 95,000 gross tons, 28,000 tons larger than the QE2 (Queen Elizabeth 2). It will carry as many as 4400 passengers and crew. As a result of the recession beginning in 1989 a number of ships were sold or retired, but as of 1994 the better marketed and managed lines were sailing 90 percent full. The cruise lines, however, were scrambling to maintain occupancy and were discounting cabins as much as 50 percent; two-for-one promotions and reduced fares for families occupying one cabin were heavily promoted.

North America accounts for 81 percent of the world cruise market for cruises of three days or more. As can be seen in Figure 6-3, four companies dominate the North American cruise industry: Carnival, Royal Caribbean, Kloster, and Princess (*Travel Industry World Yearbook*, 1993). Carnival Cruise Lines is the biggest (with 18.8 percent of the market in 1992) and most profitable. Starting with one leased ship in 1972, the company now owns the Holland American Line and its subsidiaries, Westours, Seabourn Cruise Line, and Windstar Sail Cruise. Ted Arison, the founder, rapidly capitalized on the fly/cruise concept and fed on the mass market using heavy TV advertising. The company tapped into the large California market with the fly/cruise concept and by sailing out of Florida to the Caribbean. Pricing is about 20 percent below the competition and there is heavy emphasis on the casino gambling where profits are high (David Howell, *Passport:An Introduction to the Travel and Tourism Industry*, South-Western Publishing Co., 1989, p. 128).

Once the breakeven point is reached, the marginal cost of an additional passenger is low. Food cost increases but other costs increase very little. Labor costs for service personnel increase very little. Wages and salaries remain fixed, tipped employees' income increases at no cost to the ship.

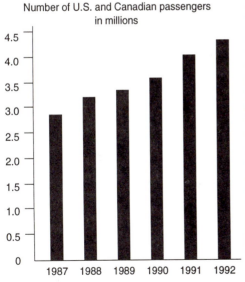

Number of U.S. and Canadian passengers in millions

1992 percent share of the passenger cruise business, by berth capacity	
Carnival Cruise Lines	18.8%
Royal Caribbean Cruises	14.6%
Kloster Cruise*	11.4%
Princess Cruises	10.3%
Chandris Cruise	6.8%
Cunard Line	4.7%
Other Lines	33.4%

*Includes Norwegian Cruise Line

Note: 26 other cruise lines make up the remaining 33.4% of the capacity.

Source: Cruise Liners International Association

Figure 6-3   Cruise Market Growth

Gambling is becoming a larger factor in cruise ship economics. Larger ships mean bigger casinos where the odds favor the ship. The new ship, Sensation, of the Carnival Cruise Line, has a casino appropriately called Club Vegas that has crammed in 228 slot machines, twenty blackjack tables, three roulette wheels, three dice tables, and three poker tables. The newest and largest cruise ship, one being built by Carnival, will afford a large casino space. The ship can carry 3300 passengers, the size of a small town's population.

Nearly all cruise ships are registered in countries other than the United States. To fly the American flag, a ship must be built in the United States, where shipbuilding costs are about 50 percent higher than in other nations. Some foreign shipyards are government subsidized to keep workers employed. Foreign ships are free to hire whomever they want and it is not unusual for a luxury ship to have a staff of twenty or more Chinese who perform the scullery work and are never seen by the passengers. The officers on Scandinavian ships are usually Scandinavians, but the staff may be nationals of several countries. The ratio of crew to passengers is about 50 percent.

Much of the potential economic benefits to the United States from cruising are lost because most of the crews of U.S.-owned companies, especially those who perform the semi-skilled jobs aboard cruise ships, are other than U.S. nationals who are eager to take the jobs at lower wages than North Americans. U.S. shipyards have not been able to compete with other national shipyards, and union costs for U.S. officers and crew are not competitive. Shore-based jobs for U.S.-owned cruise lines—marketing and reservations—do provide jobs.

Shipboard food costs are high because nearly all cruise ships feature top-of-the-line menus. Full-service meals with numerous selections are offered four times a day, in addition to soups, sandwiches, and other items almost around the clock. The larger ships have several dining areas. Dining is a major part of the cruise experience—some passengers gain 3 to 5 pounds a day. Some companies are specialists in cruise food service and operate under contract with the ship's owners.

Cruise lines and airlines have some of the same elements regarding pricing. The effort is to sail one hundred percent booked even though many of the passengers pay twenty to fifty percent less than others for the same cabin style. Factors affecting the price of a cruise are its duration, the season, the cabin size, its location, and the ship's reputation. High season for the Caribbean is the winter; the summer for Alaska. The most expensive locations aboard ship are the outside cabins (with portholes). Larger cabins and upper decks cost more. Some passengers take two adjoining cabins. A range of price categories are offered on most ships. The most expensive category can be twice as high as the economy class located inboard on the lower decks.

To reduce fuel costs, cruise lines use diesel fuel and sail to fewer ports. Sailing is often carried out at night and at slow speeds. The newer ships use aluminum in their superstructure to reduce weight.

Cruise lines depend almost exclusively on travel agencies for booking tickets; the agencies are happy to cooperate because cruise sales bring commissions of 15 percent or more. Some agencies specialize in cruise sales, working out of their homes. A cruise sale is a big ticket item; a sale of a $10,000 cruise package means $1,500 or more in commission. Around-the-world cruises can cost as much as $127,000 per couple. Travel agency sales for cruises totaled $13.6 billion in 1991. Not all travel agency relations with cruise lines are happy ones. Carnival Cruise Lines stopped accepting the American Express charge card, saying the fees charged were twice as high as other credit cards. American Express immediately dropped Carnival as a preferred supplier and cut back on Carnival sales.

The future looks promising because the cruise market is huge: Only 5 to 6 percent of the U.S. population have taken a cruise. The economics for the cruise passenger looks good also because cruise prices include a package that contains lavish food, entertainment, and interesting itineraries. Fly/cruise packages include round-trip airfare. According to the Cruise Line International Association, 85 percent of cruise passengers are extremely or very satisfied with their cruise even though cabins are tiny compared to hotel rooms.

One reason for the rapid growth of the industry is the shift to massmarketing. Whereas an around-the-world cruise on a luxury ship can cost more than $100,000 for a couple, today's average passenger makes less than $50,000 a year and the cruise may be priced at less than $300 a day including airfare.

Cruise marketing is focused on the middle to upper class. The average age of passengers dropped from 52 in 1986 to 49 in 1990. The longer the cruise the older the age group. The greatest number of cruise passengers are from the United States, followed by the British, Germans, Australians, and Canadians.

Like the airlines, ownership of cruise lines is being concentrated in a relatively few megacompanies. It is expected that by 1995 the industry will be dominated by three or four major lines, each with several distinctive brands of (larger) ships (*Travel Industry World Yearbook*, 1993).

TRAVEL AGENCY ECONOMICS

Travel agency services come at a comparatively low price: about 10 percent of the sales made for the travel suppliers (airlines, railways, rental car firms, cruise ships, etc.). If provided by the suppliers themselves, the cost would be higher, probably about 15 percent of sales.

In 1992 the 32,147 travel agencies in the United States booked $51 billion in airline ticket sales, according to the Airline Reporting Corporation. Commissions for these sales were about $5.3 billion. Total travel agency sales for 1991, according to *Travel Weekly* magazine were $85.9 billion, with $47.9 billion in airline sales, $10.5 billion in hotel sales, $13.6 in cruise sales, and $6.7 billion in car rental sales. Other sales came to $7.2 billion.

Travel agency owners and their staff work for comparatively low incomes, especially when the level of expertise required is considered. Owners of the typical four- to five-person travel agency earned about $24,000 to $30,000 a year in 1992; the experienced employee about $18,000. According to the U.S. Bureau of Labor Statistics, the average hourly wage in 1990 for travel agents was $9.14, comparatively low for the level of skill required.

The trend toward becoming a franchisee or joining a cooperative travel group continues to grow, since independents do not enjoy the override commissions negotiated by the large travel companies with carriers. These overrides can amount to an additional 5 percent commission, and can increase the travel agent's profit by up to 50 percent.

A census completed in 1991 by the American Society of Travel Agents showed that in 1990, 90.1 percent of responding agencies had gross sales of less than $5 million a year. Slightly over 60 percent of the agencies in the survey had full-time working owners and 81 percent had female managers (Eric Friedheim, *Travel Agents, From Caravans and Clippers to the Concorde*, New York: Travel Agent Magazine Books, 1992).

The independent travel agency with no affiliation is fading away, replaced by mega-agencies and franchise agreements. The independent agency can survive by joining a cooperative marketing service or a consortium of agencies that together create the clout necessary to negotiate the override enjoyed by the franchised and mega-agency. Some eleven nationwide consortiums and several regional ones represent small travel agencies. Not only do the consortiums provide override enhancement, they offer help with securing bonds, corporate rates from hotels, mutual purchasing and insurance plans, and member educational plans. Travel agencies normally are open five days a week but a consortium or franchisor can set up 24-hour, seven-day-a-week service (Nona Starr, *Viewpoint, An Introduction to Travel, Tourism and Hospitality*, Boston: Houghton Mifflin, 1993).

Many travel agencies, especially those that are part of a travel franchise, target the corporate traveler and use satellite ticket printers to produce tickets ready for pick-up at the office of a corporation. Someone at the corporation uses an 800 number to reach the travel agency. The agent makes the reservation using electronic technology and sends the ticket information to the satellite ticket printer located at the corporation. A ticket boarding pass and itinerary are ready for the corporate traveler to take to the airport and board his or her flight.

Rocky Relationship with Hotels

In the past, many hotels have been reluctant partners with travel agents. Disputes over commission payments owed to travel agents by hotels have strained relations. The president of CASH (Commissions Automatically Settled by Hotels) estimated that half the commissions due to travel agents go unpaid because of poor record keeping, expense of transmitting small commissions, foreign exchange problems, and time-consuming collection effort (*Ibid.*, p. 117).

Payments for international reservations have been a problem. Conversion costs of bank drafts nearly equaled the commissions. The time and costs of making international hotel reservations other than through some of the large international hotel chains may exceed the commission. Best Western International, with members in some thirty-five countries, has arranged for an exchange specialist to pay travel agents in their own currencies.

Travel Agency Profitability

Like most small businesses, profitability depends upon management, marketing, sales volume, and cost control. Like a hotel, a full-service travel agency requires a good location and accessibility to its clients. Many agencies serve corporate markets, where location is less important. They are connected by satellite ticket printers, or by phones or fax machines.

A travel agency with annual sales of $2 million may employ four or five persons and each needs to produce about $75,000 in commissions a year to cover costs and leave a small profit. In many agencies the owner works full time and enjoys the travel benefits provided by the carriers in the form of discounted prices and familiarization trips. Owning a typical agency is not the royal road to fortune.

Although the travel agency has been the epitome of a small business enterprise, several travel companies are huge and are getting bigger. American Express reported it sold $8 billion of airline, hotel, car-rental, and cruise bookings in 1993, 10 percent to 12 percent of which it netted in commissions (*Wall Street Journal*, February 24, 1994). The Carlson Travel Network was, in 1993, already one of the world's largest travel agencies under a single business banner with $10.8 billion in annual sales (coming from hotels, restaurants, resorts, travel agencies, travel incentive sales, and a training and promotion company). Carlson has minimized its risk by avoiding equity positions through franchising and servicing other companies. Only six of the 2200 travel agencies under the Carlson name were owned by the company, the rest were franchised. In 1994 Carlson Travel Network combined with Wagonlit Travel of Paris, creating an enterprise with 4000 locations in 125 countries.

As can be seen in Figure 6-4, travel agencies are of critical importance in booking airlines, cruise lines, rental cars, and packaged tours. They are also important, but less so, in ticketing travel for railroads. Less than 10 percent of bus ticketing is done by travel agents.

Travel agency owners must review their market position from time to time and emphasize sales that produce the highest profit. Some travel agency owners have decided to sell only tours or cruises, high ticket items. Others develop their own tours. International air sales usually produce higher commissions, in some cases as much as

Supplier Dependence on U.S. Travel Agents

	Estimated Percent of Volume Booked by Agents
Airlines:	
Domestic	80
International	85
Hotels:	
Domestic	25
International	85
Cruise lines	95
Rail	37
Bus	Less than 10
Rental cars	50
Packaged tours	90

Source: Travel Industry World Yearbook, 1993

Figure 6-4 Supplier Dependence on U.S. Travel Agents

25 percent. Owners can examine their income mix and decide to reallocate sales efforts to more profitable lines. One possible sales mix looks like this:

Air Sales	60%
Cruise Sales	15%
Hotel Sales	10%
Car Rental Sales	10%
Other Sales	5%

Further analysis shows that half of air sales are domestic, half international. Short-flight domestic ticketing may cost the agency $30 per ticket, a loss transaction if all costs are considered. Commissions on domestic flights are 10 percent; on international flights, up to 25 percent. International ticketing is much more profitable if it can be done without losing domestic sales.

Cruise sales are big ticket transactions, from about $2000 to $10,000 per ticket. The time and effort for the agent may be little more than for a short domestic flight. A hotel reservation in the United States can require but a few minutes to complete and little additional effort if the hotel pays the commission promptly. Making a reservation for a European hotel may cost more than the fee received, and, if the client is disappointed, there can also be a loss of goodwill and confidence in the agent.

Another agent-owner decision is about the desirability of taking on "outside" agents, people who usually have other full-time jobs. Arthur Frommer, a well known travel writer, states that as many as 100,000 people earn commissions and travel discounts by being part-time agents. They work without salary, but receive commissions for the sales they produce. These sales reps usually work out of their homes. Some enjoy leading tour groups, which they promote among friends and associates.

Doing the Numbers

Like most service industries a travel agency's biggest cost is labor, about 50 percent of sales. Though wages and salaries are low, costs as a percentage of sales are high. The lease arrangement with one of the airline computer systems, indispensable to a travel agency, can exceed $500 a month and is tied to sales volume. A typical statement of accounts according to the American Society of Travel Agencies is seen in Figure 6-5.

The usual travel agent in a full-service travel agency must keep busy to meet sales objectives. Small ticket sales often do not cover costs and itinerary changes are frequent. The necessary minimal per day sales figure per agent is believed to be about $400 to cover costs and provide a reasonable profit. In some locations the figure is higher.

A definite trend in travel agency operation has been the rapid growth of on-site reservations and ticketing locations. At the end of 1991 they represented 30 percent of all U.S. agency locations (Nona Starr, *Viewpoint, An Introduction to Travel, Tourism and Hospitality*, Boston: Houghton Mifflin, 1993, p. 312).

Airlines and travel agencies enjoy a symbiotic relationship: Each needs the other.

Travel Agency Financial Statement

Acct. No.	Title	January	January Last Year
_____	Commissions earned	_____	_____
_____	Other income	_____	_____
	Total revenue	_____	_____
_____	Sales commissions	_____	_____
	Total sales expense	_____	_____
_____	Salaries	_____	_____
_____	Overtime	_____	_____
_____	Other wages	_____	_____
	Total salaries	_____	_____
_____	Payroll taxes	_____	_____
_____	Retirement plan	_____	_____
_____	Group life insurance	_____	_____
_____	Employee activities	_____	_____
_____	Travel meetings and entertainment	_____	_____
_____	Automobile expense	_____	_____
_____	Dues & subscriptions	_____	_____
_____	Other insurance	_____	_____
_____	Promotion & entertainment expense	_____	_____
_____	Tour material & bulletins	_____	_____
_____	Advertising	_____	_____
_____	Postage	_____	_____
_____	Stationery	_____	_____
_____	Minor equipment purchase	_____	_____
_____	Telephone & telegraph	_____	_____
_____	Computer lease	_____	_____
_____	Legal services	_____	_____
_____	Data processing services	_____	_____
_____	Other professional services	_____	_____
_____	Equipment rent	_____	_____
_____	Office rent	_____	_____
_____	Office repairs & maintenance	_____	_____
_____	Heat, electric & water	_____	_____
_____	Depreciation furniture & equipment	_____	_____
_____	Furniture & equipment repair & maintenance	_____	_____
_____	Freight & express	_____	_____
_____	Messenger service	_____	_____
_____	Exchange & service charges	_____	_____
_____	Cash overages & shortages	_____	_____
_____	Bad debts	_____	_____
_____	Miscellaneous expense	_____	_____
	Total general expense	_____	_____
	Net before overhead	_____	_____
	Overhead	_____	_____
	Net income before taxes	_____	_____

Source: ASTA Travel Agency Accounting and Information System, American Society of Travel Agents, Alexandria, Va.

Figure 6-5 Travel Agency Financial Statement

The airlines cannot provide ticketing at the low costs that travel agencies are willing to accept. The travel agency like other businesses, assumes risks, mainly in granting credit to its customers. To be viable the agency must control credit and costs. The virtues of owning a small business and the advantage of flying at reduced prices (which are provided to travel agents by the airlines) make the travel agency business appealing to thousands of people, even though thousands of travel agencies fail each year.

In the future, the small independent travel agency is likely to be less of a factor in the travel industry, and many will probably join cooperatives or become a part of a consortium to be able to participate in overrides provided by travel suppliers. A huge company like American Express will continue to capitalize on the advantage of gaining income from its American Express credit cards, and on superior bargaining leverage with airlines and other travel suppliers.

THEME PARK ECONOMICS

Theme parks are very much a part of the tourist business, attracting millions of people, some from thousands of miles away. They are responsible for the construction and operation of tens of thousands of guest rooms, the availability of which is an important consideration in the destination decision making of millions of tourists. The large theme parks employ thousands of people. Labor constitutes the number one operating cost.

While theme parks account for only 7 percent of all U.S. amusement parks, visitors to them in 1990 were estimated at 253 million (Tom Powers, *Introduction to Management in the Hospitality Industry*, John Wiley, 1992, p. 351). Investments of billions of dollars have gone to theme park construction. According to the International Association of Amusement Parks and Attractions (IAAPA), a nonprofit organization with over 2500 members in fifty countries, there are between 600 and 700 amusement park facilities in the United States, many family owned and operated. The theme park industry includes fifty major North American parks that draw over one million visitors annually. Figure 6-6 shows that the top fifteen theme parks in the United States, each had more than 3 million visitors in 1992.

Pleasure gardens and amusement parks draw upon the ideas assembled in Copenhagen's Tivoli Gardens, a park opened in 1843. Today's theme park ideas are mostly American in origin, sparked by the huge financial success of Disneyland in Anaheim, California, (opened in 1955) and later, Disney World in Lake Buena Vista, Florida. The shining example for theme parks is Disney World, a 27,400 acre entertainment complex. Its construction was a planning and financial coup. The land covers 43 square miles, an area twice the size of Manhattan. Its first phase involved dozens of consultants and an expenditure of $300 million. Disney acquired the land in 1964 and 1965 for about $200 an acre, much of it swamp and snake-infested swampland. The swamp became part of the Magic Kingdom, built around water. By 1970 surrounding land was selling for $10,000 an acre. Disney will profit immensely from land sales in the future.

Disney convinced the Florida State Road Department to construct highway inter-

Top U.S. Theme Park Admissions - 1992

Park and Location	1991 Attendance (in Millions)	1992 Attendance (in Millions)
Walt Disney World* Lake Buena Vista, Florida	28.0	30.2
Disneyland Anaheim, California	11.6	11.6
Universal Studios Florida Orlando	5.9	6.7
Universal Studios Hollywood Universal City, California	4.6	4.8
Sea World of Florida Orlando	3.4	4.1
Sea World of California San Diego	3.3	4.0
Knott's Berry Farm Buena Park, California	4.0	3.9
Paramount's King Island King Island, Ohio	2.8	3.3
Six Flags Magic Mountain Valencia, California	3.2	3.2
Six Flags Great America Gurnee, Illinois	2.6	3.2
Cedar Point Sandusky, Ohio	3.1	3.0
Six Flags Great Adventure Jackson, New Jersey	2.9	3.1
Busch Gardens Tampa, Florida	2.9	3.1
Six Flags Over Texas Arlington	2.7	3.0
Santa Cruz Beach Boardwalk Santa Cruz, California	3.0	3.0

*Includes the Magic Kingdom, Epcot Center, and Disney-MGM Studios Theme Park

Source: *Amusement Business*

Figure 6-6 The Top U.S. Theme Park Admissions, 1992

changes off nearby major highways. Year-round warm weather was a big advantage for the Disney Corporation in California and Florida. Euro Disney's climate is much less salutary, and the $4 billion theme park outside Paris has been a financial failure, weather being a contributing factor. In 1993 the park was losing $1 million a day. Opened in 1992 at Marne-la-Valle, about twenty miles east of Paris, Euro Disney is jointly owned with local interests (51 percent), and the Walt Disney Company (49 percent). Euro Disney lost $5.3 billion francs in its first fiscal year of operation. In contrast, the Walt Disney Company had its best year in 1993. Michael Eisner, its CEO, cashed in most of his stock options and took home a check for $192 million (Mark Eliot, *Walt Disney: Hollywood's Dark Prince*, New York: Carol Publishing Group, 1993).

Euro Disney's financial picture was looking brighter in 1994 as entry fees and room rates in its six hotels were reduced. The opening of the channel tunnel between England and France and the completion of a new high-speed train that will cross France will help. A specially constructed station near the resort will be built (*Wall Street Journal*, January 13, 1994). Tokyo Disneyland has been a resounding success, generating $40 million a year in net profits for the Disney company since its opening in 1983.

Technology, say some observers, can be used to provide the thrills of Disneyland in a small space at a fraction of the cost of a theme park ("Theme Parks, Feeling the Future," *The Economist*, February 19–25, 1994, pp. 74–79). Virtual reality rides and other "virtual" experiences have a decided investment advantage. Thirty small cinetropolis-type theaters can be built in shopping malls for the billion dollar price of one theme park. The 150-seat virtual reality theater can offer up to 15,000 rides a day and the attraction can be reprogrammed to attract repeat customers. The return on Walt Disney's theme parks is believed to be little more than 12 percent, roughly half of what it was a decade ago. Anyone who has visited a Disney theme park knows that a virtual reality theater is not likely to put Disney out of business, but could cut sharply into the attendance figures and profits of Disney and similar theme parks.

Theme Park Labor Costs

The IAAPA states that full- and part-time employee salaries are the highest cost factors, followed by food and beverage costs, service, marketing, maintenance, and utilities. The large parks each employ thousands of personnel.

Operating a theme park on the scale of a Disney World is a huge, complicated undertaking. Walt Disney set the standards for all theme parks by insisting on the utmost in sanitation, police and fire protection. Theme parks are subject to large changes in attendance depending upon weather, gasoline prices, and the general economy. Seasonal labor demands force tight labor cost control and the training of thousands of employees each year. Disney employees are carefully selected. Training is continuous. Employees are cast, as in a play, for the different roles (jobs) played.

Theme parks, like airlines, hotels, and restaurants, can be highly profitable, once the fixed costs have been covered and the breakeven point passed. Each additional customer throws off a high percentage of profit. The problem comes with crowding, which brings on the point of diminishing returns. Sophisticated mathematical modeling techniques have been used to reduce the problem of long waiting lines. These techniques are described in more detail in Part III of this book.

Capital investments in theme parks is high. Unfortunately, when Disneyland was built, Walt Disney lacked the capital to buy the surrounding land. Disney World, in Florida was different and has the potential for huge capital gains from land and other sales. In 1971 Disney World was built for an initial investment of $300 million, followed by $1.1 billion to open Epcot Center in 1981, and another $500 million for the Studio Tour that opened in 1989 (Harold L. Vogel, *Entertainment Industry Economics*, 2nd edition, New York: Cambridge University Press, 1990, p. 323).

The popular theme parks are hard pressed to add rides that are bigger and more exciting than their competitors. "A roller coaster costs $4 to $6 million to build and takes up a lot of space, and there are a lot of operating costs," says Roy Aaron, CEO of Showcase, a Los Angeles maker of simulator rides. The Splash Mountain ride at Walt Disney World cost about $80 million to construct. The entertainment analyst for the Merrill Lynch stock and bond brokerage firm estimates the cost of building a "decent" theme park is $300 to $500 million (*Wall Street Journal*, February 2, 1993).

The rides of the future may simulate skiing in the Alps of Switzerland or swooshing down Mount Fuji in Japan. Virtual reality parks take up about one-tenth the space of the traditional rides and insurance costs are a fraction of the "real" thing. A million-dollar simulator can be programmed to provide different experiences and be tailored to local audiences. Insurance costs are minimal compared to risky rides such as a real roller coaster. New simulators use visual and moving theaters that give visitors sensations like flat-out acceleration, zero-gravity, free falls, and high-impact crashes (Ady Melman, "Theme Parks and Attractions," *VNR's Encyclopedia of Hospitality and Tourism*, p. 939, 1993).

Nearly all of the fifty U.S. theme parks operate (or plan to operate) one or more big simulator rides, each of which costs about $1 million to construct. Sophisticated hydraulic or electrically driven platforms form a base for most of these thrill rides. Take an imaginary ride on a submarine. For $1 a minute, travel on a mystery ride, or fly your own World War I plane and engage in a virtual reality dog fight. The Excalibur hotel in Las Vegas recovered $2 million of the cost of its virtual reality ride in eight months of operation (James R. Norman and Nikhel Hutheesing, "Hang onto Your Hats and Wallets," *Forbes*, November 22, 1993, pp. 90–98).

Theme parks are being partially upstaged by huge shopping malls like those in Edmonton, Canada, and near Minneapolis, Minnesota, where thrill rides and water slides combine shopping opportunities with restaurants and theaters—all under one roof, immune to outside weather conditions.

Theme parks are part of the entertainment business. The distinction between them has become blurred as the huge casino hotels, water parks, and Sea Worlds take on each other's characteristics. Markets for the larger theme parks are not only regional but international.

The Disney Company led the way in merging thrill rides, educational experiences, and entertainment with its Disney cartoon characters. Time Warner (owner of Six Flags), Paramount Communications, and Universal Studios have followed suit. The MGM Grand Hotel in Las Vagas has developed a new concept by combining a theme park and casino with its hotel. What will follow is uncertain when the average citizen can dial a choice of 500 movies and an array of other entertainment choices at minimum cost in the quiet and security of his or her living room. The communications revolution taking place in the 1990s may seriously detract from the appeal of theme and other amusement parks as the TV viewer will be able to experience similar emotions while safely ensconced at home watching TV, and at small effort and expense. It is doubtful, however, that the TV picture or the simulator can ever give the same thrill as seeing a huge orca (killer whale) soar twenty feet in the air, perform with its trainer, and soak the front row spectators with splashes.

CAMPING GROUNDS ECONOMICS

Camping involves millions of travel miles and the expenditure of millions of dollars each year. Some 12,000 campgrounds, public and private, provide camping spaces in the United States and are a part of the recreational vehicle (RV) business that sells or services the estimated 8.5 million RV's in the U.S. (Tom Powers, *Introduction to Management in the Hospitality Industry*, John Wiley & Sons. 1992, pp. 392–398).

Campgrounds annually cost between $1500 and $3500 in investment and operation per campsite. The rental fee for a campsite is about $12 a night. Depending upon the campsite cost, the campground owner can breakeven at about 30 percent occupancy. Labor cost is low because services offered to the camper are minimal compared to a hotel. Only a few employees are needed and in many cases the owner(s) may do all of the work. A surge in gasoline price, an economic recession, or bad weather can seriously cut revenues. Campground franchises, such as KOA and Yogi Bear Jellystone campgrounds, are sold. Compared to staying in a hotel or resort the campers can reduce the cost of food by cooking themselves, and if they are part of a family or other group it is possible to substantially reduce the cost of travel.

The cost of maintenance of public campgrounds is usually borne in part by the public. Hawaii and some other states, the Bahamas, Puerto Rico, and most Caribbean island nations prefer guests who provide greater income to the community as hotel guests. As tourists campers buy a number of items on which taxes are paid including gasoline, food and sundries. The total can be impressive. In 1991, California's Office of Tourism reported that campers in the state spent $300 million in food stores, $400 million in retail shopping, $390 million in restaurants, $350 million for lodging, $170 million for recreation, and $380 million in ground transport. Total camping spending for that year in California was almost $2 billion.

From a financial viewpoint, campground investment and operation is probably better seen as part of a real estate investment land development, with the view to land appreciation and sales, especially if the land is in the path of future housing developments.

RAIL TRAVEL ECONOMICS

Theoretically rail travel is the most cost-efficient way for tourists to travel. The energy required to pull a train, a rolling steel wheel on a steel rail, is much less than that needed to propel a car and its passengers, and much less than required to lift an airplane into the sky and return to earth. It takes 1000 automobiles to carry as many commuters as one train (Nona Starr, *Viewpoint*, Boston: Houghton Mifflin, 1993, p. 146). Given a sound roadbed, safe bridges, a reliable engineer, and closed rail crossings, rail travel is also the safest way to travel.

Why then do railroads in the United States carry less than 1 percent of all intercity passenger traffic? One answer is cost. In 1991 the U.S. Congress provided America's Amtrak rail system with a $475 million subsidy—Amtrak has lost money each year since its formation in 1970. In other words, rail passengers in the United States are, and have been, partially subsidized. Part of the reason for Amtrak's negative financial record is the fact that given a choice, North Americans prefer the privately owned, and driven, automobiles over the schedules and depots offered to rail travelers. Taking a train to a destination usually means a cab or other ride in addition to the train ride and is much less convenient.

Subsidies for rail travelers are nothing new. European and Japanese rail travel are loss-making operations. Japan has subsidized its passenger rail system some $11 billion annually; Germany, $5 billion a year; the United Kingdom, $3.5 billion a year. India is an exception, however, as the national railway system produces sizable income for the government.

In the past, rail unions drove up costs by rigid work and pay rules. Amtrak crews were paid a day's wage for each 100 miles traveled so that for a round trip between New York City and Washington, DC they received 4 ½ days' pay. This has changed.

Train travel hit its peak in the United States during World War II when every means of transportation was pressed into service. Following the war, air travel for trips over a few hours saved time and money; and, increasingly, air travel was the mode of choice for long-distance travel. Railroads saw their costs rise above revenues and decided to make rail travel a memorable experience—memorably miserable. Train windows were not washed; depots were allowed to deteriorate, and schedules were not met. Reservation service was practically shut down.

Amtrak was created to correct the situation, and there has been some improvement—but not much, compared to European and Japanese rail travel. Only on one highly traveled U.S. route is Amtrak comparable to air service in time and convenience—the Amtrak Metroliner between New York City and Washington, DC. A comparison of train and plane time between the two cities is shown below:

Train	*Time*
Amtrak Metroliner	
Cab: Midtown office to Penn Station	10 minutes
Boarding time	15 minutes
Metroliner: NYC to DC	2 hours, 50 minutes
Total	3 hours, 15 minutes

Plane	*Time*
Delta Shuttle	
Cab: Midtown office to La Guardia Airport (LGA)	45 minutes
Boarding time and security	20 minutes
Shuttle: LGA to DC (National Airport)	1 hour, 30 minutes
Cab: National Airport to downtown DC	30 minutes
Total	3 hours, 5 minutes

(Nona Starr, *Viewpoint, An Introduction to Travel, Tourism and Hospitality*, Boston: Houghton Mifflin, 1993, p. 153.)

For many leisure travelers the train ride itself is a large part of the vacation experience. The Orient Express trains in Europe (London to Istanbul), the Blue Trains of

South Africa, and trains in the South American Andes mountains are experiences travelers readily pay extra for.

Though the Amtrak network of passenger rail tracks in the United States covers 25,000 miles, the number of cars in the Amtrak fleet is small, about 2000 cars. France and Germany each have some 17,000 rail cars; Japan has 26,000 cars. The longest railways in the world are in Russia and the other members of the Commonwealth of Independent States (formerly the Soviet Union), India, and China.

In 1992 Amtrak assets were valued at over $4 billion and it had an annual revenue of about $1.4 billion. Its employees number 24,000. Amtrak proponents and many others believe that a viable rail passenger service is vital to the nation's defense. The U.S. Congress apparently agrees and votes annual subsidies for Amtrak's maintenance. Meanwhile, Europe plans to spend $100 billion during the years 1994 to 2004 for upgrading and extending its high-speed rail lines. EuroCity trains are express trains on the main lines between European countries. France opened new TGV (very rapid trains) lines between Brittany and Paris and extended service to Bordeaux and Spain. The Eurotunnel (also known as the "Chunnel"), beneath the English Channel, built by an Anglo-French consortium for $14.93 billion (its cost far exceeded its budget) went into service in 1994. Travelers can ride by rail via the Chunnel at about 60 mph for the 31-mile trip, unaffected by weather and sea sickness. Tickets cost between $330 and $465 per round trip.

One reason rail travel is more popular in Europe is the high cost of air travel, much higher per mile than leisure air travel has been in the United States. Europe's rail system provides service to almost every city, town, and hamlet.

Europe continues to upgrade its rail passenger service. In 1993 Germany opened a 155-mph link between Mannheim and Stuttgart. Switzerland and Italy are spending hundreds of millions on their railways. Japan continues to expand its famous bullet train system even though it is a huge deficit operation. Canada, on the other hand, has reduced the size of its passenger rail network by 51 percent, a move that will save taxpayers about $900 million over five years.

Expectations, not yet realized because of cost, are that Maglev (magnetic levitation) trains will one day speed travelers around Europe and North America at speeds of up to 300 mph. Maglev trains straddle a rail and are lifted and moved by a magnetic force that eliminates friction between wheel and rail.

In 1994 the German cabinet approved a Maglev railroad between Hamburg and Berlin, with service to begin by the year 2005. The $5.2 billion project could involve 10,000 jobs. Germany's Maglev will travel at speeds up to 270 miles per hour, making the 185-mile journey in less than an hour. The trip takes 3 ½ hours in regular trains. The German government will pay for the train systems at a cost of $3.28 billion.

Although Europe is laying out tens of millions of dollars to speed up and improve its railroads, rail riders even there are declining in number. Antonio Lorenzo Necci, chairman of the International Union of Railways, said that in the past two decades the European passenger market fell to 7 percent from 10 percent (of all travel modes). "Our advantage," Mr. Necci stated, "is that highways are full" (*Wall Street Journal*, February 4, 1994).

OTHER TOURISM SECTORS

Intercity Bus

Though intercity bus travel shows a flat sales volume curve, it remains vital to those communities not well served by air and rail. Increased insurance rates forced a number of small bus companies out of business. Intercity bus travel by foreign visitors, however, has increased.

Motorcoach Tours

A separate and sizable tourism segment, motorcoach tours, is robust, and goes to places like Atlantic City, Mexico, and Branson, Missouri, a thriving country music center. In 1990 more than 22,000 motorcoaches were being used for escorted tours in North America. The tours were assembled by tour operators and a few by travel agents. Nearly all were marketed by travel agents. Tour operation is a specialized business evidenced by the failure of even some of the largest tour companies.

Motorcoach tours are marketed to groups that fit the size of the motorcoach being used, mostly seating 45 passengers. Like the hotel and airline business, fixed costs are high and the goal is to achieve 100 percentage occupancy (load factor). Allowance must be made for "no shows" in selling tours as is true in the airline and hotel business. Once breakeven costs are reached, variable costs decline. Each additional tour participant above the breakeven point means the possibility of sharply increased profits.

Tour fixed costs usually include the cost of transportation, brochure costs, office expenses, and the cost of the escort. Motorcoaches are usually rented for a definite tour period, but some tour companies own their buses. Tour companies compete with several of the airlines that develop and sell tours, especially for international visitors.

Convention Centers and Visitor Bureaus

Convention centers have been built in most U.S. cities and along with visitor bureaus are charged with attracting visitors to their communities. Convention centers are usually built and funded with public money. Convention centers are often financed with a separate tax levied on hotel room sales, sometimes exceeding 15 percent of the room income. A Chamber of Commerce may fund a visitor bureau.

Tourism is a part of the hospitality and tourism industry, the boundaries of which are as yet not fixed. Recreation and entertainment, lodging and travel, merge and overlap. This book covers only what has become accepted as central tourism industries.

Part III

Quantitative Methods Applied to Tourism Economics

7

The Multiplier Effect of Tourist Spending

New money entering an economy in whatever form—investments, government grants or expenditures, remittance from workers abroad, or tourist expenditures—stimulates the economy, not once but several times as it is respent, the "multiplier effect." John Maynard Keynes, the famous British economist, and R.K. Kahn developed the idea that economic growth results from investment, which creates employment and income for the future.

Exports bring in money from outside an economy. Economically, tourism income from foreign tourists are exports for countries. Keynes called exports injections into an economy, injections that add to economic growth. An injection impacts the economy by fostering internal spending. The new money remains in the economy by being spent and respent. Some of it soon loses stimulative value in the form of leakages—savings, taxes, and imports. The greater the leakages, the lower the multiplier. Savings that are not immediately reinvested diminish the demand for goods and services. Unless taxes are respent they too reduce the economic effect of the new money. Imports are a leakage in that the money spent elsewhere no longer stimulates the domestic economy. Economic growth, said Keynes, is generated when injections are greater than leakages.

Professor Wassily Leontief added to the multiplier theory with his work on input-output theory, which showed how different segments (or industries) within an economy interrelate and effect each other. The effects of linkages between industry sectors and their measurement is seen in the study "The Economic Impact of Tourism in Hawaii," 1970–1980, discussed later. Tourist dollars have direct, indirect, and induced effects; these are also explained later.

REPORTS ON THE MULTIPLIER EFFECT

In a subsistence economy, such as one found on a less developed island, the new dollar has a negligible multiplier effect. The economy has a high "import propensity"—most of the money leaves before much of a multiplier is developed. In an advanced economy such as Canada, the leakage is low and the tourist dollar, before being completely spent, has had a stimulative effect of about 2.5 dollars (a multiplier effect of 2.5) (Adrian Bull, *The Economics of Travel and Tourism*, New York: John Wiley, 1991, p. 148). Tourism income studies almost always factor in the tourism multiplier.

Much of the computation of inputs and outputs that go into income multipliers are estimates, and it is not surprising if two researchers come up with somewhat different multipliers for the same country.

Figure 7-1 shows the tourism income multiplier for a number of countries. The multipliers are not quite comparable because of the methodologies and completeness of the data on which the multipliers are based.

Countries can be classified according to their dependence upon imported goods and services, and the degree of their tourism import propensity. Robert Cleverdon divides countries according to their degree of import dependency as shown in the list below.

Less than 10 percent: Totally import reliant (such as Mauritius).

10 to 50 percent: Heavily import reliant (such as the less-developed Caribbean and South Pacific islands).

50 to 70 percent: Import luxuries and a few necessities (such as the better developed Caribbean islands).

70 to 90 percent: Import principally luxuries and have advanced manufacturing sectors with good resources (such as Kenya, Tunisia, and Greece).

   —*(Robert Cleverdon, "The Economic and Social Impact of International Tourism on Developing Countries," E.I.U. Special Report No. 60, The Economist Intelligence Unit Ltd, May 1979, p. 32)*

The Caribbean Tourism Research Center estimated that in 1979, out of total earnings of $3.3 billion, just over a third stayed in the region. In Fiji, only 20 percent of tourist earnings stayed in the economy. A 1984 study showed that in the island of St. Lucia, in the Caribbean, 58 percent of the food consumed by tourists was imported, and for meat 82 percent had been imported (Chris Ryan, *Recreational Tourism*, London: Routledge, 1991, pp. 50–51).

Figure 7-2 shows how the dollar, when injected into an economy, produces a multiplier effect and stimulates the economy. Leakages from the economy, as spending occurs, are also shown.

What goes out of the economy after a tourist receipt depends in large part on the linkages within the economy, how the money is spent within the economy. The more spent within the economy that remains as a benefit, the higher the multiplier. A coun-

Tourism Income Multipliers

Destination	Personal income multiplier
Turkey	1.96
United Kingdom	1.73
Republic of Ireland	1.72
Egypt	1.23
Jamaica	1.23
Dominican Republic	1.20
Cyprus	1.14
Northern Ireland	1.10
Bermuda	1.09
Hong Kong	1.02
Mauritius	0.96
Antigua	0.88
Bahamas	0.79
Fiji	0.72
Cayman Islands	0.65
Iceland	0.64
British Virgin Islands	0.58
Solomon Islands	0.52
Republic of Palau	0.50
Western Samoa	0.39

Source: Fletcher, J. "Input-Output Analysis and Tourism Impact Studies," *Annals of Tourism Research, 16*(4), 514–529. In *VNR's Encyclopedia of Hospitality and Tourism*, New York: Van Nostrand Reinhold, 1993, p. 669.

Figure 7-1 Tourism Income Multipliers

try multiplier can be misleading in that multipliers vary widely from region to region, and city to city. Multipliers calculated for towns or small communities are almost always lower than when larger areas are studied. The larger areas make possible more linkages and more market units reached by the tourist dollar.

Multipliers effect industries within the area covered differently depending upon the linkages between visitor expenditure and the industries within the economy. In Mexico the linkage between visitor spending and the economy of places like Puerto Vallarta and Cancun are high, but it is negligible for remote villages. Visitor spending in New York City has a direct effect on the huge hotel and restaurant business, but has less effect, indirect or induced, on the city's garment trade or publishing businesses.

Businesses do not necessarily need to be the immediate recipients of tourist spending to be beneficiaries. Maid service companies that clean condominium rooms on a Hawaiian island, for example, may be paid from a company based in the state of Washington. Payment for the service comes from out of state; the profit made by the parent company represents a leakage to the Hawaiian economy.

Tourism income multipliers have been developed for a number of cities and regions. One reason for their popularity is that a multiplier as a number is easily understood. The multiplier says in effect that tourism spending not only brings new dollars into a local economy, but that as new dollars are circulated their effect is multiplied.

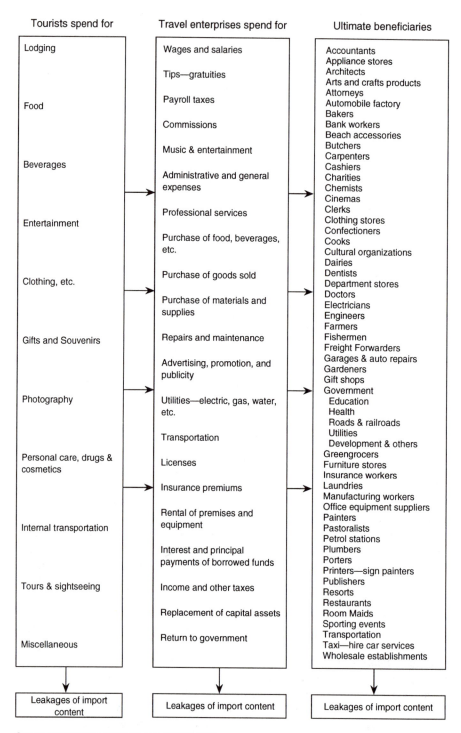

Tourists spend for	Travel enterprises spend for	Ultimate beneficiaries

Lodging
 	
Food
 	
Beverages
 	
Entertainment
 	
Clothing, etc.
 	
Gifts and Souvenirs
 	
Photography
 	
Personal care, drugs & cosmetics
 	
Internal transportation
 	
Tours & sightseeing
 	
Miscellaneous
	Wages and salaries
	
	Tips—gratuities
	
	Payroll taxes
	
	Commissions
	
	Music & entertainment
	
	Administrative and general expenses
	
	Professional services
	
	Purchase of food, beverages, etc.
	
	Purchase of goods sold
	
	Purchase of materials and supplies
	
	Repairs and maintenance
	
	Advertising, promotion, and publicity
	
	Utilities—electric, gas, water, etc.
	
	Transportation
	
	Licenses
	
	Insurance premiums
	
	Rental of premises and equipment
	
	Interest and principal payments of borrowed funds
	
	Income and other taxes
	
	Replacement of capital assets
	
	Return to government
		Accountants
		Appliance stores
		Architects
		Arts and crafts products
		Attorneys
		Automobile factory
		Bakers
		Bank workers
		Beach accessories
		Butchers
		Carpenters
		Cashiers
		Charities
		Chemists
		Cinemas
		Clerks
		Clothing stores
		Confectioners
		Cooks
		Cultural organizations
		Dairies
		Dentists
		Department stores
		Doctors
		Electricians
		Engineers
		Farmers
		Fishermen
		Freight Forwarders
		Garages & auto repairs
		Gardeners
		Gift shops
		Government
		  Education
		  Health
		  Roads & railroads
		  Utilities
		  Development & others
		Greengrocers
		Furniture stores
		Insurance workers
		Laundries
		Manufacturing workers
		Office equipment suppliers
		Painters
		Pastoralists
		Petrol stations
		Plumbers
		Porters
		Printers—sign painters
		Publishers
		Resorts
		Restaurants
		Room Maids
		Sporting events
		Transportation
		Taxi—hire car services
		Wholesale establishments

Leakages of import content	Leakages of import content	Leakages of import content

Source: World Tourism Organization, Madrid, 1982.

Figure 7-2   Multiplier Effect: How Tourism Spending Flows into the Economy

138

The implication is that the tourist dollar is somehow better than a dollar already in circulation. The tourist dollar may be no better than any other investment from the outside, an automobile plant for example, or a grant from the federal government. Both stimulate the economy when spent. Tourism income however, may be seen as "better" than other income because much of it is received for "services," payment to waiters/waitresses, tour guides, and other people who do not give tangible products in return for their services. The import propensity of services in themselves is zero.

Where opportunity costs are low—that is, where few if any other choices for securing income are available—tourism is a valued source of income. It may not be as desirable as from a high tech research firm, for example, but it is better than no income at all.

The economic importance of tourism to some island economies is very high even though the tourism income multiplier is low. For the small islands of the Caribbean the gross domestic product (GDP) derived from tourism ranges from 30 to 60 percent. The U.S. and British Virgin Islands, the Cayman Islands, Barbados, Curacao, St. Barts, St. Martin, Bonaire, Aruba, and Antigua are all examples of small Caribbean islands that have a large dependence on tourism. The larger Caribbean islands of Jamaica, Puerto Rico, and the Dominican Republic find tourism a significant part of their economy. In the Bahamas, further north, tourism accounts for as much as 70 percent of the economy. Depending largely on air connections and distance from markets, the small Pacific islands of Fiji, the Cook Islands, the Samoas, and Tonga also count tourism as an important source of income (*Pacific Island Economies*, Washington, DC: The International Bank for Reconstruction and Development/The World Bank, 1991).

DERIVING THE TOURISM MULTIPLIER

Tourism proponents love the multiplier effect. Tourist dollars are received, then respent, a process that in the course of a year may recur seven or more times before its effect is too small to measure. But there are leakages. Some immediately leaves the economy to pay for imports. In a Caribbean resort the meat served at meals has probably been shipped in; this is, as said before, a leakage, money that leaves the economy to pay for imports. Other money is said to be leaked when it is saved by people in the economy. In other words, it is not available to be respent and thereby stimulate further spending within the economy. Items within an economy have what is called import propensities, a tendency or habit of spending for imports. The U.S. economy has a high import propensity that has helped create a massive national debt.

Professors Robert W. McIntosh and Charles R. Goeldner illustrate how a multiplier is derived in their book *Tourism Principles, Practices, Philosophies* (New York: John Wiley & Sons, 1990, pp. 282–283). The illustration shown in Figure 7-3 assumes that the time period examined is one year. It also assumes that there will be seven rounds of spending before the stimulative effect of the tourist dollar is lost. Under these assumptions money saved would not be banked (where it would soon be reinvested and respent). With each round of spending the stimulative effect on the

$$\text{Multiplier} = \frac{1}{1 - MPC}$$

where

M = marginal (extra)
P = propensity (inclination)
C = consume (spending)
Suppose $1000 of tourist expenditure and an MPC ($M \times P \times C$) of ½. Then,

$1000.00
\+
500.00   ½ × 1000
\+   \+
250.00   (½)^2 × 1000
\+   \+
125.00   (½)^3 × 1000
\+   \+
62.50   (½)^4 × 1000
\+   \+
31.25   (½)^5 × 1000
\+   \+
15.63   (½)^6 × 1000
\+   \+
7.81   (½)^7 × 1000
. . .
$2000.00 (approx.)

$$\text{Multiply: } \frac{1}{1 - \frac{1}{2}} \times \$1000, \text{ or } 2 \times \$1000 = \$2000$$

Thus, the original $1000 of tourist expenditure becomes $2000 of income to the community in one year.

Source: Robert W. McIntosh and Charles R. Goeldner, *Tourism Principles, Practices, Philosophies,* New York: John Wiley and Sons, 1990.

Figure 7-3   Formula for the Multiplier

economy is reduced by savings, import purchases, and taxes, or money leaving the economy for other reasons. At the end of a year the $1000 of tourist spending as seen in the example had a stimulative effect on the economy as if it were $2000. The multiplier effect is two.

Numerous tourism studies have been conducted in which tourism multipliers have been calculated using additional criteria. Such studies are expensive and if done well must include input-output analysis. Multipliers are figured for taxes, employment, and other economic segments (known as induced expenditures).

The multiplier may be calculated by dividing a unit of exogenous expenditure (coming from outside the economy) going to savings or being spent on imports to the economy. In other words, the multiplier equals 1 divided by the leakages. In mathematical terms:

$$\text{Multiplier} = \frac{1}{(1 - C + M)}$$

where C is the marginal propensity to consume (the proportion of any increase in income spent on consumption, as a part of GDP), and M is the marginal propensity to import (the proportion of any increase in income spent on imported goods and services, as a part of GDP).

Larger economies, such as those found in a country, have their parts more closely linked and therefore money spent in the economy is more likely to remain in it and be respent. In other words, it has more and stronger linkages. The multiplier effect is likely to be larger than in small economies where a larger percentage of money goes out of the economy to pay for imports.

In 1990 the multiplier for the U.S. economy as a whole was 1.92.

$$\text{Multiplier} = \frac{1}{(1 - .63 + .15)} = \frac{1}{1 - .48} = \frac{1}{.52} = 1.92$$

This was based on the United States having a marginal propensity to consume of about .9 and a disposable income of 70 percent (.7) of the GDP. The marginal propensity to consume part of the GDP (C) was .63 (.7 of .9 = .63). Imports were approximately 15 percent of GDP ($M = .15$). In other words each dollar of GDP induced 15 cents of imports. Subtracting the M from the C (.63 – .15) left a denominator of .52 (1 – .48). The multiplier in the late 1980s declined because imports increased (Michael Parker, *Economics*, New York: Addison Wesley, p. 716, 1993).

Employment Multipliers

Tourism proponents put the economic benefits of tourism in easily understood terms: total dollar receipts, wages and salaries, jobs created, tax revenues, and new establishments. Figure 7-4 shows a study conducted in 1989 by the U.S. Travel Data Center that illustrated the annual impact of 100 additional visitors a day on the typical U.S. community.

An earlier input-output study of the economic effects of tourism in Mexico stated that forty-one jobs were created by an investment of $80,000 in tourism, twenty-five more than would have been created by the same investment in the petroleum industry, and twenty-six more than in metal products (M.E. Bond and J.R. Ladman, "Tourism: A Strategy for Development," *Nebraska Journal of Economics and Business*, 1972, pp. 37–52).

A Kentucky Department of Travel Development report shown in Figure 7-5 calculated the annual effect of 100 additional tourists per day on the average Kentucky community. In Britain, it has been estimated that for every 100 jobs created directly by tourism,

Direct Impact	Total Impact*
$1,570,000 in retail and service sales to visitors	$2,990,000 in business industry receipts
$327,000 in wages and salaries	$757,000 in wages & salaries
29 new travel industry jobs providing additional income for 23 households with 60 residents	66 new jobs providing additional income for 53 households with 139 residents
$134,000 in state and local tax revenue, enough to support 33 school children	$217,000 in state and local tax revenue, enough to support 53 school children
Two more retail or service establishments	Five more retail or service establishments

*Includes direct, indirect, and induced impact
Source: U.S. Travel Data Center, 1989

Figure 7-4 Annual Impact of 100 Additional Visitors a Day on the Typical U.S. Community

there are three to four additional jobs created indirectly (Floyd E. Herman and Donald E. Hawkins, *Tourism in Contemporary Society*, Prentice-Hall, 1989, p. 214).

Governments are interested in tourist employment multipliers and in government tax income multipliers. Tax multipliers vary, partly based on how government revenues are collected. The government of the Bahamas, for example, collects most of its taxes via import duties. The more imports are needed for construction of hotels and their operation, the more taxes collected. Governments that rely mostly on income taxes may experience a different tax revenue multiplier. Countries where tax evasion is widespread have smaller tax income multipliers. Less developed countries may levy high import duties because of the difficulty of collecting other forms of taxes.

Income from tourism taxes are significant for many places. All states impose taxes

Annual Impact of 100 Additional Tourists per Day on the Average Kentucky Community

Direct Impact	Total Impact*
$1,006,670 in retail and service industry sales	$1,778,786 in business receipts
$299,668 in wage income 39 new travel industry jobs	$529,513 in wage income 56 new jobs
$70,898 in state and local tax receipts, enough to support 37 school children	$125,276 in state and local tax receipts, enough to support 66 school children
Increase in population of 65	Increase in population of 102
24 new households	27 new households
$84,000 increase in bank deposits	$149,000 increase in bank deposits
Two more retail and service establishments	Four more business establishments

*Includes direct, indirect, and induced impact (impact as money moves through the economy)
Source: Kentucky Department of Travel Development, 1986

Figure 7-5 Annual Impact of 100 Additional Tourists per Day on the Average Kentucky Community

on tourists in one form or another. Sales taxes on food and beverages, gasoline taxes, room taxes, and landing fees at airports are examples. New York City has a special sales tax on hotel rooms that can be as much as 19 percent of room sales. Many countries charge a departure tax. Some of the taxes collected are allocated for tourism marketing. Tourist operators complain that many such taxes find their way into general funds used for a variety of purposes. Tax income, like other income to an economy, generates spending and responding as the money works its way through the economy until its effects are too small to be measured.

INPUT-OUTPUT ANALYSIS

Comprehensive studies of the economic impact of tourism necessarily include input-output analysis (IOA), the analysis used by economists to develop projections of such matters as employment or the probable effects of tax changes, or to assist in regional or national development planning.

Wassily Leontief, a Harvard professor, studied the effects of the interrelatedness of economic sectors in his work on input-output analysis, for which he was named a Nobel laureate in 1973. His technique and theory can be used to make a more informed decision about how one economic sector relates to the others. As applied to the impact of tourism on an economy, each part of the economy is measured as it effects the others and the amounts of these linkages are also measured.

An input-output table shows how transactions flow through an economy during a given time period. A matrix, the rows of which show the total value of all sales made by each sector of the economy to all the other sectors, is drawn up. The columns show the purchases made by each sector from the other sectors. Multipliers are computed to show the effect each sector has on the others. Each business effected by tourism income can be correlated with the others. As usually done, industries are aggregated into sectors and the sectors correlated ("Input-Output Analysis: Applications to the Assessment of the Economic Impact of Tourism," Chapter 10, *VNR's Encyclopedia of Hospitality and Tourism*, New York: Van Nostrand Reinhold, 1993).

Regional Input-Output Modeling System

Fortunately the U.S. government and the U.S. Travel Data Center have developed models to use in estimating the economic impact of travel within the U.S. In the mid-1970s the Bureau of Economic Analysis, U.S. Department of Commerce, completed development of a method for estimating regional input-output multipliers known as RIMs (Regional Industrial Multiplier Systems). More recently, an enhancement of RIMs known as RIMs II was completed (*The Detailed Input-Output Structure of the U.S. Economy*, U.S. Government Printing Office, 1992). RIMs II permits economic impacts to be estimated for any region composed of one or more counties, and for any industry in the national input-output table. The accessibility of the main data sources for RIMs II-based estimates are similar in magnitude to those based on relatively expensive surveys. Input-output tables are available showing multipliers for output, earnings, and employment that can be used for the study of the input of tourist expenditures.

Current tourism multipliers for a state, county, or group of counties are provided for a charge by the Bureau of Economic Analysis (BEA) of the U.S. Department of Commerce. These estimates include travel spending by foreign visitors. The model for developing the multiplier is contained in a handbook, available from the National Technical Information Service, entitled *Regional Multipliers: A Users Handbook for the Regional Input-Output Modeling System*, May 1986.

The U.S. Travel Data Center (USTDC), a for-profit organization headquartered in Washington, DC, uses its Travel Economics Impact Model (TEIM) to produce individual state estimates of employment, payroll, and tax revenues generated by travel spending on overnight trips, and day trips of 100 miles or more away from the traveler's home. The USTDC estimates do not include foreign traveler spending or multiplier effects. The travel expenditure category is derived for each state from a national travel survey, government data, and other reliable sources. The per-unit cost factors are multiplied by the activity levels to produce the expenditures in each state. The TEIM model can calculate payroll and tax revenues generated for state and local governments. Spending estimates by the TEIM model exclude day trips of less than 100 miles from home; the TEIM model does not measure the secondary impacts of travel expenditures because of the difficulties of finding relevant interindustry input data.

Methodology for Conducting Tourism Impact Studies

Tourism economic impact studies have been done for dozens of destinations around the world. Hawaii, which welcomes between six and seven million visitors a year and where tourism is its major source of income, has a number of full-time employees in its Department of Business, Economic Development, and Tourism that conduct research on the economic impact of tourism on the state. The methodology it uses for determining the economic impact of tourism on the state illuminates the process and gives an idea of the detail needed. An input-output model it developed is used as a tool to estimate the total number of jobs, income, and state and local taxes generated by what it calls the visitor industry ("The Economic Impact of Tourism in Hawaii: 1970 to 1980," Research Report 1983–92, *The State of Hawaii Data Book*, 1992, updates the original research report).

The state divides multipliers that effect tourism into two types: Type I includes only direct and indirect effects; Type II multipliers include direct, indirect, and induced effects. The direct effects are the changes in sales, employment, and income in Hawaiian businesses as a result of the purchase of goods and services by visitors. The indirect effect measures the changes in sales, employment, and income generated indirectly in other Hawaiian businesses as the tourist dollar is respent. Induced effects are part of consumption expenditure that varies with real GDP, minus imports. Import propensities for thirty-seven tourist related consumption categories were identified as listed :

1. Food purchased for off-premise consumption
2. Purchased Meals & Beverages
3. Tobacco Products
4. Shoes & Other Footwear
5. Women & Children's Clothes
6. Men's & Boy's Clothes
7. Clothes Cleaning, Dyeing, Etc.
8. Jewelry and Watches
9. Toiletry Articles
10. Barber Shops, Beauty Parlors, & Baths
11. Hotels
12. China, Glass, and Tableware
13. Other Durable House Furnishings
14. Semi-Durable House Furnishings
15. Cleaning and Other Miscellaneous House Supplies
16. Stationery Supplies
17. Telephone and Telegraph
18. Other Household Goods
19. Drugs and Sundries
20. Physicians
21. Private Hospital and Sanitation
22. Auto Repair, and Park & Rent
23. Gasoline and Oil
24. Transit Systems
25. Taxicab
26. Airline Transport
27. Other Transport
28. Books and Maps
29. Magazines, Newspapers, and Sheet Music
30. Non-Durable Toys and Sports
31. Radio, TV, and Records
32. Flowers, Seeds, and Potted Plants
33. Motion Picture Theaters
34. Theaters and Operas
35. Spectator Sports
36. Commercial Parks and Amusements
37. Other Recreation

The thirty-seven categories were aggregated into ten industry groups and employment multipliers developed for each industry group as seen below:

Agriculture	1.91
Textile & Apparel	1.64
Other Manufacturing	3.14
Air Transportation	2.24
Other Transportation	1.99
Wholesale Trade	2.07
Eating & Drinking Places	1.72
Other Retail Trade	1.53
Hotels	1.93
Other Services	1.68

Figure 7-6 shows the output multiplier and income created for each dollar of income from visitors to Hawaii. A Type I output multiplier for eating and drinking places, for example, showed that an original dollar purchase of food and beverage by visitors indirectly generated an additional 41 cents of sales. In other words $1.41 in sales was created from the initial $1.00 purchase. The Type I output multiplier was 1.41. The multiplier effect did not stop there. Another 54 cents was created by the continued spending of Hawaiian households. The induced spending plus the direct and indirect spending totaled $1.95.

In mathematical terms, this induced spending multiplier operation is expressed as:

$$TS_t = \Sigma_j(VE_{jt} \cdot M_j)$$

where:

TS_t = Total sales generated by tourism in year t.
VE_{jt} = Direct visitor-related spending in industry j in year t.
M_j = Type II output multiplier for industry j.

Source: The State of Hawaii Data Book, 1992

To estimate the effect of visitor spending on taxes it was assumed that the share of tax revenues generated by tourism equaled the share of household income generated by tourism (Thomas W. Blaine, "Input-Output Analysis: Application to the Assessment of the Economic Impact of Tourism," *VNR's Encyclopedia of Hospitality and Tourism*, New York: Van Nostrand Reinhold, 1993).

The World Travel and Tourism Council has estimated the direct, indirect, and induced effects of tourism to result in a total impact of tourism in various regions of the world. Figures 7-7 and 7-8 present the results of these studies for 1990. The world totals show that the impact of $2.9 trillion in spending resulted in a total impact of $10.1 trillion in the world economy ($7.2 trillion was indirect and induced). Similarly, while there were 118 million people directly employed by tourism industries there were another 294 million people employed as a result of indirect and induced effects, bringing the world total to 412 million people employed due to tourism.

Output Multiplier and Income Created per Dollar of Sale to Visitors

	Output Multiplier		Income Coefficient	
	Type I	Type II	Type I	Type II
Agriculture	1.31	2.21	.62	.98
Textile and Apparel	1.21	1.77	.39	.61
Other Manufacturing	1.48	1.96	.33	.52
Air Transportation	1.24	1.76	.36	.57
Other Transportation	1.34	2.06	.50	.79
Wholesale Trade	1.28	2.11	.57	.91
Eating & Drinking Places	1.41	1.95	.37	.59
Other Retail Trade	1.24	2.15	.63	1.00
Hotels	1.45	2.23	.54	.85
Other Services	1.31	2.06	.52	.83

Type I: direct and indirect effects

Type II: direct, indirect, and induced effects

Source: The State of Hawaii Data Book, 1992

Figure 7-6 Output Multiplier in Hawaii

According to worldwide historical averages, each additional million dollars in tourism sales will create $517,000 in value added (indirect effects) and $482,000 in sales to tourism industries as a result of the original tourism sales (induced effects). Utilizing the multiplier formula, the total result of each million dollars in additional sales will result in an aggregate output of $2.5 million (a multiplier of 2.5) (*The WTTC Report - 1992 Complete Edition*, World Travel and Tourism Council, London, UK, 1993).

The Multiplier Effect for Gross Output (U.S. Dollars in Billions)

Region	Direct	Indirect and Induced	Total Impact
Africa	38	95	133
North America	720	1,801	2,522
Latin America	107	268	376
Caribbean	42	104	145
Asia/Pacific	751	1,878	2,629
Western Europe	844	2,110	2,954
Eastern Europe	340	849	1,189
Middle East	59	147	205
WORLD TOTAL	2,901	7,252	10,153

Source: The WTTC Report - 1992 Complete Edition, World Travel and Tourism Council, London, UK, 1993

Figure 7-7 The Multiplier Effect for Gross Output (U.S. Dollars in Billions)

The Multiplier Effect for Employment (Rounded to Nearest Million)

Region	Direct	Indirect and Induced	Total Impact
Africa	4	10	14
North America	10	24	34
Latin America	12	31	43
Caribbean	1	3	5
Asia/Pacific	55	138	193
Western Europe	16	41	57
Eastern Europe	17	42	58
Middle East	2	6	8
WORLD TOTAL	118	294	412

Source: *The WTTC Report - 1992 Complete Edition*, World Travel and Tourism Council, London, UK, 1993

Figure 7-8 The Multiplier Effect for Employment (Rounded to Nearest Million)

8

Forecasting Tourism Demand

The twentieth century has witnessed a steady increase in tourism in the United States and the rest of the world. The level of organization, methods of transport, and the facilities available at destination points have enjoyed an accelerated pace of improvement. The arrival of information highways and visible changes in the mass media have enhanced the appeal of tourism, and there is a greater demand for quality service at competitive prices. The smart entrepreneur in the field must know how to analyze the available data and interpret it to his or her advantage.

Forecasting plays a major role in tourism planning. The promotion of tourism projects involving substantial sums of money requires an estimate of future demand and market penetration. The commitment to add another geographical area to an existing tourism business would be much easier if it is possible to analyze the current and past tourist traffic, and predict the nature of changes in tourism demand. These extrapolative approaches to forecasting require historical data. This chapter outlines several quantitative forecasting methods that make use of such historical data, and gives a brief description of the accuracy measures that help to evaluate the suitability of a given model to a known situation. They include the *naive method, simple and weighted moving averages*, and a family of *exponential smoothing* methods, all of which are popular tools. Quantitative methods in forecasting also include *causal methods* based on the mathematical relationship between the series under examination and those variables that influence that series. *Regression analysis* involving two or more variables provides the foundation for causal methods. This chapter illustrates *time series regressions* and other quantitative forecasting models that are dependent on historical data. *Seasonality* effects, *business cycles*, and other miscellaneous topics are also discussed. These concepts, briefly defined, are

Naive Method A forecasting model in which the forecast for the next period is the same as the actual value for the current period.

Moving Average A smoothing technique that averages a given number of data points.

Simple Moving Average (SMA) An unweighted average of a consecutive number of data points.

Weighted Moving Average (WMA) A weighted average of a consecutive number of data points.

Exponential Smoothing A time-series technique that uses a weighting factor to develop a forecast. This is comparable to a weighted moving average technique in which more weight is given to recent data. It gives some influence to all data points, requires minimal data, and has more flexibility.

Causal Methods Quantitative forecasting methods based upon the mathematical relationship between the series being examined and those variables which influence or explain that series.

Regression A means of fitting an equation to a set of data.

Time Series A set of historical data obtained at regular intervals.

Time Series Regression A type of regression that develops the equation from data over a period of time.

Seasonality A basic pattern that is often found in a data series. It indicates movements in a data series during a particular period in a year (week, month, or quarter) that repeat year after year. This effect may be caused by climate/weather, social customs/holidays, and business policies.

Business Cycles The up and down movement in business activity around the long-term trend.

Trend A basic pattern found in a data series over a period of time. The trend may show an increase, a decrease, or a steady pattern that remains horizontal.

QUALITATIVE AND QUANTITATIVE FORECASTING METHODS

Fluctuations in the tourism business are far too complex to be incorporated into a single homogeneous theory. However, several forecasting methods and measures are available to those who prefer to supplement intuition with some objectivity. Forecasting methods may be classified as either qualitative or quantitative. The qualitative approach relies on expert opinion and includes technological and judgmental methods.

Technological Methods Subjective approaches to project new technologies and product applications. Technological methods are primarily used for long-term forecasts. The projection is based on the expertise of the forecaster and yields a range of possibilities, rather than an unique value.

Judgmental Methods Subjective forecasting methods ranging from sophisticated wild guesses to consensus among observers. These methods rely heavily upon human judgment, and the biases of individual participants would influence the forecast.

The main focus of this chapter is on quantitative methods, where forecasters use statistical tools to examine the data in order to discover underlying patterns and relationships. The two subcategories of the quantitative approach are the time series and causal methods.

DEMAND CHARACTERISTICS

The Nature of the Demand for Tourism

The objective of forecasting is to predict future events or conditions. Mathematical models are available to describe historical events and apply past trends to project into the future. However, common sense indicates that not all future events or conditions follow historical trends, especially in the tourism business. Forecasting demand for tourism must therefore include other ingredients to complement quantitative projection techniques.

Forecasting is, nevertheless, a systematic process involving several steps: collection of basic facts about past trends and forecasts; analysis of changes in past demand trends and differences between previous forecasts and actual behavior; examination of factors likely to affect future demand; forecasting for some future period; and continually monitoring the accuracy and reliability of the forecast, and revising it if so required.

There are several methods for collecting travel data. The number of tourists arriving in and departing from the country could be a useful source of travel data. This could be supplemented with detailed information about the visitors, the excursions they make, and the amount of money they spend. These surveys are time-consuming and difficult to handle. It may be easier to conduct in-flight and on-board surveys to a given destination. The Hawaiian Visitors Bureau uses this method extensively. Where border formalities are lacking, census returns may be gathered from hotels and entertainment centers that attract tourists. Specialized household surveys may also be used to obtain information regarding their travel patterns.

The Need for Forecasting the Demand for Tourism

Forecasts provide inputs to decision making in the tourism business. Forecasting models can be cheap or expensive; simple or complicated. How much resource is spent on forecasting depends on its perceived value by the decision maker. It is an accepted fact that tourists flock in the wake of an economic boom. The entrepreneur may presume that time and money need not be expended on accurate forecasting models and consequently divert resources toward other concerns. The impact of this decision is strongly felt in the choice of forecasting models.

ESTIMATING TOURISM REVENUES

Definitions of the terms and categories used is the first step in the study to ascertain income from tourism. Some travel research publications use the term "person trip" instead of "visitor," but the terms are synonymous for all practical purposes. The term "trip" usually refers to a trip outside the traveler's home area, or at least fifty miles from the home. If commuter trips were included, particularly in places like California, the figures for travel spending would increase markedly.

In other cases a "trip" covers a distance of at least 100 miles, and the traveler stays out overnight. This is so for Canada. Some definitions exclude persons who do not qualify as "visitors" as in the case of people looking for employment. It is important therefore to know exactly how these terms are defined.

Simple Random Sampling

It is both expensive and unnecessary to survey everyone when conducting surveys of people in economic impact studies. If, for example, a study is conducted to learn how many travelers have come to a particular destination for business reasons, a random sampling of visitors would suffice. An accurate sampling is representative of the entire group. The operant words are "random" and "representative." A random sample has the same or equal chance—or probability—of occurrence for each member of a group. Care should be taken, however, to make sure that the sample represents whatever is being measured. The same is true for economic sampling.

Random sampling is expected to have a preternatural power. One person is expected to represent hundreds, even thousands, the assumption being that the "sample" has the same characteristics or elements as the whole.

Sampling is used in all political polls. The Gallup poll takes regular samples of just a few thousand from a voting public of over 50 million people. They are interviewed for their opinions, and the results normally deviate less than 3 percent from the eventual outcome. Some national polls contact less than 2000 people before accurately announcing which way the political wind is blowing.

In the design and implementation of a simple random sampling plan the following points are important.

The Population of Interest   The population of interest must be known before a random sampling is drawn. Random sampling has to be truly random—really representative of the population from which it has been drawn. If not, no accurate estimates of population characteristics can be made on the basis of sample findings. Unless the sample is randomly chosen, sample information is essentially meaningless.

Drawing a random sample is easy if a list of all the people in the population is available. Such a list can be in the form of an alphabetically arranged card file, a directory of names, or a file with hotel/motel registration forms. By selecting every tenth, twentieth, or fiftieth name—in general, every nth name—a systematic random sample is obtained. For example, in a hotel with an alphabetical file of all guests and a list of 25,000 registered guests last year, it was decided to draw a random sample of 1000 guests. Beginning randomly with any one card from 1 to 25, every subsequent twenty-fifth card was drawn until 1000 cards were collected.

Stratified Sampling   Besides the systematic sample techniques used by researchers, there are simple methods that employ random number tables for the selection process. Computer software packages like Minitab have greatly increased the ease of generating random numbers.

Another popular method is the stratified random sample technique. This breaks the population into meaningful subgroups, thereby reducing costs without sacrificing accuracy. If the spending patterns of visitors are stratified according to age, income, and gender, the time and cost expended would be reduced together with the sample size.

If a complete "listing" or some such inventory of the population is unavailable, a random sampling becomes difficult, sometimes impossible. This frequently happens when the sampling is done at a local visitor attraction. A so-called judgment sample is one method that is used in this case. The assumption is that the sample, like the true random sample, is representative of the population as a whole. Without this assumption the survey becomes meaningless and potentially misleading.

Unless a random sample is chosen mechanically, the danger of a biased sample is always possible. In statistical terms a *bias* is a systematic deviation of the estimate produced by the sample from the population mean. A bias can be demonstrated only if multiple estimates are made, and the population mean is a result of a large collection of actual estimates that are obtained from repeated sampling. In reality samples are usually performed only once and the existence of a bias remains unknown. Some judgment, therefore, is required in a study that does not make use of any random sampling technique.

No interviewer, however, can select a true random sample on the basis of judgment alone. Instead, interviewers are given strict rules concerning whom to pick in order to minimize bias, that is, in order to select a "random" sample of persons attending a particular attraction, select every tenth group entering the attraction. If the group consists of an even number of members, interview the person on the extreme left. Interviewing should be done continuously while the attraction is open, or at random times over the total time period. In practice it is probably acceptable to interview during a wide variety of times rather than at any one selected time—interviews conducted only on Saturdays in July cannot be deemed representative of the entire year's performance.

Sample Size and Sample Error   This is an issue of statistics and budget. It is necessary to work with a sample of at least a hundred persons, five to ten times as many if that can be managed. Rarely is it necessary to use samples larger than 1000.

Figure 8-1 shows an estimate of sampling errors for percentages. If sample sizes

Estimate of Sampling Errors

Number in sample	100	200	400	800	1600	3200
Percentage near 10%	6	4	3	2	2	1
Percentage near 20%	8	6	4	3	2	1
Percentage near 30%	9	6½	5	3	2	2
Percentage near 40%	10	7	5	3½	2	2
Percentage near 50%	10	7	5	3½	3	2
Percentage near 60%	10	7	5	3½	2	2
Percentage near 70%	9	6½	5	3	2	2
Percentage near 80%	8	6	4	3	2	1
Percentage near 90%	6	4	3	2	2	1

Figure 8-1   Estimate of Sampling Errors

are over 500, sampling errors are less of a problem. The focus should be on the kinds of biases that may influence results.

The science of statistical analysis allows a calculation of the size of a sampling error based on the size of a sample. As can be seen in Figure 8-1, the larger the sample size, the smaller is the sample error.

Two examples of how to utilize these sampling errors follow.

1. In order to determine the percentage of all visitors who come to a city for business we take a random sample of 400 visitors. The sample shows that 60% come for business purposes. This, according to the above table, is subject to a sampling error of 5 percentage points. In other words we know from our sample that the actual percentage of all visitors who come for business is: 60% ± 5%, or somewhere between 55% and 65%. Statisticians add the qualifying phrase "at the 95% confidence level." This means that, statistically speaking, we are 95% sure the true figure will fall in the 55% to the 65% range, and we are running a 5% risk that it will fall outside this range.

2. A random sample of all visitors to the state of California is taken. The sample size is 1600 people, and includes 10% foreign visitors. The sampling error in this case is, according to the above table, approximately 2 percentage points. In other words we can say that based on our sample results, between 8% and 12% of all visitors to California are from abroad.

For all purposes, the only factors that determine the size of the sampling error are the percentage involved and the sample size. The size of the population has nothing to do with it. A larger sample will automatically reduce the sampling error. In some cases, however, the sample size must be made four times larger in order to cut the error in half. In practice a trade-off is required between the desired amount of accuracy and the time and money available for the sampling study.

What if there is an interest in a population characteristic other than a percentage? One example is a study to determine the average total spending of all 1 million visitors to an area, applying the principles described above. Again a random sample is drawn from a few hundred to, at most, a few thousand people. The larger sample provides more accurate results, but at a substantially greater cost.

TIME SERIES ANALYSIS

An analysis of the time series involves the breaking down of past data into four major components: trend, seasonality, cycles, and random variations. Trend refers to a gradual shift in the data movement either in an upward or a downward direction over a period of time. The models are the naive method, the simple moving average, the weighted moving average, *simple exponential smoothing*, the time series regression, *linear trend smoothing*, and *nonlinear trend smoothing*. Seasonality, cycles, and random variations are explained in subsequent paragraphs.

Simple Exponential Smoothing Simple exponential smoothing (SES) is a constant-level forecasting model in which the forecast for the next period is obtained by calculating the error term for the current period and adding a fraction of that error to the current forecast. The error is the difference between the actual and forecast value. The constant level implies the absence of any upward or downward trend in the time-series. SES makes use of a single smoothing parameter, which is the same as the fraction of the error term referred to above.

Linear Trend Smoothing Linear trend smoothing (LTS) is an exponential smoothing method that recognizes a straight-line trend. This incorporates a parameter to represent the smoothed trend, in addition to the smoothing parameter referred to in SES that leads to a smoothed level. The changes in the trend is constant each period, indicating that it follows a straight line.

Nonlinear Trend Smoothing Nonlinear trend smoothing (NTS) is an exponential smoothing method that is similar to LTS, referred to above, where the changes in the trend need not be constant each period. Depending on the trend pattern, another parameter is introduced to reflect the modification in the trend. Thus NTS makes use of three parameters, while LTS uses two, and SES uses only one.

Measurement of Forecast Accuracy

Many different forecasting methods have been developed and studied over the years. Regardless of the methods used, forecasts are measured by their accuracy. There are three most commonly used yardsticks: the mean absolute deviation (MAD), the mean absolute percentage error (MAPE), and the mean squared error (MSE). This section deals with a description of these three methods of measuring accuracy.

The Mean Absolute Deviation (MAD) The mean absolute deviation is a measure of forecast accuracy obtained by averaging the absolute values of the errors. Suppose the actual tourism revenue in millions of U.S. dollars for three consecutive years is $190, $201, and $205 respectively, while a forecasting model yields $190, $200, and $210 million. In this case, the forecasting model adds $10 million each year, while the actual figures show an addition of $11 million in the second year and another addition of $4 million in the third year. There is obviously a difference between the actual and the forecast figures. This difference is called an "error" or a "deviation." It is desirable to select a forecasting model that keeps this error to a minimum.

The error term can assume any positive or negative value. During the second year, the forecast value of $200 million is less than the actual value of $201 million. Hence the error of $1 million is positive. However, the forecast value of $ 210 million in the third period is more than the actual amount of $205 by $5 million, and this difference is therefore negative. A simple sum of these error terms would not reflect the forecast accuracy, since some of them may cancel each other. This problem could be avoided by considering only the absolute values of the error, disregarding the sign. Obtaining a sum of these absolute values and dividing the total by the number of periods used, gives the mean absolute deviation (MAD). The MAD value for this sample problem is $(0 + 1 + 5)/3 = 2$

The Mean Absolute Percentage Error (MAPE)   The mean absolute percentage error is a measure of forecast accuracy that is obtained by averaging the absolute error in a percentage form relative to the actual value. The mean absolute deviation takes care of the "sign" problem explained above. However, the magnitude of the error does not reflect the error proportion in relation to the actual data from which the error is calculated. If the actual data is very large (with 50,000 tourist arrivals per day in a given city), an absolute error value of 5, that is, a forecast arrival of either 49,995 or 50,005 would be considered fairly accurate since this represents an error of one in every ten thousand or 0.01 percent. On the other hand, the same error value of $5 in relation to an actual hotel charge per day of $50, that is, a forecast of either $45 or $55 would mean a error of one in ten or 10 percent. The nature of the data handled decides whether a ten percent error is acceptable or not. In any case, the absolute deviation by itself, or the mean value derived over several data points, does not provide for this distinction.

This problem could be resolved by dividing the error term first by the actual and obtaining the absolute value of this quotient, and then converting this into a percentage by multiplying this quotient by 100. Such a value is called an absolute percentage error.

As in the case of MAD, it is now possible to obtain a sum of absolute percentage error and divide this sum by the number of error terms used and arrive at a mean absolute percentage error (MAPE). For the given example of tourism revenue for three consecutive years, the MAPE value is $([0/190] + [1/201] + [5/205]) * 100 / 3 = 0.98$.

The Mean Square Error (MSE)   The third most popular accuracy measure is the mean square error (MSE). This is obtained by averaging the square of each error term. As the name indicates, the error is squared first so that the positive and the negative error values do not cancel each other. This eliminates the need for obtaining the absolute value of any error term. The rest of the procedure is similar to MAD. The error squares are summed up and divided by the number of error terms to arrive at the mean square error. The MSE value for the problem at hand is $(0 + 1 + 25)/3 = 8.67$. Since each error term is multiplied by itself, this accuracy measure is highly sensitive to the magnitude of the error.

The Naive Method

A substantial inventory of time series methods has been developed over the years. This chapter examines the ones that are popular in the literature. Time series models make use of historical data to predict the future. They would be valid if future events could be regarded as a function of past events. The simplest one is called the naive method, since it uses the latest data point as the forecast for the next period. Even at the highest level of government it is a common practice to base budget provisions for the next year on the amount that has been spent during this year. Thus, if this year's actual expenditure amounts to $10 billion, this becomes the forecast for next year with the use of the naive method. It probably makes sense to adopt such a simple policy with minor revisions, if there is no reason to believe that the requirements for next year would be any different from the actuals this year. The tourism business may not lend itself to such a simple explanation of what could happen in the future. All the same, the approach suggests a useful *benchmark,* or yardstick to evaluate the accuracy of a forecasting model.

Moving Averages

Smoothing approaches have the advantage of removing random variations from the data by averaging the observations in some fashion. The simple, or first-order, smoothing approaches remove the irregular patterns from the data to reveal the cycle or trend. They include the simple moving average (SMA), and the weighted moving average (WMA).

The Simple Moving Average (SMA)   A moving average is an average of consecutive data points. It may be unweighted or weighted. It can be used as a forecast or simply as a base figure for use in seasonal adjustment of the data. A simple moving average is obtained by adding the last two or more actual values. For instance, let the actual demand for periods 1, 2, and 3 be 2, 4, and 6 respectively. If a two-period simple moving average is used, the forecast for period three will be $(2 + 4)/2 = 3$. Similarly, the forecast for period four will be $(4 + 6)/2 = 5$. If a three-period simple moving average is used, the forecast for period four will be $(2 + 4 + 6)/3 = 4$. Notice that in a three-period SMA, the forecast values for the first three periods are not available. This loss of information is inevitable. However, it is more common to use a moving average method over a long string of consecutive periods, to remove random variations from data. For instance, many organizations find it convenient to apply a twelve-month moving average to forecast monthly sales figures. The procedure is simple and easy to understand. It provides a rough and ready estimate of what to expect next month, next week, or next year.

The Weighted Moving Average (WMA)   A simple moving average does not distinguish between any one period and another during the averaging process. All periods are treated with equal importance. However, many analysts prefer to give more importance to more recent data. This is accomplished by the use of weights (w), which are positive fractional values ranging between 0 and 1. The weights are assigned to each period in a descending order from the current to any chosen number of periods in the past such that the total of all these weights add up to unity.

For example, as in the case of the SMA, let the demands for periods 1, 2, and 3 be 2, 4, and 6, and let the weighted moving average use two periods at a time, with values of 0.7 and 0.3 for the weights of the current period and the preceding one. The first period available for forecasting is period three. The forecast value for this period is $4(0.7) + 2(0.3) = 3.4$. The forecast for period four is $6(0.7) + 4(0.3) = 5.4$. The same data will yield a different forecast, if a weighted moving average is used with weights of 0.5, 0.3, and 0.2. The forecast in this case will be $6(0.5) + 4(0.3) + 2(0.2) = 4.6$, instead of 5.4 for the two-period WMA. Notice that in both cases, the total of all weights add up to unity. For the two-period case the sum is $0.7 + 0.3 = 1$, and for the three-period case the sum is also $0.5 + 0.3 + 0.2 = 1$. The two variables involved in the WMA model are the number of periods included for averaging, and the respective weights to be used for each period.

As in the case of the SMA, the values to be assigned for the weights would again be arbitrary, requiring a trial and error procedure involving computers. Once the weights are chosen, along with the number of periods included for the averaging process, the forecast for the current period is a simple addition of the products of the previous actual values and their respective weights.

Exponential Smoothing

Simple Exponential Smoothing   While the moving averages are easy to understand, they do not pick up trends very well. Increasing the number of periods would help to smooth out fluctuations better, but the process becomes less sensitive to real changes in data. In addition, they require extensive data storage. The problem of keeping a record of past data can be overcome by using a formula known as the simple exponential smoothing, where the latest forecast is equal to the old forecast adjusted by a fraction of the difference between the last period's actual and forecast. The difference between the actual and the forecast for any period is called the error for that period. The fraction referred to above is called the smoothing parameter, and has a value ranging from zero to one. If more weight is to be given to the more recent data, this fraction is kept closer to one and vice versa. The objective is to search for the most appropriate smoothing constant that will minimize the error between the actual and forecast values.

To illustrate, let the actuals for the first three periods be 2, 4, and 6 respectively, as before, and let the forecast for the first period be 2. Since the error is the difference between the actual and the forecast, error value for the first period is zero. Let the fraction of the error (smoothing parameter) to be added to the last forecast be 0.5. Using the formula suggested above, the forecast for period two is $2 + (0.5)0 = 2$. The forecast for period two and its error value will help to arrive at the forecast for period three and so on. The error for period two is $4 - 2 = 2$. Hence the forecast for period three is $2 + (0.5)2 = 3$. This yields an error value of $6 - 3 = 3$ for period three. Accordingly, the forecast for period four is $3 + (0.5)3 = 4.5$. This process continues from period one to the current period to obtain the forecast for the next period.

Although each period, from the start to the current one, has an influence on the forecast of the next period, the past periods exert lesser and lesser influence, as one goes further into the past. Hence this process can be defined as an exponentially weighted average of past observations. The parameter that controls the contributions of all previous values is the smoothing parameter, which is the fraction of the error term. As explained earlier, this fraction can range from 0 to 1. If it assumes the value of 0, the forecast for any period is governed only by the initial forecast value.

On the other hand, should the value be kept at 1, the forecast for next period is uniquely determined by the actual value for the current period and all other prior actual values have no influence on the forecast. In other words, the simple exponential smoothing method is reduced to the naive method.

The value of the fractional constant is therefore crucial in controlling the behavior of the forecast. In a weighted moving average method, several weight combinations and the number of periods will have to be experimented with before a satisfactory model is found. In the case of the SES approach, it is sufficient to work with only one parameter. This provides for a considerable computational advantage. By itself, however, the SES does not account for discernible trends, cycles, and seasonal effects that form part of any realistic time series. Computer-based methods are available to take these factors into account, and they form part of a family of exponential smoothing methods involving more smoothing parameters.

Linear and Nonlinear Trend Smoothing Simple exponential smoothing, as in the case of other moving average techniques, does not respond to trends. If a trend is visible in the data series, it would be more appropriate to use linear trend smoothing or nonlinear trend smoothing, depending on the shape of the trend. If the growth is steady, a linear trend smoothing model would be appropriate. On the other hand a decaying or a growing trend would require the use of nonlinear trend smoothing. Either way, these trend adjustments require an understanding of the initial level and the initial trend. Plotting a series of past data in a graph, it is often possible to draw a line that is the closest to the data points. If this is a straight line, it is called a linear trend. Statistical techniques are available to determine the angle of this straight line and the point at which it meets the vertical axis representing the variable such as the tourism revenue, while the horizontal axis represents the time. The statistical method attempts to minimize the sum of the squares of the vertical differences from the fitted line to the actual observations. This method is called a simple linear regression of the time series or a time series regression. The word linear implies that the trend is a straight line. If the actual observations suggest a nonlinear curve, appropriate curve fitting formulae should be used.

Seasonality and Tourism Economics

The second component of a time series is "seasonality." Seasonality refers to movements in a series during a particular time of the year/week/month/quarter that recur year after year. Seasonality is the result of climate, social customs, holidays, and business policy considerations.

The seasonal index is the average seasonal fluctuation expressed as a fraction of the average value of the time series that repeats itself from one period to another. A time series may be deseasonalized by dividing each data point by the seasonal index. This is known as seasonal adjustment. Correspondingly, the expression "seasonalize" refers to reinfusing seasonality into deseasonalized data. It is done by multiplying each deseasonalized data point by its seasonal index.

A seasonal pattern may be additive or multiplicative. If the seasonal fluctuations are of a constant size, they are additive. If they are proportional in size to the data, they are called multiplicative. As the trend increases, the seasonal fluctuations become larger.

Seasonal adjustment is a straightforward procedure in which the unadjusted actual value is divided by the seasonal factor in its decimal form. Seasonality and smoothing may be combined to arrive at a more realistic forecast.

The fact that readily identifiable tourism businesses—airlines, hotels, motels, resorts, and car rental companies—are subject to seasonal variations in sales makes forecasting and labor cost control particularly important for them. Resorts in New England enjoy summer seasons beginning in June and ending on Labor Day. Managers often manage hotels in Florida during the winter season and return north during the summer. For them it is important to extend the seasons with group bookings in the off season. Most hotel markets change with the season. Florida, for example, attracts upper income markets in winter, and a less affluent clientele during the hot summer months. Resort hotels have lulls between seasons called "shoulder periods," during which the occupancy falls sharply. Marketing is used to fill the low period. Bermuda has several "college weeks" during April. Atlantic City hosts the Miss America Pageant in September, normally a period of low occupancy.

Hotels and motels depend on forecasting to estimate future sales. Sales figures are used to schedule the right number of employees, a minimum number becoming a part of the fixed costs of operation.

Some resort locations—Hawaii is an example—have minimal seasonal changes. Holidays mean full houses for some resort properties; holidays like Christmas and Thanksgiving find few guests at commercial hotels.

The airlines base their fares upon the season. Summer is the high season for transatlantic flights. Thanksgiving and Christmas are peak periods for domestic travel. Flights go full or empty according to their scheduled departure times. Morning flights from Los Angeles to New York are usually full, while afternoon and weekend flights have empty seats. When Pan American Airways was operating its Pan Am One and Pan Am Two flights around the world, the planes sometimes carried as many crew as passengers. Losses ran into the tens of thousands for each flight, yet they continued to be scheduled. Today airlines change schedules and cancel flights practically on a daily basis. They withdraw from unprofitable markets giving way to carriers that fly smaller planes.

The car rental business is usually slow on weekends, fluctuating with business week travel. Leisure rentals are pushed to fill the weekends, and fleets are shifted to meet seasonal demands. Popular events such as the Rose Bowl and baseball and football playoffs require rental cars to be moved to airports for customer pick-ups. Summer is high season at theme parks, weather being the prime determinant in the number of visitors. Euro Disney has proved a big financial disappointment as Paris winters are too cold to attract the expected number of visitors. Cruise lines can beat the seasonality factor to a large extent by positioning ships to take advantage of the weather. Alaska cruises are popular in summer; Caribbean cruises are popular the year round, but have the greatest appeal to northern residents in winter.

Capital and operational budgets are made annually, and may be updated weekly or more often. They represent the peaks and valleys of income and costs. Most tourist operations have little choice in remaining open even with skeletal crews, as fixed costs like insurance, some utilities, taxes, and lease costs continue.

Commercial hotels cannot close though costs may exceed income for relatively long periods. An airline cannot stop flying during the off season. Chain restaurants can cut staff but are not likely to close down. Marketing often produces surprising results. A catchy marketing slogan—Wendy's "Where's the beef?"—can give a sudden boost to sales, although food and service remain unchanged. A little old lady screaming "Where's the beef?" was a sure-fire way to draw public attention to the high quality of Wendy's hamburger.

Seasonal fluctuations can be reduced if businesses promote off-season events and reduce off-season prices. Florida offers reduced prices during the hot summers and late spring and fall seasons. Bermuda has a series of college weeks for college students, mainly from East coast schools, during their spring breaks.

The construction of large malls like the one at Edmonton in Canada or the indoor facilities in Tokyo are physical ways of overcoming seasonality.

Cycles

The third component of a time series is "cycles," patterns in the data that occur every few years. These are fluctuations caused by conditions outside the control of an individual business. General economic conditions, saving and consumption habits in the society, mutual generation of errors, and similar happenings can cause fluctuations in economic activity that in turn affect the tourism business as explained in previous chapters. The cyclical value of a time series is computed by dividing the moving average of each period by the trend value of the same period.

Random Variations

The last component of a time series is the random variation. These are variations in actual data, such as the tourism revenue, that cannot be tied to the trend or the cyclical components. If the data is also discernible in terms of seasonal fluctuations, this should be isolated before analyzing the random component. These random fluctuations are supposed to be caused by unusual events that do not repeat themselves. For instance, political instability in a country or a particular state in that country can cause a temporary setback to tourism revenue. If the situation were to persist, there may be a significant shift in the tourist traffic. Many natural disasters such as earthquakes, hurricanes, floods, volcanic eruptions, and droughts can cause a considerable drop in the tourist traffic to and from the affected regions. On the other hand, tourists flock to vantage points to witness some unique event such as the coronation of a monarch, international Olympics, world sports events, or the observation of an astronomical phenomenon.

Expanded Versions of Exponential Smoothing

There are other time series models, such as *adaptive filtering, Winter's method, Census II*, and *Box-Jenkins*, that are expanded versions of exponential smoothing. In adaptive filtering, extra weight is assigned to the more recent data as in the case of exponential smoothing, but a formalized process involving a series of iterations is used to determine the value of each weight.

Winter's method is a sophisticated exponential smoothing model that allows both seasonal and trend influences to be incorporated into the forecast. As new information becomes available, the forecasting equation is continually updated.

Many consider that Box-Jenkins is the most effective method to identify past data and make allowances for them. This is a very costly and complex time series approach, requiring a great deal of past data. Computer access and a sound knowledge of statistics are prerequisites to use this model. The three stages of Box-Jenkins are identifying, estimating, and testing. To begin with, a tentative model format for the forecast is identified by an extensive analysis of the pattern of the variable's past behavior. This is followed by a selection of the initial parameters. Finally, the forecasting accuracy of the model and its parameters are tested. Should the model be judged as inappropriate, the entire sequence is repeated.

Census II also separates data into the four components described earlier in a more sophisticated way. It involves a large number of steps during which the data is continually refined. Census II has been undergoing several changes in tune with more user-friendly software. An increasing number of businesses are beginning to make use of this method for forecasting purposes.

CAUSAL MODELS AND OTHER TOPICS

Quantitative models consist of time series and causal models. Causal models are models that use variables and factors in addition to time for purposes of forecasting. Causal models work on the principle of association between any two or more variables. If, for example, the currency of any country is devalued, foreign visitors would crowd there in order to enjoy a cheaper vacation. This relationship was discussed earlier, while dealing with currency issues. The underlying assumption of a causal model is that changes in the value of any one variable, such as the currency exchange rate, are closely related to changes in some other variable such as tourist arrivals. If it is possible to obtain information about one variable, the future value of another variable can be forecast through the process of association. By and large, the most frequently used models of association come under the family of regression models. If only two variables are considered, and the fitted line can be approximated to a straight line, the approach is called simple linear regression. If three or more variables are involved, and the linearity assumption still holds good, then the models belong to multiple linear regression. Relaxing the linearity assumption leads to nonlinear regression.

Econometric Analysis

Regression analysis is a special case of *econometric* modeling, that makes use of *endogenous* and *exogenous* variables. Endogenous variables are those variables whose values are determined within the system. For example, in an econometric model of the tourism business, the price of a vacation package may be determined within the model, thus making it an endogenous variable. On the other hand, an exogenous variable is one whose value is determined outside the model or the system. For example, in an econometric model, the currency exchange rate might be an exogenous variable. An econometric model is a set of equations intended to be used simultaneously to capture the way in which endogenous and exogenous variables are related. It is very important to study the assumptions underlying the model equations before these sets of simultaneous equations are used for forecasting purposes.

Input-Output Analysis

At the macro level, tourism planning can benefit from input-output analysis, which deals with the modeling of a total system in terms of the relationship among several variables. For example, the demand for hotel accommodation at a tourist spot is a function of a number of tourists arriving there. But hotel accommodation consists of beds, rooms, the lobby, restaurants, swimming pools, parking facilities, travel agencies, shopping malls, and other infrastructure facilities. Thus, an increase in demand for hotel accommodation also results in an increasing need for these components. This results in a chain reaction, with commensurate demand for the materials that make up these items, eventually leading to a spurt in orders for steel, aluminum, copper, wood, and so forth. Thus a change in demand for an end product such as hotels influences the demand for various intermediate products that make up the end product. The usefulness of input-output analysis stems from the identification of these linkages, all of which help the forecasting process. The three principal components of an input-output model are the transaction table, the direct requirement table, and the total requirement table.

The transaction table represents monetary movement among different sectors of the economy, where each industry is represented by a row and a column. The column refers to the purchases by each industry in the form of inputs. The row represents the output of each industry. The name "Input-Output" is thus derived from the transaction table. The values in the transaction table are then converted into percentages in the direct requirements table. This is done by obtaining the sum of all inputs for a sector, represented by a column, then dividing each input value by this total, and multiplying the ratio by hundred to get the percentage. The direct requirement table can also be shown in fractions instead of percentages, in which case the fractions shown in each cell of a column should add up to unity. The total requirements table takes into account the direct and indirect effects of final demand on each industry. In order to produce $100 of a product, a given industry may have to produce $12 (as an example) for its own consumption. Thus the total output of this industry has to be much more than the output shown in the direct requirements table. This difference is due to the indirect effect, which is reflected in the total requirements table. This analysis could be very valuable to the tourist industry, since it could gauge the impact on its growth from extensive changes in other industries or industry segments. A major problem in the use of input-output analysis is the collection of reliable and timely data to make up the transaction table.

Economic Indicators

Economic indicators provide an understanding of the direction in which an economy is progressing. An economic indicator is a time series that has a reasonably stable relation to the average of the whole economy, or to some other time series of particular interest. It identifies short-term cyclical turning points based on one or more component series. A major shortcoming of these indicators is that while they can provide the direction of economic activity, they cannot quantify the magnitude of the movement. While there is a constant search for a series that would signal changes in economic activity by turning upward or downward before the overall economy turned, no single series has such a relationship on a regular and consistent basis. Several series usually lead at the turning point, while others lag at these points. These are known as leading and lagging series respectively.

Diffusion Indexes

Economic time series do not all move uniformly up or down in any stage of the business cycle. Diffusion indexes are therefore used to gauge the relative strength of the forces of expansion and contraction over a time span. The diffusion index is the percentage of the series in any group under study that is expanding in any period of time such as a month or a quarter. A diffusion index fluctuates between hundred percent when all components are expanding, and zero percent when all are declining. An index of fifty percent implies that there is no change in the aggregate series.

CAPACITY PLANNING FOR TOURIST FACILITIES AND SERVICES

Tourism facilities and services have to be planned to match the demand for such facilities and services. Excess capacity is wasteful. Inadequate capacity leads to customer dissatisfaction. The problem is one of matching the arrivals with services. Even when well-matched, it is almost impossible to avoid delays in attending to customers while some facilities and servers remain idle. When a server is busy, any arrival during this period has to wait, thus a waiting line gets formed. The theory of waiting lines, also known as the queuing theory, is well developed and several mathematical models have been formulated to examine different queuing situations. Since tourism is the largest service industry in the world, the analysis of queues is an important aspect of the tourism industry.

The economic implications of understanding and manipulating queues in the tourism industry are manifold. Disgruntled customers can cost the management dearly, for they might decide to go elsewhere for the same service. A long waiting period to be seated at a restaurant for example, or long lines at a theme park, might antagonize regular customers. And word gets around.

Queues form whenever clients arrive in a random manner for a given service. Examples are frequently seen at airline check-in counters, fast-food restaurants, drive-up counters, trains held up at railway stations, and planes waiting for landing clearance from the control tower at busy airports. Even if an adequate amount (an average) of service is provided over a period of one day, queues form because customers arrive on a random basis. The "adequate amount (an average) of service provided" is usually calculated by incorporating the total number of customers arriving over a given period (usually one day). This assumes that customers arrive at evenly spaced intervals.

The goal of the queuing theory is to minimize economic costs while handling the problem of waiting customers. The economic impact of customers refusing to wait or not returning in the future are difficult to quantify. Another element of economic costs is the cost of extra hands to meet the unexpected demand. When a service element is not being utilized there is a third element in the cost of idle capacity. The key in the mathematical analysis of economic costs is the determination of what service capacity results in the lowest total costs. The economic implication of this model is that profits can be maximized by satisfying an optimum number of customers at a minimum cost.

9

Analysis of Tourism Projects

Tourism projects usually have the goals of maximizing profits and minimizing risks and costs. Costs such as marketing and market development are almost inevitable, and management must decide where and how much to spend on these costs.

This chapter illustrates how project analysis can be applied to a complicated tourism project using system analyses that have been developed in complex businesses and the military. The illustration used is hypothetical: Lome Tours Project is located for illustrative purposes in Togo, West Africa. The techniques and system analysis have universal application.

The project analyzed in this example is assumed to be part of a very large tourism conglomerate, one that has several specialists who must work together and who are familiar with the system analysis used by large enterprises. Careful control is maintained over the timing and sequencing of events in order to ensure that these events are kept on paths that reach predetermined goals at specific times, and follow in the order that promotes maximum efficiency.

The Lome Tours Project is delineated in considerable detail to show the complexity that can be a part of tourism project development. It assumes that the parent company is large and multifaceted, and ready to carry the cost of such intensive analysis. Few companies of this nature—American Express to name one—exist in 1994, but others will develop as globalization of tourism continues.

The Lome Tours Project

GlobeLand is a tourism-related enterprise with headquarters in Los Angeles and branch offices in major cities in the United States, Canada, and a few selected capitals in Europe such as London, Paris, Rome, and Athens. GlobeLand matured from a $2 million to a $100 million tourism business between 1965 and 1990. GlobeLand's strength lay in its ability to work with the tourist in the North American continent. Its reputation for quality service far exceeded the local competitors' reputations.

Most of GlobeLand's clients in the early seventies were employed by large companies in and around Los Angeles, New York, and Pittsburgh. They were willing to use GlobeLand for both official and private travel, and pay the extra price for quality and service. With the recession of 1975, GlobeLand found that, unless it penetrated the competitive but lucrative foreign travel and exotic tour package market, its business base would decline. This resulted in a network of branches in European capitals, initially established to serve American clientele and later expanded to absorb local tourism markets. From operating package tours they emerged as investors in tourism-related entities such as hotels and entertainment centers.

In 1990, GlobeLand inaugurated its West African operations by opening a branch office in Abidjan, the capital of Ivory Coast. Until recently, tourism operations were confined to short bus tours within the Ivory Coast and bordering countries such as Ghana and Liberia. Once in a while, special trips were also organized to the Republic of Togo. Currently, there is a proposal to offer regular coach and air tours to Lome. This city is the capital of the Republic of Togo, a French-speaking country, on the West African coast. Togo shares a common border with the Republic of Benin, a former French colony, on the east and with Ghana, a former British colony, on the west. Directly to the north lies Burkina Faso. Togo has a population of about four million people, one-fifth of whom are Roman Catholics and one-eighth, Sunni Muslims. French and eleven local dialects are spoken. Lome is the biggest of the ten cities that have sprung up along the narrow vertical spread of the countryside. Major industrial activity relates to mining of phosphates and limestone. The city of Lome has a beautiful stretch of coastline dotted with coconut plantations, and luxury hotels with casinos and fine restaurants offering French and Italian cuisine. Hotels are filled with vacationers from neighboring Ghana and Nigeria, and chartered flights bring crowds of tourists seeking escape from the rigors of winter in Europe.

Togo provides a gateway to a world far removed from the stress and cacophony of the average metropolis. The change in the scenery is total: blue skies, golden sand, lush greenery, and clean air. The climate is temperate, ranging from a low of 72°F to a high of 86°F. Water-skiing, wind-surfing, scuba diving, and other aquatic sports are a popular pastime.

Should GlobeLand offer regular coach and air tours to Lome from its branch office in Abidjan? If it does, how should the project be organized? What are the aspects that have to be considered in the planning and estimation process? How should it keep track of the progress? What are the special considerations that have to be given in view of the international nature of the project?

CHARACTERISTICS OF TOURISM PROJECTS

The Nature of Tourism Projects

The tourism business is a highly competitive one. The traditional bureaucratic structure needs innovative reorganization to respond to the changing environment. Prospective tourists are constantly looking for new ventures, new thrills, and new places
to see. In spite of natural disasters like the 1994 earthquake that followed in the wake
of forest fires and urban riots, Los Angeles continues to be a favorite destination,
thanks to tourist attractions such as the Universal Studios and Disneyland, where new
entertainment ideas are constantly generated and implemented.

The 6.6 (on the Richter Scale) quake at Northridge in early 1994, followed by continuous aftershocks for months, caused an estimated damage of $15 to $30 billion to the
greater Los Angeles area. According to Michael Collins, senior vice president of the Los
Angeles Convention & Visitors Bureau, the only significant obstacle facing visitors who
wanted to make the usual round of attractions at the time was the traffic congestion due to
the damaged roads. Even that was not as crippling as initially feared. Remarkably, none of
Southern California's major tourist draws—Disneyland, Universal Studios, Knott's Berry
Farm, and Six Flags Magic Mountain—sustained major structural damage in the quake.
Mr. Collins' estimate shows that only a small number—perhaps 500—of Los Angeles
County's 91,000 hotel rooms were put out of commission by the tremble, and many re-
opened for business in less than a fortnight. Although it suffered from some financial
aftershocks for a month or so before the tourist flow improved, the tourism industry in the
Los Angeles area successfully weathered a major disaster that contributes over $10 billion
a year to the local economy. Safety is a major concern for a tourist. Those who manage the
tourist attractions and the infrastructure facilities had to initiate inspection and repair
work, and give wide publicity to these efforts.

Los Angeles is not alone in its endeavor to woo the prospective tourist. In every
country, managers of tourist attractions constantly seek unique and innovative presentations to lure the tourist. Even places of historical interest like the Colosseum, the
Eiffel Tower, and the Louvre call for renewed efforts to satisfy the tourist. Visitors
want more at less cost (real as opposed to nominal) and competition with a variety of
alternate tourist choices necessitates improved services.

Today "people costs"—expenditures on personnel—have become more inflationary
than the cost of equipment and facilities. Hence emphasis is increasingly placed on
finding internal rather than external solutions for problems. The tourism business is
characterized by innovative methods of restructuring the management . The traditional
structure was highly bureaucratic and could not respond to the changing environment.
The current trend inclines towards the adoption of project management which is highly
organic, and responds rapidly to the changing environment. The project management
approach helps to reduce bureaucracy and coordinate complex efforts.

What Is Project Management?

Project management means different things to different people. But people generally
agree that it involves making better use of existing resources by getting work to flow

Line managers

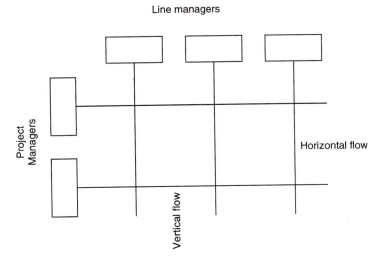

Figure 9-1   Vertical versus Horizontal Flow

both horizontally and vertically within a company. While the vertical flow is normally the responsibility of line managers, the horizontal flow is dependent on the project managers (Figure 9-1). The **Project manager** is the manager of a group who shoulders the responsibility for a project, not a function. Other designations include project coordinator and project engineer, each having a different degree of authority over the project. In other words, the project manager ensures proper communication and coordination of activities horizontally between the line organizations.

A *project* is a series of activities and tasks that have specific objectives, with defined start and end dates. Many projects have funding limitations. A project consumes resources such as people, equipment, facilities, materials, money, information, and technology (Figure 9-2).

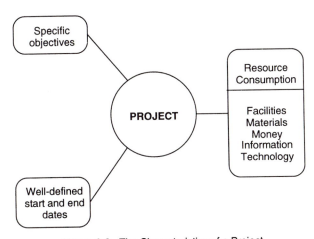

Figure 9-2   The Characteristics of a Project

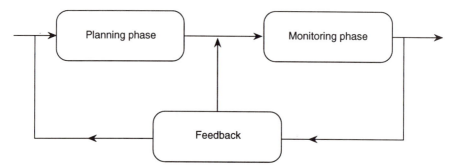

Figure 9-3 The Two Phases of a Project

Project management consists of two phases: planning and monitoring (Figure 9-3). In the planning phase, the work requirements are defined. This should lead to an assessment of the amount of work involved and the needed resources. The monitoring phase involves the tracking of progress and the making of necessary adjustments. It helps in analyzing the impact and comparing actual to predicted values in the areas of time, cost, and performance.

A project such as Lome GlobeLand is considered successful if it is completed within the given time and cost at the desired level of performance and technology, while utilizing assigned resources effectively and efficiently, and adhering to the ever-changing environmental provisions. The environmental assessment alone may have legal, social, economical, political, and technological consequences that cannot be overlooked. The proposal to organize regular tours to Lome is based upon the ready availability of infrastructure, such as improved road conditions leading to a well organized resort complex with all the modern amenities. Nowadays it is not acceptable to build a resort complex without convincing proof that environmental safeguards are strictly adhered to. The resort complex has to blend with the natural surroundings. As tourists come and go, the activity level in and around the complex increases. If tourist-related businesses flourish—providing jobs for local people— they generate a wide range of air and water pollution that has to be controlled and kept within acceptable limits.

Benefits Derived from a Project Management Approach

Since projects have to be planned, it is possible to measure accomplishments against plans. This leads to an early identification of problems, so that corrective action may follow quickly. Experiences gained in this manner improve the estimating capability for future planning. Knowledge is gained of circumstances when objectives will be exceeded, and when they cannot be met—as in the case of a tour operator unable to charter enough flights to a West African tourist resort. Managers will know when to draw a time limit to scheduling, and how to achieve a meaningful trade-off among competing resources—perhaps providing a balance between sea resorts and hill stations in a limited package tour.

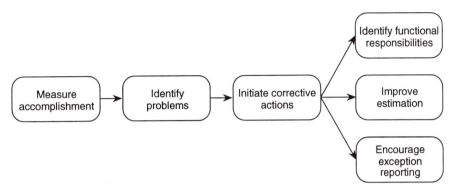

Figure 9-4 Usefulness of Project Management

Project management helps to identify functional responsibilities, such as marketing and finance, ensuring that all activities are accounted for regardless of personnel turnover. Project management encourages "exception reporting"(reporting events and situations that are significantly different from routine operations), such as hotels becoming unavailable to tourists due to an unscheduled local conference. Exception reporting minimizes the need for a continuous watch on all activities. Figure 9-4 shows the sequence of actions related to project management and their outcomes.

When Do We Need Project Management?

The project management approach is more appropriate when the job at hand is large and complex, such as Disneyland in Japan or France, requiring the integration of several activities with tight constraints and many boundaries to be crossed, particularly if they involve important environmental considerations.

In many organizations projects are few and far between, and the requirements for project management vary from one project to another. Tour companies are generally reluctant to invest in proper training. Executives who do not have sufficient time to manage projects frequently refuse to delegate responsibility. Excessive delays occur when approvals have to follow the vertical chain of command. Consequently, project work is delayed for too long in functional departments. When the project staff is limited to a particular area of operation, only a section of the organization understands project management, and problems can surface much later in the project. This makes correction more expensive. The project risk also increases proportionately. Heavy dependence upon subcontractors and outside agencies for project management expertise does not help in solving the structural deficiencies within an organization.

It is therefore imperative to ensure that there is sufficient technical capability to execute the project. This is critical for project success. A systematic effort should be made to integrate the ongoing program with key personnel from both the potential customer and the performing organization. The accessibility of a modern resort complex along the West African coastline, for example, should be appealing to the vacationers from the North American and European continents, particularly during the cold winter months, and to the performing organization, the organization that arranges the air and bus tours. The project design is custom-made to fit the required specifications—retaining the native beauty of the coastline and preserving local customs and traditions, while providing easy access to modern amenities such as overseas communication, hygienic living conditions, and emergency medical facilities.

TOURISM OBJECTIVES AND PRIORITIES

Analysis of Threats, Opportunities, Weaknesses, and Strengths (TOWS)

Tourism projects should be implemented only after the establishment of strategic goals and objectives. It is the chief executive who should initiate the planning process, clearly identify the goals, and guard against the nonessentials. Involvement of top management is necessary for the development of an effective strategy. A strategy is a plan designed to complete a mission. The mission should be planned within the perimeters of the threats (T) and opportunities (O) in the environment, and the weaknesses (W) and strengths (S) of the tourist organization. A systematic analysis of TOWS is intended to help the organization identify the opportunities that match the available strengths, while avoiding exposure of its weaknesses and environmental threats. This should lead to a plan that provides the firm with a competitive advantage.

The environmental opportunities and threats may have several dimensions: political, economic, cultural, legal, demographic, technological; and persons who influence the business—investors, creditors, suppliers, distributors, customers, employees, and competitors, as listed in Figure 9-5. The strengths and weaknesses of a tourist organization are affected by the capability and performance level of management, the amount of capital required, the current utilization of existing capacity, productivity, technical competence, the innovative abilities of employees, profitability, and the market share of its products and services, for example, how many of the current and future flow of tourists going to West Africa are likely to use the resort complex in Lome?

Strategic decisions are based on a set of strategic alternatives generated with the help of a mission statement that takes into account the prevailing opportunities and threats in the environment, and the weaknesses and strengths of the firm (Figure 9-6).

Analysis of the competitive situation for GlobeLand would involve an understanding of the environment in which the tourism business is to operate, the expectations of the traveling public, an identification of the economic characteristics and critical factors of the tourism industry, an evaluation of current and future threats from competitors, and new opportunities arising from the disintegration of the iron curtain in eastern Europe.

The company situation analysis should include a detailed evaluation of its performance, its relative competitive strengths such as wide contacts in destination cities, an identification of the weaknesses of the company such as a lack of information in many parts of Europe and America about emerging tourist spots on the West African coast, and strategic issues that need to be addressed for the company to overcome its weaknesses.

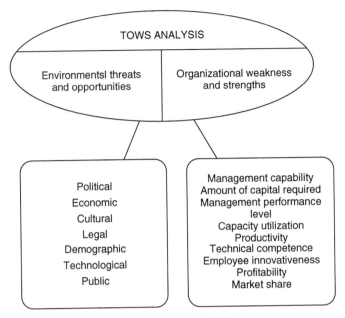

Figure 9-5 A Framework for TOWS Analysis

Mission Statement and Strategy Formulation

Let us suppose that GlobeLand has been able to formulate a mission to pursue a diversified, growing, and profitable worldwide tourism business involving air, land, and sea transportation from major cities in North America and western Europe, hotel accommodation, local travel and sightseeing tours at destination cities, and a variety of tourism-related information services. Gaining expertise in all areas of the primary business of tourism, including the design and packaging of tour services to new territories, could be a sub-mission of GlobeLand. Another sub-mission could be to attain the exceptional quality consistent with the overall marketing objectives of the agency, with close attention given to tour design and careful selection of destination services, including investment in tourism-related facilities at destination points.

Generation of strategic alternatives can be achieved by matching the strengths of GlobeLand with the opportunities in the marketplace, and by anticipating competi-

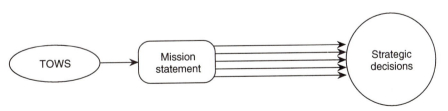

Figure 9-6 Generation of Strategic Alternatives

tors' moves and responding quickly to build a competitive advantage and attract tourists. If the market research team in GlobeLand comes to know of an elaborate scheme by Mitsunobi, an entertainment giant from Japan, to build a waterpark along the West African coastline in Cotonou, the capital of the Republic of Benin, which is fairly close to the resort complex in Lome, GlobeLand can plan a competitive attraction and/or modify its strategy. It may be that a waterpark in the neighboring city of Cotonou would be a more popular attraction than any current facilities available in a Lome resort complex. Is the construction of a waterpark nearby an opportunity or a threat? Perhaps the majority of tourists attracted to the waterpark may also make use of the resort complex. There could be an interchange of information about the facilities offered by both parties so that the combined effect is to attract more tourists to these spots, complementing and reinforcing tourism-related businesses to serve a larger clientele. GlobeLand may consider introducing water skiing, scuba diving, and other water-related sports to strengthen its base. The CEO of GlobeLand should be satisfied that this is the best course to take because the potential benefits are many, and the risks involved are worth it. In such situations, the chief executive should not plunge into a quick decision without evaluating neighboring tourist attractions such as a theme park.

Force Field Analysis of Project Objectives

The project objectives of tourism projects can be set with the aid of a force field analysis, which helps to diagnose a dynamic situation. The analysis consists of listing the driving forces that will push a tourism project toward success, and the restraining forces that may induce failure as illustrated in Figure 9-7. A workable plan would be a driving force. Other items such as clarity in specifications, goals, expectations, responsibilities, and interface relationships among the executives may be taken into account. Technical

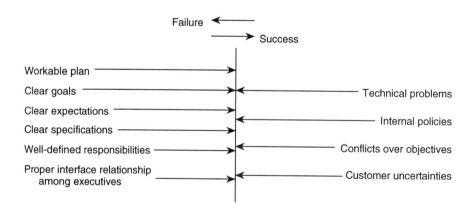

Figure 9-7 Force Field Analysis of Project Objectives

problems, internal politics, conflicts over objectives, and customer uncertainties would be restraining forces. In a steady state environment, the driving and restraining forces are in balance. Changes in the driving or restraining forces would, either individually or collectively, cause a shift in the current equilibrium.

Establishment of Project Priorities

Some common factors influence the establishment of project priorities. For example, Lome Tours is one of many projects under consideration by GlobeLand. Other projects include expansion of tourism to eastern Europe, Japan, Australia, New Zealand, Thailand, and Indonesia, and a variety of other investment proposals, including resort developments and theme parks. Some of these investments include joint ventures in collaboration with major airlines, hotel chains, and local investors. The impact of Lome Tours on other projects and other affiliated organizations should be studied carefully. Project priority is also influenced by the risks GlobeLand will incur technically, financially, and competitively; the expected savings and return on investment; the nearness of the scheduled completion date; and the penalties for delayed completion.

ORGANIZATION FOR TOURISM PROJECTS

Project management is organized to achieve a single set of objectives through a single project of finite lifetime, as in the case of Lome Tours. The company has many other projects in the pipeline. Each one has its own policies, procedures, rules, and standards. During the initial years of GlobeLand in the 1960s and 1970s, the organizational structure was traditional, with the three vice presidents for operations, marketing and public relations, and finance and administration reporting to the president. Each vice president had two or more divisions, and the divisional managers supervised several departments as shown in Figure 9-8.

Initially this organizational form worked well. It provided continuity in the functional disciplines; policies, procedures, and the lines of responsibility were easily defined and understood. It provided good control over personnel, since each employee of GlobeLand had only one person to report to. Communication channels were vertical and well established. The functional managers maintained absolute control over the budget. They had manpower flexibility and a broad base from which to work.

However, the phenomenal growth of the organization could not be sustained with the traditional form. While many new projects were initiated, there was no strong central authority or individual responsible for the project at hand. The integration of activities that cross functional lines became more and more difficult, and the vice presidents had to get involved with the daily routine. Coordination became more complex, and additional lead time was required for the approval of decisions. There was no customer focal point, and the response to customer needs was slow.

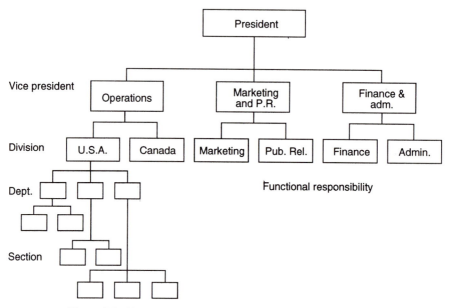

Figure 9-8 Management Structure of GlobeLand Before Expansion

This led to separation of the project management function from the controlling influence of the functional managers using a line-staff organization pattern (Figure 9-9).

The solid lines show the formal authority, while the dotted lines indicate informal authority and/or information flow between the project manager and department managers. For some projects, the project manager served only as a focal point for activity control. The project manager kept the division manager informed of the project status. The manager had no formal authority and had to depend upon technical compe-

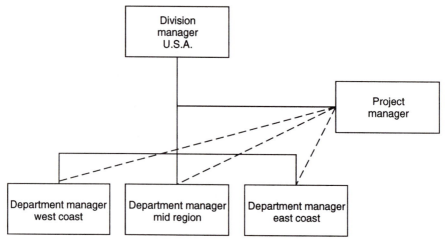

Figure 9-9 GlobeLand Line and Staff Organization

tence and interpersonal skills to influence department managers toward timely completion of activities. For other projects, the project manager maintained monitoring authority only. The division managers were not ready to cope with the problems arising from shared authority. The line-staff project manager who reported to the division manager (U.S.A.-Operations) did not have any authority or control over portions of a project in other divisions (Canada-Operations, Marketing, Public Relations, etc.).

The matrix organizational form is an attempt to give power and authority to the project manager, who has total responsibility and accountability for project success. This form was adopted by GlobeLand after they opened their services to European capitals. The revised organization chart of GlobeLand is shown in Figure 9-10.

While presenting the new organization chart, the president of GlobeLand emphasized the importance of sharing information through both horizontal and vertical channels, and declared that the respective managers should be willing to negotiate for resources. The horizontal line was to operate as a separate entity except for administrative purposes. All managers had an input into the planning process. The project manager would maintain maximum project control over all resources, including cost and personnel, through the line managers. The functional organizations provided basic support to the projects. Policies and procedures could be set up for each project independently, provided that they did not contradict the established policies and procedures of the company.

This led to the development of a strong technical base, and much more time could be devoted to complex problem solving. Knowledge was available for all projects on an equal basis. Since key personnel could be shared, program cost was minimized.

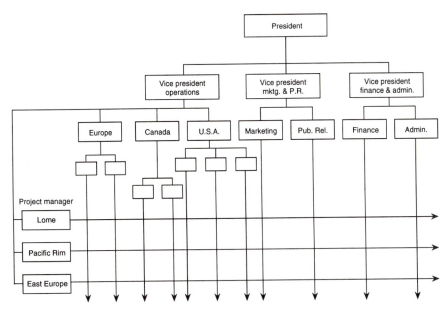

Figure 9-10 Matrix Management Structure of GlobeLand

People could work on a variety of problems, paving the way for better people control. However, with multiple managers and personnel reporting in two directions, conflicts over administration surfaced during the transitional period. Long-range plans suffered as the company became more involved in meeting schedules and fulfilling the requirements of various temporary projects, such as consolidation of financial reporting, updating payroll systems, mechanization of personnel records, and introducing on-line costing.

The project managers were given on-the-job training, working with experienced professional leaders and supporting functional activities. Special courses and seminars were organized to improve their conceptual understanding of the profession. Project management directives, policies, and procedures were established, along with a project charter to provide a thrust to proper project organization. This helped project managers to assume overall project leadership, build project teams, resolve conflicts, manage multidisciplinary tasks, plan and allocate resources, and interface with customers and sponsors. It enabled GlobeLand to cope with the complex, rapidly changing environment of the tourism business.

The assumption of overall project leadership was facilitated by a desire for accomplishment, effective communication, work challenge, group acceptance, experience in task management, and assistance in problem solving. Project managers understood that the strong restraining forces were the lack of technical knowledge, lack of self-confidence and credibility, personality problems, and uncertainty about the role to be played.

Project managers were given training in team motivation, since this was crucial for the successful completion of any project. This required clear role-definition, professional interest in the project, integration of team and project objectives, a desire for achievement, a common goal, good interpersonal relations, clear objectives and reward, strong leadership, high commitment or ownership in the project, and facility of communication.

THE TOURISM PROJECT PLANNING PROCESS

Planning and Control Functions

Project management methods have undergone drastic changes during the past three decades. What managers used to do with rough paper and pencil prior to launching a project can now be done in a more scientific form—a form that is more explicit and communicable. Empirical evidence of these changes in management techniques have been on the increase. Technological growth warrants division of intellectual and physical activities among several enterprises with attendant complications in coordination. The planning functions of these programs involve a deep probe into the nebulous future.

A plan that cannot be executed is useless. Execution involves proper control. Planning cannot remain static if control features indicate suitable revisions. The planning and control of gigantic projects is no easy task, especially if the projects involve the coordination of a large number of subcontracts. Project managers are often confronted with far too much information with very little time to examine it. In many cases, such information does not require their attention or decision. The complexity of the job, therefore, requires an elaborate, explicit, and systematic approach that pinpoints the essentials among a maze of activities. This has led to the emergence of an integrated network as an effective basis for scheduling and controlling projects.

A project usually consists of a chain of activities that do not form a recurring cycle. Launching a new tour is a project, as is the construction of a factory, or the building of a highway. A project is characterized by a definite commencement and completion, within which a clearly defined goal is achieved as a result of the accomplishment of a finite set of activities.

A project manager is like a traveler who has a specified goal to reach and who is not familiar with the terrain. The traveler, therefore, seeks a road map, which contains the relevant information about a given route. If the destination is specified, the alternative routes may be examined carefully and the most convenient route may then be selected. The details required may vary according to the circumstances. But the route map is there to provide the necessary guidance. Apart from calculating the distance from the origin to the destination and estimating the approximate duration of travel, corresponding figures can be obtained for important intermediate stations as well.

Similarly, in the case of a project, the end objectives may be clear to the manager but he or she may not be fully aware of the intricate details of all the activities that make up the project, unless he or she has the project map at hand. This map is similar to the road map. It shows how the project evolves from stage to stage.

Lome Tours Project

Consider, for instance, GlobeLand's effort to promote tourism in Lome. They have already established an office in Abidjan, the capital of Ivory Coast in West Africa. So far, they have been catering for tourists who would like to make an overland journey to Accra, capital of Ghana, driving along the beautiful coastal highway. They are now considering a modified bus tour package that would extend the tour to the exciting coastal holiday resort in Lome, the capital of Togo. The company is also considering an air tour package for those passengers who have a limited vacation period and who would prefer to enjoy the scenery in and around Lome. The five major activities relating to this Lome Tours project of GlobeLand are shown in Figure 9-11 below. This figure also includes the duration of each activity. The basic principles of project planning and control are illustrated through this example.

The project described above can now be represented in the form of a bar chart, also known as a Gantt chart, as shown in Figure 9-12. The bar chart is a convenient way to

Activity	Description	Duration (weeks)
I.	Find tour operations that benefit most	8
II.	Develop a modified bus tour package	19
III.	Develop a new air tour package	12
IV.	Consolidate tour packages and arrange publicity	5
V.	Conduct dedication ceremony	1

Figure 9-11 Lome Tours Main Activity Table

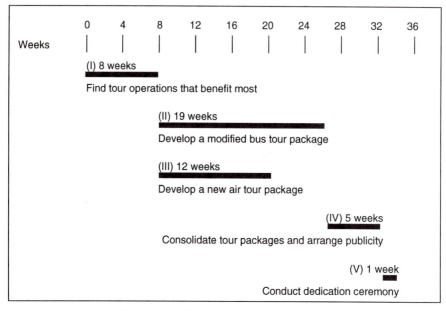

Figure 9-12 Bar chart of Lome Tours Project

represent all activities in a project, provided one is aware of the precedence relationship among activities: for example, the commencement of some activities such as II and III depend upon I. Before developing air (III) or bus (II) tour packages, it is necessary to examine all feasible alternatives and recognize tour operations that yield maximum benefit (I). Similarly, consolidation of tour packages and arranging for publicity (IV) requires completion of both types of tour packages (II and III). Finally, the dedication ceremony (V) can be conducted only after the consolidation of tour packages and the completion of publicity arrangements. Figure 9-13 includes the precedence relationship described above.

Although the bar chart (Figure 9-12) does not show the precedence relationship among activities, their interdependence is indirectly reflected in the horizontal time scale. Activity (II) commences in the ninth week, since the first eight weeks are required for the feasibility study (I). The commencement of activity (IV) depends upon the completion of both activities (II) and (III). Activity (II) requires nineteen weeks.

Activity	Description	Duration (weeks)	Preceding Activities
I.	Find tour operations that benefit most	8	Nil
II.	Develop a modified bus tour package	19	I
III.	Develop a new air tour package	12	I
IV.	Consolidate tour packages and arrange publicity	5	II and III
V.	Conduct dedication ceremony	1	IV

Figure 9-13 Activity Relationship in the Lome Tours Project

Hence this activity will not be completed until the end of the twenty-seventh week (eight plus nineteen) from the start of the project. Activity (III) requires only twelve weeks, and it is completed by the end of the twentieth week (eight plus twelve) from the start, and this represents a gap of seven (twenty-seven minus twenty) weeks between the completion of activities (II) and (III). In view of the precedence relationship explained earlier, activity (IV) cannot begin before the twenty-eighth week. This activity is completed by the end of the thirty-second week, since its duration is only five weeks. Finally, the last activity (V) with a one-week duration begins at the end of the thirty-second week and the whole project is completed by the end of the thirty-third week. The project duration of thirty-three weeks is indicated in the time scale of the bar chart.

From Barcharts to Networks

A bar chart is a convenient way to represent all activities in a project, provided the precedence relationship among the activities is known. The precedence relationship implies that some activities, such as a bus trip from an airport to a hotel as part of a tour package, cannot begin until all the tourists arriving by the chartered airline take their seats in the bus. First they need to get their luggage cleared. The chartered plane has to arrive at the destination point before the tourists can disembark. Other activities can be performed concurrently. When the luggage arrives at the baggage clearance center, the members of the tour group can identify and clear their respective belongings simultaneously. If customs clearance is involved, they may do so in parallel, depending on the number of such channels.

A **network** is a graphical presentation of project activities exhibiting their sequential relationships. The origin of the *network* approach can be traced back to two separate projects, one undertaken by the private sector and the other by the U.S. government, the latter being much larger in magnitude and in the degree of uncertainty than the former. Both groups advocated the use of a network, depicting explicitly the relationship among various activities. This was indeed a significant change from the then-existing practice of using bar charts. The smaller of the two projects related to the construction industry where, by virtue of extensive experience, the activities could be well defined at the planning stage and unique time values ascribed to each one, as in the case of the Lome Tours project of GlobeLand. This type of network can be classified as *deterministic* and *activity-oriented*. A **deterministic network** is a project network in which the data used has an element of certainty, implying that the probability of its occurrence is one. An **activity-oriented network** is a project network that is described by placing each activity in a node with arrows connecting these nodes to indicate the precedence relationship only.

The method consists of drawing a network of the project portraying the interrelationship among the activities and assigning time values to each activity. The network yields several activity sequences known as *paths* from start to end of a project. Obviously, the project cannot be completed until the longest sequence of activities has been completed. This path is called the *critical path*. It is the longest path in the network. The method used to identify the critical path with deterministic activity duration is commonly known as the *critical path method* (CPM). Every activity along the critical path is called a *critical activity*. Any delay along this critical path would result in a corresponding delay in the project duration. It is easy to show that every network should contain at least one critical path, if not more. Among other benefits derived from this approach, the critical path provides for management by exception. While the identification of the critical path is important, it is useful to study other paths—known as *slack paths*—to ensure timely completion of a project. **Slack** is the extra time that an activity (or an event) can be held up without delaying project completion. Depending on network details, each path from the start to the end of a project has a different amount of slackness. The critical path, by definition, has no slackness.

In contrast to the CPM approach, where activities are familiar and their duration easy to estimate, large projects involving several contractors and subcontractors are difficult to plan and execute. In such cases, the estimation of activity duration requires a different approach involving probabilities and *event orientation*, where a node (or a circle) represents an *event*, and an arrow represents an activity. Every activity is characterized by a unique predecessor event, and a unique successor event. Information is obtained for every activity in the form of three time estimates—*optimistic, pessimistic*, and *most likely*—which are combined to arrive at the *expected duration* of that activity. The critical path is then identified as before. This approach is called *Program Evaluation and Review Technique* (PERT).

A Network Approach to the Lome Tours Project

The activity-oriented network for the Lome Tours project would have five activities, represented by five boxes (or circles) connected to each other with appropriate arrows, showing which activities have to be completed before others can start (Figure 9-14).

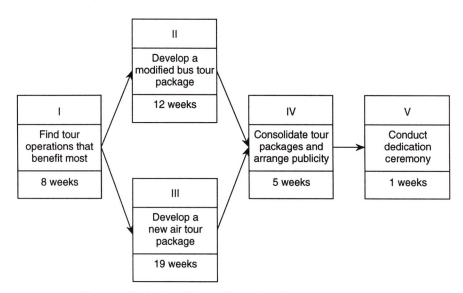

Figure 9-14 Activity-Oriented Network for the Lome Tours Project

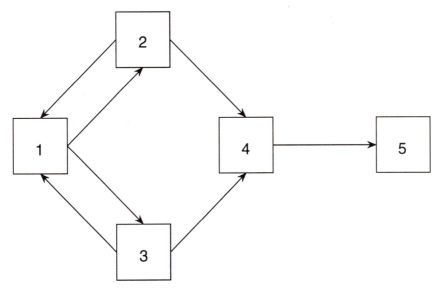

Figure 9-15 An Activity-Oriented Network with Feedback Cycles

The network is *directed*, showing clearly the precedence relationship. The network is also *acyclic* in the sense that the directed arrows do not form a loop. There are situations requiring repetition of certain activities in a network, in which case there would be one or more loops, and the network becomes *cyclical* as shown in Figure 9-15 where more alternatives have to be considered if the proposed tour packages are not satisfactory.

An event-oriented network of the "Lome Tours" project is given in Figure 9-16. While an activity consumes time and resources, an event, represented by a node, depicts a point in time only and does not consume any resources. In an event-oriented network (EON), arrows represent activities and every activity is characterized by a

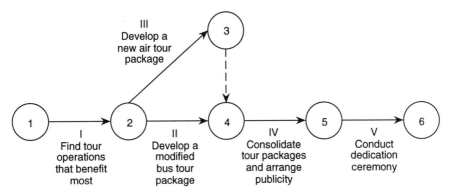

Figure 9-16 An Event-Oriented Network (EON) for the Lome Tours Project

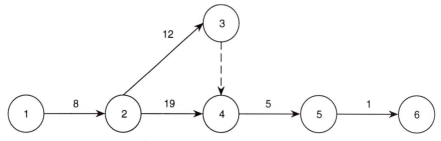

Figure 9-17 Activity Durations for the Lome Tours Project

unique *predecessor event* and a unique *successor event*. In order to facilitate this unique identification of each activity, a *dummy activity* is introduced between events (3) and (4). A dummy activity is used mainly to show the precedence relationship among activities. It does not consume either time or resources.

The network shown in Figure 9-17 has two paths from the *start event* (1) to the *end event* (6). They are [1-2-4-5-6] and [1-2-3-4-5-6]. If the duration of each activity along the first path is added, the total duration comes to [8 + 19 + 5 + 1 = 33]. Similarly, the second path yields [8 + 12 + 0 + 5 + 1 = 26]. Since the first path is the longer of the two, it is the critical path. Any delay in any activity along this critical path will cause a corresponding delay in the project duration. Accordingly, the critical activities are (1,2), (2,4), (4,5), and (5,6).

Each activity is defined by a unique combination of a predecessor and a successor event. The earliest occurrence of each succeeding event is based on the *earliest finish* time of the intervening activity. If two or more activities have to be completed before an event can occur, the activity that has the highest value as the finish time, determines the earliest occurrence of that event. Beginning with the start event, this logic is repeated for every subsequent event, until the end event is reached. This is called the *forward pass*.

The forward pass calculations yield the earliest occurrence of each event from start to finish, in a sequential manner. Since the events and activities are interconnected in a network, it is equally important to compute the *latest finish* and the *latest start* of each activity as well. This set of calculations is known as the *backward pass*. This is a mirror image of the forward pass calculations, beginning at the end rather than at the start event, and going backward rather than forward. The important event requiring attention in the forward pass is the *merge event*, where two or more activities merge into that event. The earliest occurrence of that event is determined by the highest finish time among the activities merging into it. In the case of a backward pass, the important event is the one from which two or more activities emanate; this event is called a *burst event*. The latest occurrence of a burst event is therefore determined by the lowest of all late starts among its successor activities. The late start of an activity is computed by reducing the late finish of that activity by the activity duration. The late finish of an activity is the same as the latest occurrence of its successor event. Beginning with the end event the backward pass proceeds to the intermediate predecessor event through the activity link, and the procedure continues until the start event is reached. For the purposes of this calculation, it is normally assumed that the latest occurrence of the end event is the same as its earliest occurrence. This enables the backward pass to arrive at the same date of project commencement as originally assumed while performing the forward pass. Accordingly, the longest path is determined by tracing a sequence of events and activities whose earliest values are the same as the latest values. The forward pass gives the earliest values, while the backward pass gives the latest values. Since the longest path is the critical path, this approach identifies the amount of slackness in each path, including the critical path. A network may have more than one critical path, depending upon the network configuration and activity durations.

Resource Allocation and Cost-Time Trade-Off

A study of the slackness can provide a basis to reorganize common resources in the most efficient manner. Sometimes it may be possible to divert resources from a slack activity to a critical activity and shorten the corresponding critical activity. This would result in a tighter resource schedule, but the project could be completed in less time without consuming extra resources. There are many ways in which several resources can be allocated to one or more projects. The resource allocation procedures leading to the best schedule depend upon the criteria used. *Activity floats*, the amount of slackness available for a given activity in a project network, can be utilized in non-critical activities to arrive at a more even allocation of resources over the project period.

The allocation of resources often implies additional expenditure. There is an inverse relationship between time and direct cost. Project duration can be compressed by diverting additional resources to the least expensive critical activities. However, completing a project ahead of time may mean reduction in certain indirect costs such as equipment rentals, indirect wages, and other overheads, as well as incentive payments accruable due to early completion, if built into the original contract. The decision to compress or expand the overall project duration may depend upon several such factors. This approach is called *cost-time trade-off*.

Project Condensation, Integration, and Detailing

In the preparation of a network, it is possible to include a large number of basic activities or represent just a few, both approaches being equally valid. However, the actual choice of details will depend upon several factors, including the level at which the network is analyzed, the need for precise definition of events and activities, and the number of dependencies upon outside agencies in the completion of various subcontracts.

At the outset, a *work breakdown structure* is prepared, including the major project phases and the key events that are known as the *milestones*. Each subcontractor will have a network relating to his or her portion of the overall project. When a large number of such networks are collected together for a complete picture of the project, suitable methods of integration have to be devised to link these independent networks.

Progress Review

A project network is essentially a planning and control device. The information derived from the network makes scheduling possible. Whenever the network is so used, the corresponding schedule should be realistic and made fully operational. This requires a periodic review of the progress achieved. The staff should be committed to meeting the schedule, and should become aware of possible delays and their consequences. No ambiguity should exist in the definition of activities and events. Proper milestones should be established as targets and given their due importance. Above all, communication between people forming the project team, the outside agencies, and the managerial personnel should be well established, so that information flows smoothly and without interruption.

Project Management Software

Attempts have been made by various authors to standardize the network logic, when different projects of similar types are to be programmed. Advances in computer hardware and software during the last two decades have made a considerable difference in the management of large-scale projects. There are over seventy project management software packages available in the commercial market. These programs are continuously being revised and updated, so it is useful to keep in touch with the respective vendors. The program characteristics alone can be analyzed in terms of the number of tasks per project, number of resources per task, project linkages, sub-projects, overlapping tasks, gaps between tasks, dynamic scheduling, and calendar modification.

IMPLEMENTATION GUIDELINES

A project network is nothing more than a list of activities with explicit representation of their interrelationship. The activity sequencing may be dictated either by technological dependencies and/or by resource constraints, including cash flows. An initial network is just a plan based upon the need to accomplish a specific objective. At the preliminary stage, it is necessary to define the nature and scope of the work to be done. There are several questions to be answered at this stage of implementation:

1. What is expected from the execution of the project?
2. What are the sources of information relating to the project?
3. Who will take charge of the control of the project? To what extent will that person be given the authority to execute the work?
4. What is the existing condition of the planning and reporting procedures? What changes will be required to make the new system effective?
5. To which parts of the project is the network going to be applied, and how much details is to be shown?

Selection of the Initial Project for Network Application

An organization not familiar with the use of networks should exercise sufficient care in the selection of the initial project for network application. Usually, the first program for implementation is also used for training purposes; hence, the total duration of the first project is an important factor in the training given for network implementation. Project performance reports may be on a monthly or other periodic basis, and unless a sufficient number—at least four to six to begin with—of these reports are brought in for examination and managerial action, the full implication of the project reporting system will not be understood. Undertaking huge projects without proper training and understanding of the technique will result in waste and frustration.

Guidelines for Activity Detailing

Although the breakdown of a project into activities depends upon the nature, size, and importance of the project and the computational facilities available to the project manager, some guidelines should still be established. In general, planning to a certain level of detail is meant to supply sufficient information to enable the project personnel to take appropriate action in time. If the details incorporated in a network are excessive, a true prediction will not be available. In many cases, a single activity may be easily expressed in terms of a whole network. It is possible to improve upon the performance of certain activities by such a detailed analysis. However, a mass of details will create an imbalance between the amount of reporting to be done and the amount of work actually executed.

Cycle of Operations Implementation of network techniques requires an understanding of the cycle of operations pertaining to the project. Beginning with input information from contractors who are responsible for the project, weekly or monthly adjustments are made not only to the flow diagram but also to a file maintaining all the events relating to the flow diagram. The elapsed time estimates for activities are also fed into the system, whether manual or automatic. Such a system yields a variety of reports, some of which are sent to the senior management and others to technical and operational personnel. The level of details included in these reports has to match the needs of these individuals. Based on the current information made available to these people, changes may be warranted either in the network diagram itself or other items fed into the computational system.

Periodic Review The dynamic character of a project plan requires that all information relating to the project network should be kept up-to-date. This is possible if the respective personnel are required to submit periodic reports on a weekly, monthly, or quarterly basis, and changes can be posted.

At the output end, periodic requests for extra information may have to be confined to the critical areas, thus allowing for special reviews of specific events only. By supplying estimates of time values of critical activities, emphasis is given to tight areas, and such a selective analysis enables a more accurate data collection.

Frequency of Reports Some reports must be produced more often than others. Emphasis must be placed upon these reports, which have to be submitted once every two weeks. In submitting a report of prior happenings, the manager may state anticipated changes and indicate problem areas in order to enable appropriate corrective actions. On the other hand, an updating of currently most critical activities may perhaps be done once a month.

It may be necessary to evaluate the entire network on a quarterly basis. This review is similar to the setting up of the initial project network. All events and activities in the existing networks are critically examined by a team of representatives. Whenever necessary, revisions and new estimates are prepared. These changes are then brought together in a well-defined procedure and incorporated for future use.

As more and more projects are brought within the purview of the network approach, it becomes necessary to devise a system of reporting that will account for a suitable flow of data and analysis. Perhaps report cycles may have to be staggered for various parts of the project, with biweekly, monthly, or even quarterly schedules. This equalizes the load upon the staff week after week.

Scheduling Bias Network calculations lead to scheduling of activities on a calendar basis, taking into account holidays and shift work. If the scheduling is done simultaneously with the time estimates, a bias will be introduced in the realistic estimation of activity duration. On the other hand, by providing the estimates without any indications of project delays, the time calculations will show a fairly realistic approximation to the actual time consumption. Network calculations are based on reliable estimates of individual activity durations. If a bias is introduced at this initial stage, the repercussions will be felt throughout the project execution phase.

Organize a Project Office

Many organizations are functionally oriented, the functions being represented either in terms of departments or divisions such as sales, purchase, or finance as originally conceived by GlobeLand. The network approach in project management, on the other hand, integrates various activities in accordance with their dependencies, regardless of their functional nature. In this respect, the stress is laid on the tasks to be performed, and many organizations are not fully responsive to such functional synthesis. Yet coordination is absolutely essential for the successful completion of a project.

Regardless of the nature of the project being initiated and the methods of computation involved, it is desirable to form a centralized agency to oversee the project. At the time of network formulation, it is necessary to have a joint meeting between the scheduling personnel, the program managers, and the technical personnel. The engineers concerned may assign the single-time (as in CPM) or the three-time (as in PERT) estimates when the skeleton network has been prepared.

The interrelationships among activities are also reviewed by the whole group. Organizational responsibility for work performed should be indicated by appropriate code numbers for each activity. It may be a division or a department or any other existing unit within the organization. The central project agency (or office) should review the completed network for appropriate logic. The group then assigns numbers for events and activities, and several computations follow. The central agency again plays a vital role in the analysis of reports and the dissemination of appropriate information to various levels of general and program management. Similarly, the information from various management levels flows through the agency for revisions to the current network.

Maintain Flexibility

Network-based project scheduling is intrinsically a flexible device. This flexibility should not be lost by rigid ground rules and procedures that are time-consuming and expensive. Each organization places different demands upon its project staff. Networks should be adapted to the idiosyncracies of each case. Making changes should be confined to important items. While reporting is essential, an insistence upon exactitude would be improper. Network scheduling requires explicit statements that relate to objective planning. Thus a situation is created wherein management personnel, like project engineers, appear to be subservient to a systemic framework. Such a perception would be detrimental to the expression of individual initiative.

One of the difficult problems in the successful implementation of network-based project management is the supply of necessary information from operating personnel, particularly at the network formulation stage. Time estimates given by project personnel are based upon an instinctive understanding of a job yet to be performed. Misinformation may arise out of suspicion that a firm commitment by various members of the group may be enforced against their wishes. Miscalculation can and does occur. Operating conditions may have changed considerably since the original time estimates. There should be room for people to rectify the situation without losing face.

Although explicit commitments have their drawbacks, there are some specific advantages. Every member of the team knows his or her place in the total picture. He or she comes to understand the importance of his or her role. In many organizations, changes in the operating personnel are common. Unless there are explicit statements concerning the role of individuals or departments in relation to a project, transfer of personnel will augment difficulties in communication and necessitate special training. Finally, explicit commitments result in a clear delineation of responsibilities, and an incentive for successful completion of respective workloads. This makes possible the granting of incentives on the basis of concrete achievements. When several outside contractors are involved, these conditions are inevitable.

Promote Teamwork

Project management is founded on teamwork. The emphasis is on the accomplishment of tasks, regardless of the nature of functional specialization. The project team should consist of people disciplined in more ways than one. Specialists in various fields involved in the project as a whole should have a place in the team—people in cost estimation, accounting, production, planning, scheduling, engineering, or administration. In particular, the team leader should be fully familiar with the capabilities and limitations of the network approach, and should have undergone a fairly thorough training in its operations. The team may also consist of people in purchasing, data processing, organizational methods, manufacturing, marketing and so on, and staff may occasionally be asked to advise on specific issues of the projects. The team as a whole should be sufficiently familiar with the techniques. The team should have sufficient information and understanding to train a number of operating personnel who will be eventually responsible for the implementation of the system. In addition, they may take on the preparation of reports and the maintenance of the whole filing system, beginning with network formulation and ending with the implementation process. The team may participate in the preparation of the proposal, and assist managers who are responsible for different areas of the projects in the identification and analysis of defects pinpointed by the reports.

The role of such a team should be well defined, whether it is executive or advisory in nature. As in other managerial situations, it is important to observe unity of command. The ultimate responsibility for project execution should rest with the project manager in charge of the project, with the team providing the necessary guidance.

The experience gained in the successful completion of a maiden project should help the implementation team to form part of a more permanent central staff group that could play a continuing role in the execution of subsequent projects. It is not necessary that all members of the original team should form part of this permanent setup. In any case, the team should report directly to corporate management, or to any one of sufficient authority to bring together various functional specialists as and when required.

BENEFITS DERIVED FROM PROJECT NETWORKS

Listing of Activities

Network formulation requires a proper listing of all activities related to the project. The extent to which details are incorporated may vary according to the requirements of the plan, but a list of activities covering the whole project is required in order to proceed with the project. This systematic listing process at the initial stage pinpoints a variety of activities that would otherwise have remained obscure. Should there be any logical inconsistency, it is now made explicit, and a proper network is then formulated.

Project Scheduling

By assigning a time estimate to each activity, an explicit calendar-based schedule can be developed. The workload can be translated to manpower needs and skill profiles. Overtime requirements can be effectively budgeted. Holidays and maintenance shutdowns can be included in the schedule.

Resource Utilization

Apart from a close supervision of critical activities, the network allows for an intensive utilization of resources, including manpower, equipment, money, and raw materials. This can be effected by directing common resources from slack activities to critical ones whenever possible.

Simulation

By introducing synthetic time reduction, management can simulate a change in the program in relation to consumption of resources and also network design. The merits of various alternative plans of action thus formulated can be compared in order to obtain an optimum and workable plan. This search for the best plan need not be confined to the initial stage of the project. As project work progresses, new opportunities and/or constraints become visible, and it becomes necessary to effect appropriate changes in the plan for the remainder of the project. Current software capabilities in project management can easily accommodate a variety of such "what if" analyses.

Functional Synthesis

Since project planning and control is centered around a logical network showing the interrelationship of the activities, the language of the network brings together numerous employees in a large organization to work for well-defined objectives. In particular, it encourages increased communication and cooperation among the various departments on the critical path, cutting through the traditional organizational barriers. Thus the individuals involved in keeping their activities on schedule are prompted to do so indirectly by group pressure. By making the nature of relationship among the functional groups explicit, the network also enables identification of areas of doubtful responsibility and those areas that are yet to be assigned.

Forecasting

Finally, project networks help in forecasting performances against schedules in probabilistic terms wherever applicable. A comparison of actuals versus targets—whether relating to time, cost, or performance level—may show slippages, requiring attention to the root of the problem. If timely corrective action is not taken, the situation may further deteriorate. The project network approach enables development of several scenarios, forecasting the consequences of specific actions. For instance, during a peak tourist season, it is important for a tourism operator to ensure that all related facilities are in good working order. If proper maintenance is not carried out in time, or if the load on the facilities exceeds given specifications, the chances of a breakdown increase, causing unnecessary interruption. This may lead to substantial loss of revenue, customer goodwill or the like. Thus the network approach can forewarn management about trouble spots well in advance, and ensure that preventive actions are taken at the appropriate time.

CONCLUSION

In conclusion, tourism is a multibillion dollar business. Decision at the top level of a tourism-related organization could involve major capital investments. These decisions set in motion large projects with complex interrelated functions. Management has to face challenges arising from these complex projects with foresight, organizational skill, and sound internal communications. Network-based project management provides valuable guidance for management in this arduous task.

The network approach to project management is dynamic. It has become indispensable both at the planning and execution stage of a project. More and more user-friendly computer software packages are now at the disposal of the project manager. Ample demonstrations of successful applications of the network approach have occurred in military and civil contracts and in public and private sector corporations dealing with manufacturing and service operations. The tourism business has a great deal to gain from its usage.

As we have seen, tourism is variously defined, a fact that makes its measurement and consequences, its economics, far from precise. That tourism is increasing in volume and economic significance is unquestioned. Its differing effects, especially the social impacts on a community is not uniformly welcomed. Its economic impacts are often difficult and expensive to quantify, a common problem for economists.

This book has highlighted a few industries that are well established as being parts of tourism. We have briefly discussed their economics and some of the quantitative methods that have proved useful for tourism development projects. Tourism, domestic and international, is almost certain to grow dramatically in the future. So too, will the need grow for more accurate tourism statistics and their implications.

Index